T0355456

Theater and Martial Arts in West Sumatra

This series of publications on Africa, Latin America, and Southeast Asia is designed to present significant research, translation, and opinion to area specialists and to a wide community of persons interested in world affairs. The editor seeks manuscripts of quality on any subject and can generally make a decision regarding publication within three months of receipt of the original work. Production methods generally permit a work to appear within one year of acceptance. The editor works closely with authors to produce a high quality book. The series appears in a paperback format and is distributed worldwide. For more information, contact the executive editor at Ohio University Press, Scott Quadrangle, University Terrace, Athens, Ohio 45701.

Executive editor: Gillian Berchowitz
AREA CONSULTANTS
Africa: Diane Ciekawy
Latin America: Thomas Walker
Southeast Asia: William H. Frederick

The Monographs in International Studies series is published for the Center for International Studies by the Ohio University Press. The views expressed in individual monographs are those of the authors and should not be considered to represent the policies or beliefs of the Center for International Studies, the Ohio University Press, or Ohio University.

Theater and Martial Arts in West Sumatra

Randai and Silek of the Minangkabau

Kirstin Pauka

OHIO UNIVERSITY CENTER FOR INTERNATIONAL STUDIES

MONOGRAPHS IN INTERNATIONAL STUDIES

SOUTHEAST ASIA SERIES NO. 103

ATHENS

Library of Congress Cataloging-in-Publication

Pauka, Kirstin, 1963–
    Theater and martial arts in West Sumatra : Randai and silek of the
Minangkabau / Kirstin Pauka.
        p.   cm. — (Monographs in international studies. Southeast
Asia series ; no. 103)
        Includes bibliographical references and index.
        ISBN 0-89680-205-1 (pbk. : alk. paper)
        1. Randai.   2. Theater—Indonesia—Sumatra—History—20th century.
3. Minangkabau drama—History and criticism.   4. Minangkabau
(Indonesian people)—Social life and customs.   I. Title.
II. Series.
PN2904.5.R35P38   1998   98-19143
792'.09598'1—dc21   CIP

Für meine Eltern, Dagmar und Johann Pauka

Contents

Illustrations

Maps

Photographs

Diagrams

Acknowledgments

I WOULD like to thank all the wonderful Minangkabau people who had a part in this study. My gratitude goes especially to the members of the randai groups Palito Nyalo, Cindua Mato, Sago Sejati, and Rambun Pamenan, as well as to the members of the silek schools Puti Mandi, Sungai Patai, Harimau Sakti, and Bungo. Their willingness to share their art forms with me made this study possible. I am most grateful to the organizers of the Fifth West Sumatra Randai Festival, especially to Pak Chairul Harun, Ibu Ernilitis, Pak Damrah, and Pak Maadis Datuk Putih. Their help in gathering data and their insights into randai proved most valuable. Many thanks also go to the members of the performance groups Binuang Sakti and Teater Kita, as well as to the teachers at the Indonesian Academy for the Performing Arts (ASKI), the Indonesian School of Music and Arts (SMKI), and UNAND, especially to Mursal Esten and Pak Zulkifli. Edy Utama deserves special acknowledgment for his continued interest in my research and his support and friendship during many adventurous tours to the most remote performance locations imaginable. I would like to thank most of all my dear colleagues and good friends Tatang and Tri Iman Prasetyono, who indefatigably helped in the search for ever more scripts and more performances. Special thanks also go to Dr. Christine Martins for her hospitality and friendship.

The documentation of a most unusual event, the Pauleh Tinggi Ceremony, is a part of this study thanks to the clan elders and village chiefs in Sincincin, Pariaman district, especially Datuk Mudo, who graciously granted me access to this secretive all-male ceremony.

I gratefully acknowledge the following organizations for their support: the Indonesian Institute of Science (LIPI) for their assistance in securing the visa and other vital documents; the Henry Luce Foundation for a grant for preliminary research; the German Academic Exchange Service (DAAD) for a grant during the field research; the American Association of University Women (AAUW) for a doctoral fellowship during the writing of this study; and the Peace Education Organization for the support through its International Peace Scholarship. Without their assistance this project would have been impossible and I am most grateful for their trust, interest, and financial support.

I would also like to thank the editors of the *Asian Theatre Journal,* the *Drama Review,* and the *Journal of Asian Martial Arts* for their permission to reprint some of my material on randai and silek that was previously published in their journals.

Here in Hawaii, a warm mahalo goes out to my colleagues Elizabeth Wichman-Walczak, James R. Brandon, Ricardo Trimillos, Alice Dewey, and especially to my mentor, Roger Long, for ongoing guidance and support. I also owe thanks to my friend Koji Lum for his care and understanding throughout this endeavor.

And finally, I would like to thank my editors Gillian Berchowitz, Nancy Basmajian, and Robert Furnish for their help, constructive criticism, and advice. Mahalo and aloha to all of you.

Chapter 1

INTRODUCTION

Randai, folk theater of the Minangkabau, is a unique and exciting Southeast Asian performance art. This chapter introduces the basic characteristics of randai and provides background information on the Minangkabau people of West Sumatra. Their history, customs, and religion all contribute to the understanding of randai theater as a cultural expression of the Minangkabau people.

What Is Randai?

Most readers, even those familiar with the performing arts of other areas of Indonesia and Southeast Asia, probably have heard of randai only in passing. Due, perhaps, to the predominance of Java and Bali in the realm of Indonesian performance studies, the Sumatran form of randai has been somewhat overlooked.[1] However, randai theater is the principal folk performance art found throughout a large area of Sumatra and has been performed and cherished for decades by the Minangkabau, the largest ethnic group in West Sumatra. It is a highly refined dance-drama form, comparable to (better-documented) Southeast Asian theater genres such as the Malay *mak yong,* Thai *likay,* Javanese *ludruk* or *ketoprak,* or the Philippine *komedya.*

Randai theater—until recently an all-male tradition—is a unique blend of martial arts, dance, folk song, instrumental music, and acting. Its most outstanding feature is its close link to the indigenous Minangkabau martial art form called *silek.*

If a visitor today was to come across one of the randai performances that are staged throughout West Sumatra, he or she would instantly be alerted to the impending event by the commotion created by villagers from the surrounding areas who walk in small groups toward the performance space, chatting animatedly in anticipation of a long night of entertainment. An exciting tapestry of instrumental music played on gongs, horns, flutes, and drums welcomes the spectators and announces to everyone around that the troupe has arrived and a performance is about to start. Once the audience is assembled around the open lot in a tight circle (kids crowding in as close to the center as they are permitted), the performance commences. An even number of dancers, arranged in two rows, enter the performance space with an initial dance consisting of martial arts steps. In this opening dance a transition from the two rows into a circle takes place. The resulting circular martial arts dance is called *galombang* and it is the basis of all following dances. As the first galombang ends, the dancers sit down in a circle. One or two performers step into the center of the circle to sing a greeting to the audience, ask forgiveness in case they should make any mistakes, and announce the story to be performed. Another circular galombang follows, accompanied by an introductory song that sets the mood for the first scene. Then two or more performers step inside the circle to deliver the dialogues of the first scene. The dancers again sit in a circle around the action and quietly watch until, after the last word is spoken, they rise at once at the vocal cue of the leader and perform a different circular dance to a new song. This continues for several hours, with alternating scenes and circular galombang dances, and typically culminates in a major fighting scene through which the conflict that was laid out in the story is resolved. A final closing dance is then performed to a standard tune, indicating the end of the performance. The performers file out of the circle in two rows, the musicians play a closing tune, and the spectators scatter to the nearby food booths and coffee stalls to exchange their views on the story and discuss the skills of the performers, especially their proficiency in the martial art silek.

Silek was seminal to the emergence and development of randai. It still serves as a major topic in randai scripts; and it exercises a continuing influence on randai's current performance features, including staging, costumes, music, acting, and most important, movement repertoire. Since martial arts are a prominent feature of randai and are also part of many other theater arts throughout Asia, an examination of the relationship between martial arts and theater in randai is relevant in the larger context of Asian performance studies. The fact that the martial arts have played a crucial role in the development and shaping of randai and are still prominently featured as part of each performance today makes randai stand out among the performing arts of Asia and invites comparison with other martial arts related theater forms such as Indian *kathakali,* Javanese *sandiwara,* or Thai *khon.*

As a matrilineal society, the Minangkabau have been the subject of many anthropological studies. These, however, have not been extended to include a look at the fascinating performance arts that have developed as an outward expression of the unique traits of this ethnic group, a look that might likely enrich the understanding of the Minangkabau from an anthropological point of view. The fact that randai was until recently an all-male tradition linked to the indigenous martial arts is a case in point. The traditional matrilocal social structure and the segregation of living quarters into the *rumah gadang* for women and the *surau* for unmarried men most likely furthered the practice of silek and randai as initially all-male activities which were practiced in the proximity of the surau. The fact that living arrangements have slowly been changing over the past 30 years and female and male spheres of influence have begun to overlap more is reflected in the way randai now integrates female performers.

The following chapters present randai as a living performing art of the Minangkabau and focuses on its relationship to silek. I therefore include an examination of silek, especially its training methods, techniques, and aesthetics, and investigate how they influence randai. Randai itself is then presented in all its key elements including scripts, staging, costume, music, acting, and dance —again, with highlights on the influences of silek on each of these features.

In addition, a brief survey of active groups will be included to provide an overview of the current state of randai in regard to group composition, repertoire, and performance schedules. In this context the emerging role of women in randai is also addressed. The phenomena of their recent integration into this formerly all-male tradition and their rising importance as active performers might shed light on changes in the Minangkabau society.

In a sense, we are witnessing changes in randai that reflect changes in the society as a whole. The integration of women is just one aspect of this change. Other changes are related to the spreading of modern life styles and urbanization. These developments in turn influence the creation of new scripts dealing with issues of modernization, the political situation in Indonesia, and the conflicts between traditions or customs (adat) and modernity. Modern technology and staging methods are altering randai performances in a very real sense. Staging methods move away from the traditional open-air, level, circular performance space to a raised, roofed, single-focus, proscenium stage. The ever-increasing reliance on electronic amplification alters performance values and aesthetics and puts pressure on troupes to adjust to their new dependence on technology.

Despite all these changes and outside influences, randai seems to be able to persevere and preserve its traditional link to the Minangkabau culture, to a large extent through its strong bond with silek.

The Minangkabau People

The densely populated central highlands of West Sumatra are the original home of the Minangkabau people, the largest ethnic group on this westernmost island of the Indonesian archipelago. Ethnically they are Deutero-Malays, a subdivision of the Malay ethnic group that populates a large area from the Malay peninsula to the eastern islands of Indonesia. Their language, Bahasa Minang, is part of the western division of the Austronesian language group, closely related to Bahasa Malayu and Bahasa Indonesia. The Minangkabau comprise the second largest matrilineal society in the world and at the same time are devout Muslims, at fact that has invited much interest and debate among scholars.[2]

The name Minangkabau, according to a popular folk legend, is derived from the words *menang* (to win), and *karabau* (water buffalo). According to this folk etymology, when the Javanese under Adityawarman invaded the island of Sumatra in the middle of the fourteenth century, the Minangkabau struggled to retain their autonomy. At one point in the ensuing war, the opposing military leaders decided to let two *karabau* fight to determine the victor. The Javanese selected the strongest bull they could find, whereas the clever Minangs devised a trick. They starved a calf for ten days, then, on the day of the tournament, they mounted a sharp iron point on its nose. The calf, confused and desperate for milk, charged at the bull, piercing its belly with the iron horn. Thus the Minangkabau won, and named themselves after the victorious water buffalo that aided them in their struggle for autonomy.[3]

Taking tremendous pride in their ethnicity and distinct culture, the Minangs cherish their arts. The cradle of their culture lies in

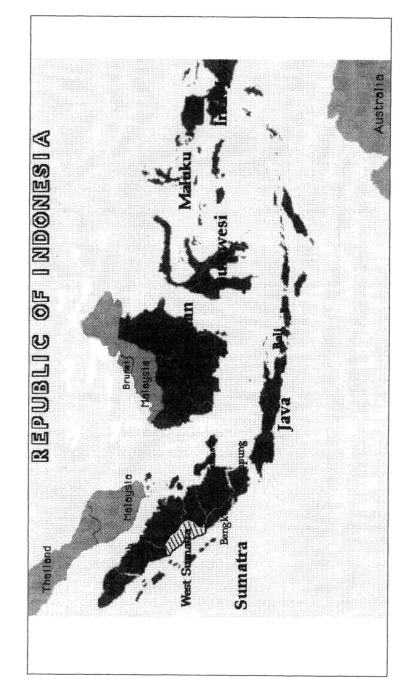

REPUBLIC OF INDONESIA

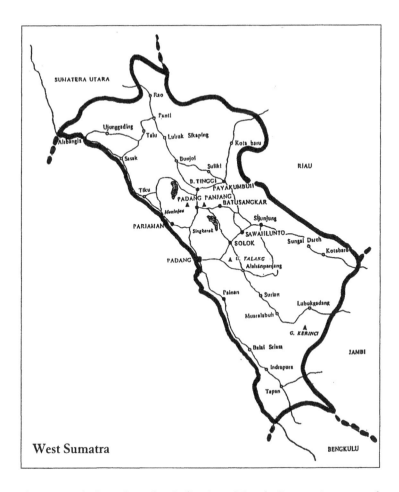

West Sumatra

the original three heartland districts (Tanah Datar, Agam, and Limopuluah Koto), known as *darek* (upland, hinterland). The remaining districts of West Sumatra were in the past considered *rantau* (outer reaches, frontier) but today are part of the Alam Minangkabau (world of the Minangkabau).

A distinguishing feature of the Minangkabau has to do with this rantau. *Merantau* (to go to the rantau) refers to a voluntary and temporary migration. Originally it implied going to the "frontier" areas surrounding the central darek, but increasingly, the destinations for this temporary migration expanded to include other areas of Sumatra as well as parts of the Indonesian archipelago and the Malay Peninsula. Merantau always implies that a return to the homeland is planned.[4]

Merantau is an institutionalized activity primarily for young Minangkabau men. They are required by custom to leave home for a period of time before marriage in order to seek further education, experience, employment, wealth, and, of course, adventure. Success during their travels typically raises their status within the Minangkabau society and improves their prospects of finding a bride upon their return. However, some young men do not return home, but establish permanent settlements abroad (Murad 1980, 34). Merantau is an institutionalized activity so deeply ingrained in the culture that it is a prominently featured topic in most of the indigenous folk arts and is an integral part of almost every randai story.

HISTORICAL BACKGROUND

The Minangkabau are basically a rural society relying on agriculture in the fertile plains of the West Sumatran highlands, and on trade. Evidence of a Minangkabau kingdom can be found in inscriptions as early as the fourteenth century. The Minangkabau kingdom was seen as an expansion of the Malayu kingdom that was founded by Hindu colonists in mainland Southeast Asia around the seventh century A.D. A second source, a poem from 1365 A.D., lists Minangkabau as one of the countries that paid tribute to the Javanese kingdom of Madjapahit under King Adityawarman.[5] Although he lost in the legendary buffalo fight mentioned earlier, the Minangkabau "allowed Adityawarman to become their king as long as he respected their *adat* [customary law]" (Frey 1985, 68). Nominally, the Minangkabau kingdom ruled over all of central Sumatra and collected tribute from the rantau areas of West Sumatra, but the actual power of the ruler was limited. Even before colonization by the Dutch, the kingdom was weakened by internal quarrels, a lack of heirs, and, most important, by the warfare with the Padri movement (fanatical Muslim puritans) set on converting the Minangkabau heartland to their version of Islam, and in the process dividing the region into warring factions. The Dutch appeared on the scene in 1821 and, by allegedly supporting the legitimate authority of the remaining members of the royal family against the Padri, the colonialists gained access to the Minangkabau heartland and subsequently included the Minangkabau lands in their "possession" of the Dutch East Indies. The Minangkabau kingdom formally existed until 1815, when leaders of the Padri sect persuaded members of the royal family and their officers to attend negotiations at Saruaso, where the Padri assassinated most of them. A few escaped and fled to other regions. The last Minangkabau ruler died in 1844 far away from the royal palace, which in the meantime had been burned to the ground. By then, Islam was firmly established in the entire coastal region, and in most parts of the highlands.

The Dutch retained their control over the region, especially over trade, along with the rest of the Dutch Indies until the occupation of Indonesia by the Japanese during World War II. After the war, Indonesia declared its independence on 17 August 1945, but had to endure a prolonged and bloody struggle for almost five years until it finally reached autonomy as a nation. A treaty establishing the Republic of Indonesia as a sovereign nation was signed in 1949. Thus, West Sumatra became one of the twenty-seven provinces comprising the republic, and today is subdivided into administrative units *(kabupaten)* in accordance with the central government in Jakarta. The republic's motto, Diversity in Unity, as part of the national *Pancasila* program is embraced by the Minangkabau. Diversity in Unity is intended to recognize the diverse ethnic groups that live in the Indonesian islands and acknowledge their cultural differences, while at the same time honoring the national unity of the Republic of Indonesia that transcends ethnic differences. Accordingly, the Minangkabau take pride in their unique culture, which is distinct from that of other ethnic groups in Indonesia, and cherish their various traditions and performing arts, including randai.

Adat refers to the indigenous customs and traditions of the Minangkabau.[6] One aspect of adat was mentioned earlier, the custom of merantau, or temporary migration. Merantau is just one of the unique elements of Minangkabau adat; on a larger scale, adat is the foundation of the social and cultural life and dictates relationships between individuals and society. Adat comprises laws and guidelines regulating and prescribing all aspects of life; they are permanently encoded in vast collections of oral literature.[7] These traditional stories *(kaba)*, legends *(tambo)*, proverbs *(pantun)*, and wise sayings *(pepatah-pepitih)* continue to be used to educate and advise the younger generations about adat. Adat prescribes basic life principles that are necessary to help maintain order, balance, and harmony in the community, including the principle of consensus that guides all kin group decision making *(mupakaik)*.[8]

Adat establishes codes for the proper behavior for all members of society: for example, younger members have to obtain permission from their elders before undertaking important activities like going to the rantau. Adat laws outline the relationships among kinship groups (clans, subclans, lineages, and families) and regulate property ownership and inheritance. Adat regulations provide a framework for proper decorum from birth to death. Ceremonies like circumcisions, weddings, installations of lineage heads, and burials follow strict protocols dictated by adat. For all ceremonial gatherings there are set, highly formalized speeches *(pidato)* that celebrate the link between the participants and their ancestors, a bond upheld by the continued practice of the appropriate customs. It is considered essential by the Minangkabau to know one's adat well and behave accordingly.[9] If the bond is broken, the community will fall into chaos. The importance of adat as the fundamental sociocultural fabric that holds the community together is reflected in randai, where adat is the underlying fabric of its plays. The single most distinguishing aspect of adat is the fact that it prescribes a matrilineal and matrilocal social structure. The smallest matrilineal unit is the *sabuah paruik* (one womb), consisting of one female elder, and all her direct descendants, including her brothers and younger sisters. They traditionally live together in one house, the *rumah gadang* (big house). A household is identified by the name of the most senior female of the family. This house and the family compound are owned by the eldest female and upon her death are passed on to her daughters. This practice also applies to the family's land, and a variety of other precious family heirlooms, all of which are considered *harto pusako,* heirlooms that cannot be sold and have to be handed down the female descent line. Women have considerable power in inheritance and ownership of property. Besides being responsible for the day-to-day management of domestic affairs, they also hold essential public, economic, and ceremonial roles of importance (Prindiville 1985; Tanner 1985).[10]

Males derive their importance from their relation to their female relatives.[11] A woman's oldest brother, her *mamak* (uncle), has two functions. To the outside society, he is the family representative; within the family, he shares responsibilities for matters such as the maintenance of the house, compound, and fields, as well as the education of his nieces and nephews *(kemanakan)*. While the uncle has traditionally significant influence in family matters, the father has much less. A husband *(urang sumando)* holds local residence in two places; only at night does he visit his wife, where he is considered a guest of honor. During the day he is expected to function as uncle and be available at his sister's house to assist with work and the education of her children. As husband and father a man remains an outsider to a well-established and strong family unit that is centered around the female descending line. This is not to say that there are no strong emotional bonds between husband and wife or father and children; indeed there are. But if a marriage does not work out, it can easily be terminated by either side.

Although in recent years the traditional rumah gadang has given way to smaller family residences that house subunits centered around one mother and her children, plus the father, the matrilineal social structure remains intact. Property continues to be inherited along the female descending line, as prescribed by adat. In sum, despite the fact that Islam in now the major religion of the Minangkabau people, adat—and with it the matrilineal system— have survived from pre-Islamic times.

In the context of randai theater, however, the traditionally strong role of women is often de-emphasized, and the plays focus more on the roles of men as uncles, fathers, teachers, or religions leaders. Considering that randai was until recently an all-male tradition, this is maybe not too surprising.

RELIGION

Two major religious forces are of importance when considering the Minangkabau: animism and Islam. Animism as the indigenous religion of the Minangkabau has today been largely supplanted by Islam. However, many animistic traits still remain and deserve our attention in the context of the martial arts and the theater.

According to animistic beliefs, each living being, as well as inanimate objects, possesses a spirit or soul, called *semangat*. A complex belief system surrounding these spirits led to the rise of a spirit specialist or shaman, called a *pawang*. The pawang's obligation was to control and appease the spirit world, often with the help of magic. The belief in spirits is still widespread today, as is the belief in the magic powers of individuals. Pawang are still consulted to cure illness, predict the future, influence the weather, and otherwise communicate with the spirit world. However, since Islam has become the dominant religion, many of the spirit beliefs are now condemned as blasphemous and backward. Nonetheless, some of the beliefs in ghosts, spirits, and magic have been incorporated into a more mystic branch of Islam, and pawang often expand their important spiritual positions by incorporating Islamic teachings, especially in the more remote inner highlands of West Sumatra. Randai troupes from these regions typically still have a spiritual guide that ensures the well-being of the troupe. He is responsible for making offerings for favorable weather and for assuring that no black magic will interfere with a performance. He will typically include prayers to both indigenous spirits and Allah.

The advance of Islam into the Minangkabau lands was slow, which might also explain the persistence of older animistic practices. Due to the relative isolation and inaccessibility of the heartland of the Minangkabau culture, Islamization here took a different path than in Java, where the rapid conversion focused on the power center of the royal palace, the *kraton* (Abdullah 1985, 148). In West Sumatra, Islam first took hold in some of the rantau areas along the coast, mainly in the small port towns on the West coast, and via the east coast rivers by seafarers and traders who came from the other parts of the Malay world and from as far away as India. This early formative period of the Islamic tradition concentrated on these coastal regions and had little impact beyond. It eventually spread further inland via the institution of the surau, or men's house. The surau were traditionally an integral part of the matrilineal system, providing young unmarried males of a clan with a place outside their mothers' house, which was reserved for women and children. The communal surau therefore had always been a place of learning for young men, where they were instructed in silek and the rules of adat. It is easy to see how it became a place to study the teachings of the Qur'an as well.

> This was made possible by the fact that, in the early Islamic centuries, Muslim brotherhoods *(tarekat)* had sprung up in response to a popular need for a more intimate communication with God than that provided by the dry legalism of the official doctors of Islam. Devotees of these brotherhoods, called Sufis, concentrated on following the *tarika* (Arabic: path, way) laid down by a teacher of *syekh,* in whose school they gathered, often for many years. These *tarekat* and their schools could fit into the existing *surau* system of the Minangkabau without the least disruption and so become an

acceptable addition to village life in certain villages. (Dobbin 1983, 121)

These small centers of learning had no major impact on the traditional way of life and existed more or less on the fringes of Minangkabau society until the extremist Padri movement spread from the Middle East and penetrated into the Minangkabau hinterland via pilgrims that returned from their hajj to Mecca in the late eighteenth century. With their return and their increasing power more and more of the Alam Minangkabau became engulfed in a violent struggle and was thoroughly Islamicized, often under considerable military pressure from the well-armed and well-trained Padri cadres (Dobbin 1983).

Today, most Indonesians consider themselves Muslims and Islam is the most widespread and dominant of the religions officially recognized by the government of the Republic of Indonesia.[12] Among the many ethnic groups that find themselves a part of the Indonesian state, the Minangkabau are among those who most strictly adhere to Islamic teachings.

The presumable incompatibility and resulting conflicts between Islam and adat have been constant topics of discussion among scholars. However, the two systems continue to coexist.[13] As Abdullah (1966) points out, the Minangkabau society is comprised of many conflicting systems, of which adat and Islam are just two.[14] The effort to harmonize opposing systems and to integrate new influences is in fact a central element of Minangkabau adat itself. It recognizes the continuous need to adapt to change.

Over time, the relationship of adat and Islam has been redefined. The earliest written manuscripts on adat, from the nineteenth century, already incorporate references to Islamic law: they state that "adat is based on propriety, and religion is based on religious law" (adat basandi alur, syarak basandi dalil), implying the mere coexistence of the two systems. Later texts determine that "adat is based on religion, and religion is based on adat" (adaik basandi syarak, syarak basandi adaik). Here, an interdependent relationship is established between two equally positioned systems. The latest aphorism decrees that "adat is based on religion, and religion is based on the Qur'an" *(adat basandi syarak, syarak basandi kitabullah)*. This now attempts to transform adat into an outward expression of the Qur'an (Abdullah 1970, 12). At the same time, it legitimizes the continued importance of adat from the viewpoint of Islam.

These transformations and changes in the relationship between adat and Islam are also reflected in other aspects of Minangkabau culture. An example is that silek, the indigenous art of self-defense, originated well before the arrival of the first Muslims. However, in an effort to integrate Islam into the foundations of Minangkabau society, some of the first Islamic teachers are now credited with introducing this martial art form into Sumatra.

CHAPTER 2

ORIGIN AND HISTORICAL DEVELOPMENT OF RANDAI

THIS CHAPTER introduces the reader to various conflicting origin theories of randai and outlines why the theory that pinpoints silek as the origin is the most plausible. It then traces the further development of randai from its humble silek origin into a full-fledged dramatic genre and looks at some of the more recent influences and significant changes that have occurred. As with other theater forms in Southeast Asia, these important changes are the emergence of female performers and the impact of modernization.[1]

Origin Theories

Three distinct indigenous folk arts predate the emergence of the composite art form randai: martial arts, storytelling, and song-dance. Since the first record of a randai performance in its current dramatic form dates from 1932 (Nor 1986, 18), no details about its emergence out of the other art forms prior to the 1930s are known for certain. Three major schools of thought exist: one claims song and dance, one storytelling, and one silek as the point of origin.

According to the first theory, one supported by local practitioners, *tari ilau* (mourning dance) is a possible origin for randai. Nicknamed *embryo-randai* by local scholars (Maadis 1988), tari ilau is a dance accompanied by mourning chants prevalent in the Solok district of West Sumatra. It was said to have originated during the burial ritual for the first legendary ancestor of one of the two original Minangkabau clans. The chants and the slow circular dance are done exclusively by women. A single singer is seated in the center of the circle, chanting the song of mourning. The dancers move around her with slow steps, and they clap and yell out periodically while stamping their feet. According to the leader of the few remaining groups who perform tari ilau, this form has always been done by women and at some point in history it inspired men to do a similar dance using movements with which they were familiar, silek moves. Supposedly, the male version eventually developed into randai, while the female version remained virtually unchanged.

No other specific details can be found, and, at best, this theory is fragmentary. It gives no explanation for the fact that only the male version developed further while the female did not, and it lacks an account of how exactly the song lyrics were modified into dialogue form.

According to the second origin theory, the art of storytelling was the starting point for the evolution of randai, while silek and dance were added later. *Bakaba* (storytelling) or *sijobang*[2] (sung narrative poetry of one specific Minangkabau epic) is the single most prominent art form in the Payakumbuh region of Limopuluah Koto. According to this theory, sijobang originally featured a single, seated male storyteller singing narrative poetry. He was accompanied by a *rebab* (or, in its most simple form, by a box of matches which he rapped and shook to accentuate high points in the story). It is postulated that at some point in time the storyteller included one or more of his disciples in the delivery of the sung narration and so the dialogue form was born. Then the music became more elaborate and other instruments were added. According to the local legend, the narrators eventually became bored with sitting and merely telling a story, so they got up to enact the scenes. Then, looking for additional visual elements to enhance their performances, they included circular dances.

This second theory is also somewhat fragmentary and not convincing. It does not explain the complete disappearance of the rebab from the randai once it was fully developed, and it offers no explanation for the silek moves used in the circular galombang dance.

The third theory claims that randai evolved out of silek.[3] To teach basic silek moves, many silek masters traditionally employ a circular constellation with an even number of students. In this formation, they all face the inside of the circle and monitor the movements of the leader (a teacher or senior student who is part of the circle) from the corner of their eyes and imitate his moves as closely as possible. Silek is traditionally accompanied by several musicians who sing and play flutes or metal gongs. In the circular formation, this underlying musical accompaniment especially helps the students to move in time and closely follow the teacher's rhythm. Once the students become proficient in the basic movements of this circular form, they advance to a more mystical level, known as *dampeang* or *dampeng*,[4] a circular martial arts dance that promotes the enhancement of their sixth sense or premonition, and serves as the foundation for the aestheticized martial arts movements employed in randai.

> *Dampeng* dancers entered into a state of trance during which they were able to perform abnormal physical feats which made the display more exciting and impressive. Especially in pre-Muslim times (and also to a degree since Islam became the dominant religion), it was believed that dancers in a state of trance were able to contact the spirits, especially the spirits of the ancestors, for the sake of obtaining clairvoyance and spirit blessings for the common good and to avert calamities from happening. (Kartomi 1981, 15)

Dampeang dance with such mystical quality can still be found in the coastal Pariaman area.[5] Dampeang in Pariaman is based on the martial arts styles that prevail in this region, mainly the *ulu ambek* style (which in itself is one of the more mystical and secretive martial arts) and the *silek mangguang* style.[6]

Circular martial arts dance dampeang, also called randai ulu ambek. *Here performed during the Pauleh Tinggi Ceremony in Sicincin, Pariaman. (Photo by Edy Utama.)*

Another dampeang dance during the Pauleh Tinggi. The teacher in the foreground initiates a new movement sequence with a vocal cue. (Photo by Edy Utama.)

The songs that traditionally accompanied the dampeang contained lyrics honoring nature, ancestor spirits, and brave martial arts masters. Over time these lyrics became more elaborate and incorporated other preexisting Minangkabau stories *(kaba)* that told of ancestors, warriors, and heroes. With this inclusion, one further significant step was taken toward a more complex form of randai.

Another crucial addition to this nondramatic martial arts dance came when some members reputedly stepped inside the circle to enact a fighting scene described in the song lyrics.[7] During this enactment, the other members stopped their silek dance and sat down to watch in a formation that is now the basic spatial composition of randai acting scenes. After the fighting scene, they resumed the circular martial arts dance. Over time, other scenes (besides fighting scenes) were also acted out. But even in these nonfighting scenes, the actors used silek moves. In the beginning of this new development, the story was still told by the singers, but the actors quickly took over and transformed the narratives into simple dialogue sections. While the mystical quality of dampeang diminished, the composite dramatic form of randai supposedly emerged as a more secular form of entertainment.

Also, at that time, the silek participants were still all male, so the chosen stories logically centered around the adventures of male heroes and villains. Progressively the stories became more complex and additional preexisting folk tales and stories were incorporated. Female roles became necessary but were enacted by males. Chosen for their beauty and grace, these actors became known as *bujang gadih* (boy girls). This tradition can still be seen today, although the number of all-male groups is declining rapidly.[8]

This third origin theory seems the most substantial and convincing. It gives a believable account of the evolution of movement from silek to dampeang to the circular dances in randai.[9] Most importantly though, the name *randai* itself was associated with the circular martial arts dance (interchangeably with dampeang) as early as 1891 and possibly much earlier, before complex stories (kaba) or dramatic elements were incorporated. The term *randai silek* is still today used to describe the circular martial arts practice formation. Additionally, the word *randai* is believed to have derived from *berhandai-handai* (to be intimate, be friends with), a concept central to the group practice of silek (Harun 1992, 72). Another theory suggests that *randai* traces its meaning to *barandai* (to dance in a circle), also lending credibility to the theory that movement, and not storytelling, was the starting point of randai.

Further Development

Although the two other folk forms, storytelling and folk songs, cannot convincingly be traced as the origin of randai, they nonetheless played an important role in the formative stages of randai. A specific type of folk singing, a tradition called *saluang jo dendang* (flute and song), was especially influential. Exactly when this musical tradition was incorporated into the silek dance randai is unknown. However, it is believed that it was easily incorporated into the circular formation by allowing a group of three performers (two singers and a flute player) to enter the center of the randai circle to accompany the silek movements of the dancers, thus broadening the audience appeal and adding a more refined musical quality to randai.[10]

It is reasonable to assume that by the turn of the century, randai in its basic form consisted of circular martial arts dances, poetic storytelling, and songs. Possibly a simple form of acting and dialogue was also already part of it.[11]

Another major advancement of the form was then made possible through an outside influence. The Malay *bangsawan* comedy appeared throughout Sumatra and Java at the beginning of the twentieth century. It was introduced via itinerant troupes from Malaysia (Harun 1992, 77) and became instantaneously popular with local audiences in Indonesia. Consequently, it spurred the development of local theater forms (mainly ludruk and sandiwara in Java) in an attempt to imitate and localize this popular import.

Quickly becoming a popular folk entertainment in the West Sumatra region as well, bangsawan is believed to have influenced the further development of randai, especially its acting style. The first documented randai performance with bangsawan elements was given in 1932 in Payakumbuh (Nor 1986, 18–19).

Despite the increasing dominance by the Dutch colonial forces, randai thrived in the thirties under the patronage of the village elders and lineage heads. Frequently, these performances included covert satire and commentary ridiculing and criticizing the Dutch, whose continued presence in West Sumatra was increasingly opposed by the Minangkabau. Under the brief Japanese occupation in the early 1940s randai was suppressed, together with most theatrical activity, when gatherings of large groups of people became illegal. Starting with the Indonesian liberation period following World War II, randai regained some foothold in the village communities. It was again supported by village elders and tied into the traditional community life styles. Randai groups were invited to perform at harvests, weddings, inaugurations of lineage heads, and similar communal events.

A new source of support and at the same time a major outside influence appeared after Indonesia gained its independence from the Dutch. In the long struggle to attain national unity among the many ethnic groups that now comprise the Republic of Indonesia, performing arts all over the archipelago were used by government officials as a tool to educate the populace, and randai was no exception.[12]

Advance of Female Performers

Another major change came in the middle to late 1960s, when female performers started to act the female roles. This was a result of at least three separate developments.

First, female performers had long been popular as folk singers in the art form saluang jo dendang, which was adapted into randai.

More and more female singers started to sing in randai, replacing or complementing the male singers, and bringing with them a new repertoire. Once women were part of a randai company, the move from singing to acting one of the female roles became possible. In this manner, dendang singers are believed to have become the first female actresses of randai.[13]

Secondly, this development was, if not openly welcomed, at least quickly accepted by the religious leaders who had condemned the phenomenon of the female impersonator (bujang gadih) as a perversion. According to Islamic practice in West Sumatra, public performances by women were similarly condemned; however, female actresses grew more and more popular and replaced the female impersonators in many groups.[14] Today, very few all-male troupes are left; audiences have grown to expect female actresses.[15]

A third reason for the advance of women in randai can be found in the fact that the new Indonesian government established academies for the performing arts, open to both male and female students, throughout the archipelago, and in Sumatra these schools started to teach regional folk arts, including randai. For the first time, females were allowed to learn and practice all aspects of randai. Together with other government messages and rules about the equality of men and women, the acceptance of female performers in randai rose further. At the same time, silek schools started to accept female practitioners, permitting them to learn the movement skills necessary to perform in the galombang martial arts dance in randai. As a result, almost half the troupes today include female galombang performers.

The inclusion of female performers has been a slow process, one that is continuing today. But all-male troupes with female impersonators are almost extinct. Of 181 active randai troupes I surveyed in 1994, all but two now include female performers, although many of them had been all-male in the past.[16] In most of these formerly all-male groups, women became members during the 1980s. This seems to contradict the fact that the move toward including women started in the late sixties and should have had its greatest impact in the seventies. However, most of the groups from that period are no longer in existence, and therefore are not accounted for in the current statistics. It might also indicate that the seventies were still a transitional phase, with groups waiting to see what the general tendency would be. Once the female performers were received positively by the audiences, groups formed in the 1980s recruited more and more girls to learn randai.

Randai's Response to Modernization

Randai throughout its history has always readily adapted to changes in society, such as the occupation by the Dutch and the Japanese as well as the new challenges posed by the formation of the Indonesian State after World War II. Randai today is faced with the impact of Western popular culture, especially its films and television programs that are seen by larger and larger audiences in Indonesia.

In response, performers and troupe leaders seem to feel the need for more "realism" in their performances, as evidenced by many subtle and not so subtle changes over the last ten years. One indication of this increase in "realism" is the growing preference for women acting in female roles. Troupes also incorporate a more realistic acting style; for instance, actors and actresses actually shed tears instead of expressing their sadness through a song. While the more traditional randai performances used highly stylized movement and speaking styles, the more "realistic" versions eliminate the silek moves or restrict them to the fighting scenes. Often, some of the stylized rhyming proverbs are replaced or supplemented with outbreaks of realistic sobs, curses, and ad-libbed phrases to express highly emotional states.

Another Western influence has changed the acting and speaking style of randai: the advance of modern technology. Almost all groups today use microphones and amplifiers. Since these microphones are hand-held, they limit the performers in their use of gesture and body movement. And although they allow the performers to project their voices farther and to play to larger audiences, vocal training is increasingly neglected. Most performances have to be canceled if the electricity supply fails because none of the performers today have the vocal skills necessary to perform without a microphone.[17] Limited in their movement range, leashed by rather short microphone cables, the performers often merely stand in one spot delivering their lines. Often a group can afford only one microphone, so the performers have to hand it back and forth frequently, which again interferes with the smooth flow of the dialogue. Many performers feel handicapped by the microphones and even frequently joke about it within the performance.[18]

CHAPTER 3

THE MARTIAL ART SILEK

As we have seen, silek is the most plausible origin of randai theater, and randai continues to feature silek elements prominently in its current performance. Randai performers are required to be proficient in silek, and typically practice both forms actively (see graph 8 in appendix A). A silek master is a leading member of each randai group as trainer, supervisor, and choreographer. Often the silek practice location also serves as a rehearsal space for randai. For these reasons, a description and analysis of the silek traditions in West Sumatra will be included here to familiarize the reader with the most important characteristics and concepts of the Minangkabau martial arts. To appreciate the performance features of randai, it is necessary to be familiar with the movement repertoire and training methods employed in silek. To further clarify the strong presence of silek as the underlying foundation of randai, I include a brief orientation of the basic philosophical and aesthetic concepts of silek and its close link to magic.[1]

Silek Styles and Their Origin

The art of silek is ubiquitous in West Sumatra. Almost all villages, down to the smallest hamlets, have their own silek organizations, referred to as *aliran* (school), each headed by a *guru silek* (martial arts teacher). There are many different indigenous styles throughout West Sumatra.[2] Hiltrud Cordes lists a total of seventy-eight styles, and classifies ten of them as major styles according to wide distribution (1990, 92–95). These are *kumango, lintau, silek tuo, sitaralak, harimau, pauh, sungai patai, luncua, gulo-gulo tareh,* and *silek baru.* According to my findings, we should add *ulu ambek,* a style dominant in the entire coastal Pariaman area, and well known throughout the entire Minangkabau region. Other styles of silek are found only in small specific locations, often only in one village. In these cases I will refer to them as schools rather than styles. Many of these schools bear only the name of the village or region from which they originated, while others bear fancy names like *harimau lalok* (sleeping tiger), *gajah badorong* (charging elephant), *kuciang bagaluik* (playful cat), or *puti mandi* (bathing princess). Tracing their unique secret style back over many generations most schools pride themselves on being very different from and better than the eleven major styles.

The origins of silek cannot be traced sufficiently, due to the lack of written documentation, but one of the most compelling origin theories is that Indian martial arts found their way to Sumatra around the eighth century, during the Srivijaya kingdom.[3] The Minangkabau themselves have their own origin myths that differ greatly from the theories of Western researchers (Cordes 1990; Draeger 1969, 1972; Alexander et al. 1970). Minangkabau origin myths are abundant and colorful, as is often the case in oral traditions. Generally speaking, there are three types of origin myths for silek.[4]

Some schools trace their specific origin back to a historical person, between three to ten generations ago, passing his skills down to sons and grandsons.[5] This often includes information that the original teacher received his skill through some magic power, acquired either while sleeping, after having fainted, or perhaps during a thunderstorm or some other natural disturbance.

Other schools, citing the epic origin myth of the Minangkabau people, credit the two legendary ancestors with the invention and development of silek. A third frequently heard origin myth is based in religion. Some silek teachers credit Adam, or Cain and Abel, or even the Archangel Gabriel with the invention of silek.[6] Then, the story goes, they passed it on in some mysterious way to one of the ancestors of a specific aliran. Often, they employed the same device of sleep-teaching, fainting spells, and other magical devices. One can see how these devices can easily be linked to the more indigenous origin myths mentioned above in an attempt to connect Minangkabau history and Islam. This religious origin myth highlights the strong desire of the teachers to synthesize and to weave a historical tapestry that connects religion and Minangkabau history and legends about martial arts. In many villages, one location, the communal surau, is used for teaching the Qur'an and silek. The surau was traditionally the place where boys slept once they became too old to live with their mother's family. In the surau they were taught silek, and after the arrival of Islam the surau was converted into a part of the mosque that now serves a multitude of community functions, including Qur'an lessons and silek and randai training.

Training Methods

The training settings for silek and randai are closely linked. Almost all randai groups expect proficiency in basic silek as a prerequisite for joining the group and also expect that members continue their silek training actively and regularly.[7] This silek practice is the foundation of randai dance training.

Silek sessions take place in the *sasaran,* an open, empty space either in front of the surau building, close to the teacher's house, or in some other communal space. Training is almost exclusively held at night, after the *magrib* (evening prayer) and dinner around eight o'clock, and lasts for two to three hours—sometimes until after midnight.[8] Most practice sessions are held in very dim light, often only relying on moonlight, a small gas lamp, or a single ten-watt lightbulb. This is not done for lack of stronger lights, but to train the eye as well as the intuition (or inner power). Often there will be village elders around the training ground, casually chatting and playing music, mainly *talempong* (hand-held metal gongs) and *saluang* (bamboo flutes).[9]

Training typically includes none of the warm-ups known in other Asian martial arts. In silek, two partners of approximately the same physique and level of skill are paired and start "playing" (*main silek* is the standard term used for the training; *main* meaning "to play"). All this takes place under the close scrutiny of the teacher. Normally, only one pair plays at a time, while the other students watch. Before starting, each pair goes through a standard opening ceremony that includes bows and stylized greetings, first toward the teacher and then toward each other. Then they start with the basic silek steps. Depending on the level of their skill, they will remain with the basics, often being interrupted and corrected by the teacher, or they will move on into a more advanced freestyle exchange of techniques. After ten to twenty minutes they stop, and go through another greeting ceremony that consists of the same elements as the opening greeting, but in reversed order. Then a new pair comes up to the practice ground. The atmosphere during practice is normally relaxed; strenuous physical activity is not considered a high priority, nor is it indicative of effective training.

All aliran have slightly different training schedules, but most of them meet regularly several nights per week. It is up to the students as to how frequently they participate. Often, they only come to the practice to watch. The average time considered necessary to learn the basics of silek is between six and eight months. To develop a solid foundation, a student must train regularly for two to three years; and to become a *pandeka* (master), one has to train for at least fifteen years. Although silek was traditionally practiced by males only, today many aliran are open to females as well. A female student will always be paired with another female, never with a male student, because physical contact between the sexes in considered improper; nonetheless, the male teacher often functions as training partner for both.

For the training most students wear normal street clothing or the traditional silek outfit that consists of *galembong* (black long trousers), *taluak balango* (long-sleeved black shirt), and the *deta* (batik head wrap). In addition, a complete outfit includes a *sampiang* (batik hip sash). Very often, the students wear the galembong with only a regular shirt or T-shirt during practice.[10] For more formal occasions (joint training with other aliran, performances, or when visitors are present) the full costume is worn.

The learning process involves observation and imitation, as well as physical correction of the position or execution of a movement. Rarely does a teacher explain a technique or an underlying concept to the student during practice.[11] However, after the training is over, most students linger around the teacher for quite some time, and he will often relate proverbs and tell jokes or anecdotes related to silek.

Students practice the same basic moves over and over again in several steps. First they merely watch the senior students and the teacher. Then they imitate the teacher, who executes the movements close to the students. Several aliran use a circular formation to simultaneously teach several students the basic steps. The teacher will be one of the circle members and all students glance at him from whatever angle is possible from their different positions, following his moves closely. Direct eye contact is discouraged; instead, the students are encouraged to use their peripheral vision and intuition to pick up the teacher's movements. Often the teacher uses vocal cues or other sound cues, called *tapuak,* to indicate a change of direction or a new step. For this he claps his hands *(tapuak tangan)* or slaps his leg with one hand *(tapuak galembong).*[12]

At a more advanced level, the student and his or her partner are on their own, with no visual guidance; they have to remember the techniques and rely on each other to complete the sequence. At this level the teacher will often interrupt the sequence and give corrections. When he feels that both students have sufficiently grasped the technique and are able to remember it, he will move on and demonstrate a new sequence. Once students have learned the basics, they are encouraged to practice with other partners as well, thereby learning to adjust to a different anatomy, behavior and level of skill each time.

At this point, the students will be encouraged to "play continuously" *(main terus-menerus)*. The basic strategic concept in this training is *garak-garik,* best translated as "appropriate action and reaction." As in chess, each new move has to be considered in relation to possible reactions. Each partner has several options at all times and has to consider the most effective one. One tries to anticipate the possible reactions of the partner and manipulate him into positions where he has fewer and fewer good options to move. The game ends when one partner can no longer respond with a technique and is stuck in a position without an option to get out; he then is declared *mati* (dead). The better and the more equally skilled the students are, the longer this kind of game can go on. In addition, unlike in chess, the timing of each move is crucial. Each move has to be fast and precise and must come as a surprise, otherwise the partner can anticipate and intercept the action before it is fully executed.

Once students have reached a high level of physical skill and are considered worthy of the teacher's trust, the teacher will call students to him one at a time to give each a specific and personal technique. While giving a student this secret, the teacher might recite mantras and prayers to insure that the technique will be used only in self-defense and will be successful. Another level of training includes sending the student into the forest on his own to meditate, conquer his fears, and survive for several days on his own. Another less threatening way of exposing students to outside forces is to let them participate in joint training sessions and tournaments with other aliran. However, this is a recent development, and during these meetings all participants are reminded not to show their best techniques, because they might be learned by outsiders. Mutual friendly suspicion seems to prevail. At the highest level a student can learn powerful techniques. The most feared are *gayueng angin* (hit by the wind), long-distance magic techniques that can be fatal, and *kebal,* a kind of inner strength that makes the person invulnerable.

Techniques and Strategies

The circular martial arts dance and the fighting scenes in randai rely on silek techniques that are generally referred to by the same names in both art forms.[13] The foundation of all silek moves are the steps called *langkah.* Each new student must master the basic steps before any other technique is taught. The first step instantly brings the practitioner from the neutral upright standing position into the basic stance of silek. Placing the left foot forward and the right foot backward he will glide into a low horse stance called *kudo-kudo,* the signature stance of silek. In this stance, the feet are about two shoulder widths apart, the left foot pointing forward, and the right turned to the outside at 45 to 90 degrees (depending on the style). The knees are bent and the weight is mostly on the back foot. Some styles emphasize an extremely low stance in which most of the weight is on the rear foot and the practitioner seems to be hovering just barely above the ground; other styles prefer a higher stance with the weight more evenly distributed onto both feet.

In both versions, the torso is slightly bent forward at the waist, the right arm is extended forward in a soft inward curve at shoulder level, the left arm is held close to the body in a bent, guarding position. The head is straight, with the eyes not focused on any particular point, but rather taking the entire environment in through

A silek student demonstrates a light-footed stepping technique. The right arm shields the torso. Style: kumango.

A silek teacher demonstrates how to glide into a kudo-kudo stance. Style: bungo.

peripheral vision. This basic stance is used in the greeting and the stylized opening in which both partners step around each other and the training place before any advances or physical contact between them occur. Depending on the style, this opening sequence can include three, four, nine, or twelve such steps. Most schools classify themselves as belonging to either the *langkah tigo* (three steps), *langkah ampek* (four steps), *langkah sambilan* (nine steps), or *langkah duo-baleh* (twelve steps) styles. But some schools may use more than one langkah style depending on the context. The variations with just three of four steps are used for self-defense or in practice sessions where both partners step around each other between attacks. The more elaborate step variations are often found in the opening of performances of silek and in fighting scenes within randai.

To move from one stance to the next, the weight is smoothly shifted onto the front foot, while the back foot is lifted off the ground. Often the practitioners will remain poised on one leg, before committing to a direction with the next step. This position is generally not considered a stance like the solid kudo-kudo, but a transitory station. It is called either *pitunggua,* if the lifted foot is slightly in front of the supporting leg, or *tagak itiak,* if the raised foot is tucked behind the bent knee of the supporting leg. In silek, especially in self-defense, both versions are very brief, whereas in performance contexts and in randai they feature prominently and are held for longer periods to display the skill of the performers at keeping their balance. This is especially difficult on the uneven natural terrain on which silek and randai are customarily performed. In addition, silek masters often perform this technique on top of broken glass or ceramic pieces, where they balance for several seconds, with all their weight on one foot.

The second basic stance besides the kudo-kudo is called the *gelek.* This stance is most easily reached directly from the kudo-kudo by merely twisting the upper body quickly from one side to the other and by shifting the center of weight of the entire body toward the front while the feet stay in place. The importance of the

A silek teacher demonstrates a fast turn into the cross-legged gelek stance. Style: silek tuo.

gelek is that it closes the body against a possible attack through the twist, and the front arm can easily execute a block or parry. In many styles this stance is even lower than the kudo-kudo.

A characteristic quality of all stepping techniques in silek is that they are executed very lightly and carefully, primarily to maintain agility and the ability to quickly position oneself for attack or defense movements. Also, the practitioners are never permitted to look at the ground as this would distract them from the opponent. Therefore they have to explore the terrain with their feet, scanning it for obstacles like roots, rocks, or crevices. "We have to see with our feet," as one proverb of the *kumango* style aptly describes this technique called *pijak baro* (light step).

Jurusan (partner drills) are standardized attack-defense sequences that are also used in the fighting scenes in randai. They differ from school to school, but some shared foundations can be outlined here. For practice purposes, both partners assume different ready stances depending on who will execute the attack. The designated attacker will take a high stance with the left foot forward and the right hand in a cocked preparatory position *(sikap pasang)* to indicate whether he will attack with a punch or strike.

Two silek students engage in a jurusan (partner drill). The student on the left has just attacked with a punch; his partner counters with a wrist lock and a kick to the knee of the attacker.

Most schools use four basic initial attacks: a straight fist punch *(dorong)*, a strike with the hand blade aiming for the temple or neck coming in on a curve *(cokak rambah)*, a strike onto the top of the head coming down in a straight line *(cancang)*, and a front kick aiming at the center of the body *(antam)*. The defender will assume a different stance, either the kudo-kudo, exposing his center by opening both arms horizontally and offering the attacker his torso as a target, or a totally upright, neutral position. In either position he has to be aware of the body parts that are most likely to be targeted for an attack. As soon as the attacker initiates the attack, the defender has to decide on one of two main defensive options: moving either to the outside of the attacking limb or to the inside. In both cases he will use the basic turning step, the gelek. This initial decisive move dictates what subsequent countertechniques he will be able to use. Beginners are first generally taught to move defensively to the outside, which is considered a safer position in regard to a possible follow-up attack by the second hand of the attacker. After the first evasive move to either side of the attacker, the defender will attempt to apply a lock or hold on the attacker, rendering him immobile and thereby ending the attack. If the lock or hold is not sufficiently effective, the attacker will continue to attack with different techniques, until a final lock is reached.[14] The typical jurusan is always ended with a defensive hold, pin, or lock, or with an evasive move, never with an attack technique.

A practice session consists of several jurusan, typically starting with a simple type and progressing toward more complex and difficult variations. The basic pattern normally starts with a straight fist attack and consists of only two or three follow-up techniques, while the more advanced sequences are longer and include more difficult kicks and often ground techniques.

The ground techniques are considered the most difficult. Moving on hands and feet, the practitioners have to assume and emulate the fluidity and quality of animal movements to move smoothly and effortlessly. Masters of most styles (with the exception of *ulu ambek*)[15] claim that the ground position is actually superior, and gives the practitioner better control over the situation than a standing position. This becomes clear when one sees how effortlessly these silek masters move low to the ground, and how easily they can throw an opponent off balance through a leg sweep from underneath. In randai fighting scenes these low ground techniques are prominently featured.

Philosophical and Ethical Principles

Fighting scenes in randai not only display silek techniques but also their underlying philosophy and ethics. Virtuous fighters in randai performances function as bearers of these values. Generally, each teacher has his own unique interpretation and philosophy about the appropriate ethics and aesthetics of silek. The most consistent and recurring aspects concern the defensive nature of this martial art, and the ultimate achievements and qualities of a true master.

The most important aspect of silek, one that is universally emphasized, is its defensive character. Silek may only be used to defend oneself or others in case of an attack, never to harm or coerce a nonaggressor, to gain power, or merely to impress others. This is expressed in one of the many proverbs about silek: "I do not seek trouble, but if I am met by an adversary, I shall not run away."[16] The movement structure of silek is sometimes interpreted as reflecting this philosophy of nonaggression. The *langkah ampek* (first four steps) have to be purely defensive movements consisting of blocks or parries.[17] Only if an aggressor attacks a fifth time is the defender allowed to use a counterattack with a strike or kick. Should there be a sixth attack, he is allowed a more lethal technique to actually stun or even kill the attacker.

The langkah ampek also have religious and philosophical significance. Generally, the first four steps of any silek practice are intended to honor four entities in the following order: Allah, ancestors, elders, and teachers. This greeting is repeated in randai, where the first actor to enter the circle executes the langkah ampek to show respect toward the four entities that are part of the audience.[18]

Students are reminded that before a physical confrontation ensues, they should attempt to deflect a potentially dangerous situation verbally. This is referred to as *silek lida* (martial arts of the tongue). This practice is also present in randai, where the hero typically tries (in vain) to reason with the aggressors before he resorts to physical fighting techniques.

Aesthetics

In randai, silek is transformed into theatrical scenes and into circular martial arts dances, and it is, therefore, subject to aesthetic evaluation. In silek itself, however, aesthetic concepts are also at work, although on a different level. In silek, the beauty and function of movements are interrelated. Because silek is foremost an art of self-defense, only an effective technique is considered aesthetically pleasing. However, silek is also practiced and perceived as a performance art, and therefore secondary aesthetic values exist that relate not to its function but to its appearance. However, these primary and secondary values frequently overlap, and both sets of aesthetic values are applied simultaneously. Generally, the secondary values are the ones adopted by randai, where appearance dominates function.

When asked how to define a well-executed silek technique, most teachers list the following nine qualities: effectiveness, precision, control, speed, focus, balance, effortlessness, light-footedness, and fluidity. Generally, the first five are most important in relation to a technique's function, the last four are more relevant for the outward appearance. All nine qualities are mandatory in either context; only the ranking of importance is different. For example, effectiveness is most crucial in self-defense; without this quality silek cannot serve its purpose, even if all the remaining eight qualities are present. To render a technique effective, obviously one has to execute it without losing one's balance or focus, so it is clear that all nine qualities are tightly interrelated. All teachers claim that a well-executed technique looks beautiful and feels good; the aesthetic is both external and internal. The students develop the perception of what is aesthetically correct as well as effective as they observe their senior students and masters.

Magic

As mentioned in the introduction, beliefs in spirits and magic are still widespread in West Sumatra, and many individuals are believed to possess magical powers and to be able to communicate with the spirit world. *Pawang* (shamans) are often silek practitioners as well. To various degrees, all silek styles include the use of magic, called *kebatinan.* Some of the magic practices also exist outside and apart from silek, but here I will examine exclusively those that are found in the context of silek. Generally, magic is not displayed publicly, and access to information about magic practices is very limited. I was very fortunate to be able to witness a rare ceremony of ulu ambek, a martial arts form that relies heavily on the use of magic. In it, the practitioners fight with each other almost exclusively without physical contact. Although they come close to each other in combat, an attack always stops several inches before actually touching. This phenomena is explained as magic coming from an inner power source *(tenaga batin)*, which is achieved through years of meditation, exercise, fasting, and strong faith. This inner strength enables the defender to stop any attack before it can reach his body and do harm. The use of magic is purely defensive, and it may be best described as an invisible shield that the defender creates around his body. Often, a master of ulu ambek can extend this protective shield to include his students or close relatives and protect them against physical harm or black magic intended to manipulate the victim's behavior. During the ceremony I witnessed, the younger performers were protected through the magic shield of their teachers, who sat at the edges of the stage and chanted mantras, thereby transferring some of their magic power to the students.[19]

The knowledge and application of magic *(ilmu batin)* is divided into evil (black) and good (white) magic. The protective shield used by ulu ambek practitioners is classified as white magic *(ilmu putih)*, and so are most other magic practices used within the context of silek. Besides the inner power that can be developed by gifted individuals through meditation, fasting, and exercise, there is also a vast outside power field that some individuals can access. According to pre-Islamic animistic beliefs, this outside field is inhabited by positive and negative spirits that can be called on for help, but this contact with the spirit world is considered dangerous and can only be established by the most proficient masters.

Several silek masters I met were also pawang, or *dukun* (traditional shamans, healers, and masters of *ilmu putih*). Some of their magic abilities included the summoning of spirits of deceased persons who would enter their bodies and speak with their voices. In one case, one dukun claimed to be able to summon the spirit of his ancestor, also a silek master. This spirit could upon request enable him to perform extraordinary silek techniques.[20]

Other magic activities include the fabrication of amulets (jimat), which are given to their students for protection along with mantras. On another occasion, I witnessed the performance of dabuih, the Minangkabau version of a kind of self-mutilation (called dabus in other regions of Indonesia) in which the performer uses a sharp sword to pierce and slash himself and his students, but without inflicting injuries. The performer was a member of the tarikat, a secret mystic brotherhood of Islamic scholars. He claimed that his magic ability was based on his strong faith in Allah. In this incident, pre-Islamic practices and orthodox Islamic beliefs are intertwined. Performances of dabuih also occur in randai, where performers slash themselves or their opponents with a sharp weapon.[21] Magic weapons and magic silek techniques are often portrayed in randai, but are generally theatrical enactment and not truly magic acts because magic techniques are generally kept secret and not displayed publicly for mere entertainment.

Summary

Silek's basic techniques consist of low stances, light and fast steps, and standard partner drill sequences called jurusan, which consist of a series of defense movements made in response to various different attacks. In addition, there are advanced ground techniques. The strategies of silek are based on anticipation, appropriate response, and proper timing. Its most essential ethical principle is that of nonaggression; silek should only be used for self-defense. Aesthetics and function are interrelated, but depending on the context either one can be more dominant. Magic is sometimes employed in the form of highly developed inner strength or through outside forces like spirits or magic weapons.

Silek is one of the main origins of randai, and indisputably the most important one in regard to the evolution of its movement repertoire, its circular formation, and its combat scenes. Silek techniques and aesthetics constitute the foundation of randai's circular martial arts dance and the movements utilized in its fighting scenes. Strategies and basic philosophical concepts surface in the choreography of fighting scenes as well as in the way fighting scenes are incorporated into the larger context of randai plays.

CHAPTER 4

PERFORMERS OF RANDAI

THIS CHAPTER gives an overview over the composition of randai troupes and highlights the various roles and functions that members of a group share. It also includes information on the framework of performances such as the setting, duration, and performance occasions.[1]

Composition of Randai Troupes

There are an estimated 250 active randai troupes in all of West Sumatra.[2] Each randai group is structured according to the functions and obligations of its members (Harun 1992, 78–79). Typically, the group is headed by the *pangkatuo randai,* an elder who no longer actively participates in the performance but who in the past had considerable performance experience. He possesses knowledge about many aspects of the art form; he knows the lines, the songs, the lyrics, the proper execution of the dances, and so forth, and he is consulted regularly concerning changes in or improvement of the performances. The next two important positions are held by specialized teachers: one for the martial arts and dance, the *guru-tuo silek;* and one for the songs, the *guru-tuo dendang.* Like the pangkatuo randai, they teach the active members and normally do not participate in the performance themselves.

All active performers of the randai are generally called *anak randai* (children of randai). Among them several other positions are held by the more experienced performers. The leader of the circular dance (galombang) is the *pambalok galombang* (leader of the circle) who is often also referred to as *tukang goreh* (master of shouts) due to his ability to vocally cue and coordinate the dance. Most frequently a male senior silek practitioner,[3] he guides the dancers, initiating his movements by yelling out syllables like *hep, ta,* and *ai* so that the other performers can synchronize with his movements. Often, two performers share the position of the pambalok galombang, since the frequent and forceful yelling is rather tiring, and often the galombang performers also act in the scenes and cannot rest between dances. Another responsibility of the galombang leader(s) is the choreography and arrangement of any silek fighting sequences within the scenes.

The main singer holds the title *pambalok gurindam* (leader of lyrics) or *tukang dendang* (master of songs) and is often female. Generally she or he is supported by a second singer, called *tukang jajak;* both alternate in singing the verses. The remaining members of the anak randai frequently function as a chorus and join in the refrain of each verse. The remaining leading position is held by the *pambalok curito,* the senior actor or actress. Although not necessarily acting the lead, he or she is nevertheless responsible for the proper delivery of the lines and the acting style.[4] Overseeing the overall routine training is the *pelatih,* the coordinator and practice leader, who is responsible for arranging practice sessions, notifying the members of performance arrangements, and so on. This position is often held by one of the pambalok. In recent times some troupes also have a playwright, who is often one of the actors. New stories are constantly written and old ones are adapted and rewritten.

In addition to the actual troupe members, many groups have an official advisor and protector, in former times normally the *panghulu* (village chief)[5] or a high-ranking *datuak* (head of a lineage). At present, this position is also often given to government officials like a mayor or governor (*kepalo desa* or *camat*). In response to a questionnaire, all but 9 percent of groups stated that they receive support and advice from government officials in their village, district, or even on the provincial level.[6] The most consistent support comes from the village head, and less frequently from higher offices like the district chief, provincial governor, or the local officers of the national Ministry for Education and Culture (DepDikBud; Departemen Pendidikan dan Kebudayaan) and the Ministry of Information (DepPen; Departemen Penerangan).

Another guardian besides the officials or clan elders is the *sipatuang siriah,* a shaman (pawang) and more intimate protector of the troupe. His responsibility is to ensure the safety of the members and the success of their performances. His duties include arranging pleasant weather, inducing benevolent behavior in the audience, and deflecting any black magic that might endanger the troupe.[7] This is especially true for the more traditional troupes from the remote highlands. Troupes from the larger towns in the rantau regions (especially the capital Padang) and troupes sponsored by government offices generally dispense with the shaman, mainly because it would be considered backward. For troupes from the central darek regions, the sipatuang siriah is especially indispensable when a performance is scheduled in a faraway location, where the danger of black magic is believed to be greater than in the home community.

Groups today typically are highly flexible entities. Female members normally stop performing as soon as they are married and take on more responsibilities in their family. Male performers, due to the Minangkabau tradition of merantau, frequently leave to search for adventure, experience, or employment in a different region. Therefore, groups constantly search for and integrate new members. Often, several important members of a group leave, so that the group disbands. Former members then seek other groups, where they replace those that have left for the rantau, or else they form a new group. All this accounts for a highly flexible art form and for vivid exchanges of story material, song melodies and lyrics, silek and dance techniques, and overall performance styles.

Performance Occasions and Duration

Performances today are normally commissioned to celebrate a wide variety of social occasions, which can be divided into four broad categories. The first type of performance occasion is closely linked to adat celebrations. In this context, randai is commissioned by an individual host to entertain guests during private festivities, the most common being weddings and inaugurations of village headmen or clan chiefs (panghulu or datuak). This type of occasion can also include farewell parties for young men leaving for the rantau or welcoming parties when they return. A second type of performance occasion is traditionally linked to larger, seasonal community events, such as planting and harvesting. Here the performances are sponsored by the village chief or by a group of wealthy members of the community. The third type is linked to religious festivals, as when randai performances are commissioned to celebrate Idul Fidri (indicating the end of the fasting month of Ramadan) and other Islamic holidays. The fourth type are typically sponsored by the government and are commissioned for national holidays, such as the Indonesian Independence Day, or other national events, such as National Education Day.

In all these cases, the performances are paid for by a private or community host, and the performance is free to the public. Tickets are sold only when troupes donate their performance for a fundraising event, for instance to collect money for the building of a new communal surau or school building, or the improvement of roads or irrigation systems. Such fund-raising performances go hand in hand with the Indonesian concept of *gotong-royong* (mutual assistance), in which all participants are expected to volunteer their time and labor. Randai performers in this context volunteer their time and entertainment, and the villagers are encouraged to buy tickets and otherwise contribute to the common project. This fund raising through ticket sales is a recent development in both West Sumatra and throughout Indonesia.

Another recent addition to the performance occasions has arisen in the form of randai festivals. Major festivals, with over 150 participating groups, are typically organized every three to five years, smaller ones, with under twenty participating troupes, are put on throughout West Sumatra almost every year.

Depending on the popularity of the individual troupes the frequency of their performances vary greatly. On average they perform once or twice a month, although during seasonal, religious, or national celebrations there tend to be more invitations to perform. Half the troupes surveyed perform once or twice a month. A smaller percentage (18%) perform more than twice a month. A few of these groups are so popular and famous throughout the region that they frequently tour and perform up to three times a week in many different locations (see graph 4 in appendix A).

The duration of performances is flexible, depending on the performance setting, the preference of the host, and other circumstances. About half the performances last between two and three hours, while some last four to five or more (see graph 5 in appendix A). On special occasions, such as the inauguration of a village chief, a performance can extend to a maximum of two or three nights, with each segment lasting over four hours. Popular troupes that frequently go on tour often spend several hours traveling to the site. The artists typically arrive two to three hours before the scheduled performance time, and are served food and drinks by the hosts and have a chance to rest before preparing for the show. After the performance they normally return home, unless they have been performing in a faraway village, in which case the host will be expected to provide sleeping quarters for the artists.

None of the performers is a professional and traditionally troupes are paid very little for their efforts.[8] They receive a small donation to cover their transportation costs, in addition to food, coffee, and cigarettes. Money donations do not go to individual performers, but to the troupe, and are used to buy and maintain costumes and headdresses and, nowadays, to acquire better sound systems.

CHAPTER 5

RANDAI SCRIPTS

BEFORE LOOKING at the individual performance elements, it is helpful to familiarize oneself with the stories which are told through randai.[1] Therefore, this chapter gives a detailed description of the structure, language, and story material of randai scripts. This will facilitate the understanding of the structure of the actual theater performances and the various features, especially the interplay of songs and dialogues. This chapter also outlines how various aspects of Minangkabau culture—especially adat and Islam—are reflected and expressed in different randai scripts.[2]

Structure of the Scripts

A randai script is episodic and loosely structured. The story is arranged into parts that are acted out in dialogue form, and parts that are narrated through the song lyrics, called *gurindam*. This arrangement allows for a highly flexible performance. The content of scenes that cannot be performed for lack of time or because an actor is unavailable can easily be incorporated into song lyrics, so that the sense of continuity is preserved. Also, scenes that are not strictly consecutive can be woven together by the song lyrics.

The following example will illustrate the loose and episodic structure of a randai performance. It is the story of the young man Magek Manandin, who follows an invitation to a gambling tournament and through ill fortune is imprisoned, tortured, and separated from his family. Through the resourcefulness of his fiancée and with good luck, he is rescued and reunited with her and his family. The following detailed synopsis gives a first impression of the distinctly colorful character of a randai play and illustrates the division of the story material into song lyrics (gurindam) and dialogue scenes.

> prelude gurindam:
> We extend greetings to our honored audience and elders. Please forgive us should we make any mistakes, after all we are just children. The story we are presenting for you tonight is *Magek Manandin*.

> gurindam I:
> There were the father and mother of Magek, Datuak Bandaro (Chief Treasurer) and Puti Linduang Bulan (Full Moon Maiden), kind and peaceful rulers in their district. They have two children, Magek Manandin and Puti Bungsu (Youngest Maiden), who is a fair and beautiful girl. In another district, there rules Rajo Duo Baleh (King Twelve), whose younger sister, Puti Nilam Cayo (Fragrant Light Maiden) will soon be of the right age to be married. King Twelve is deep in thought and finally calls his *dubalang* (guard-retainer).

> Scene 1:
> King Twelve summons his guard, Bujang Salamaik, and orders him to organize a gambling tournament to find a fiancé for his sister. The guard obeys and leaves.

> gurindam II:
> Bujang Salamaik goes to carry out the king's orders. After two

months, the festivities are about to begin. The handsome Magek Manandin receives the invitation to the tournament and seeks his father's permission to attend.

Scene 2:

Manandin visits his father and asks his permission to join the tournament. His father is worried that something might happen to the young and inexperienced boy and warns him about the dangers of traveling. Manandin replies that, according to adat, he is obligated to follow the invitation or else his whole family will be disgraced, and that he intends to win at the tournament, thereby bringing good fortune to his family. His father finally grants permission and advises him to respect the adat of the foreign place, to be kind, and to mind his manners. He also instructs Manandin to obtain permission from his fiancée, Puti Subang Bagelang (Maiden with Ornaments). Finally he gives Manandin a beautiful fighting cock and five gold coins, and they bid farewell.

gurindam III:

All is said and permission is granted. Now Manandin is on his way to his true love and fiancée. He rides his tall horse to her house.

Scene 3:

Manandin and his fiancée bid farewell; she is worried and wants to hold him back, but without success. With a heavy heart, she lets him go.

gurindam IV:

The handsome Manandin is on his way, he urges on his horse. Meanwhile, in another part of the forest, three robbers are gathered at Bukit Simpang Tigo (Hill with the Forked Path). Manandin comes closer and finally they meet.

Scene 4:

The three robbers challenge Manandin and demand his clothes and possessions. They act rough to intimidate him, but he tries to convince them that their way of life is wrong. He is unsuccessful and finally they fight. After the robbers are subdued by Manandin, they apologize and vow to become good Muslims. Manandin gives them some cloth and money and lets them go free.

gurindam V:

The robbers have been beaten and beg for mercy, which is granted, along with cloth and money. Manandin continues his journey and finally arrives at the arena. People stare at his handsome face and wonder who he is. He is greeted by the guards.

Scene 5:

The guard welcomes Manandin and brings him before King Twelve. Asked why he comes so late, he explains about the robber attack. The rules of the gambling are explained and then they start the cock fights. Manandin loses.

gurindam VI:

Manandin's luck is abysmal! He has lost at all the games and is left with nothing, even his expensive garments and horse are gone. Embarrassed, he leaves the arena on foot and wanders until night falls. Exhausted, he falls asleep in an empty barn. In the morning, villagers find him and accuse him of having stolen a buffalo. They beat him and bring him before the ruler, King Twelve. In the meantime Manandin's uncle Rajo Kuaso (King Mighty), makes plans to travel.

Scene 6:

King Mighty is in council with Manandin's parents and tells them about his intention to go to Singkarak (where Manandin has already gone) to buy a buffalo for the harvest season. He asks them to look after his daughter Subang Bagalang, their future daughter-in-law, to which they agree gladly.

gurindam VII:

Manandin is in jail, abandoned and starving. In the meantime, his uncle, King Mighty, is about to meet with King Twelve.

Scene 7:

King Mighty meets King Twelve and inquires about a buffalo he wants to buy. King Twelve offers to show him one and presents him with the captive Manandin as a joke. The uncle is shocked and humiliated. Manandin tries to explain the misunderstanding, but the uncle just scolds him for ruining his reputation and drags him home.

gurindam VIII:

The uncle returns home and tells his relatives about Manandin's crime. His fiancée, however, believes he is innocent.

Scene 8:

Manandin's uncle and parents debate what to do. His mother and father want to repay the debt and even things out, but the uncle (who has lost face before King Twelve) ignores their opinion and plans to punish Manandin by imprisoning him in a deep gorge. Manandin bids farewell to his sister and parents and is dragged off by the guards.

gurindam IX:

The fiancée's pet parrot flies unsuccessfully in search of Manandin, who lies bound in a deep gorge.

Scene 9:

King Mighty tells his daughter that her former fiancé is a criminal and that he will instead marry her to King Twelve. She resists, but her father forces her to agree. She summons her parrot again and asks him to search for Manandin.

gurindam X:

The parrot finds Manandin, frees him from the ropes, and consoles him.

Scene 10:

Manandin talks with the parrot about his love for his fiancée and says that she should wait for him.

gurindam XI:

The parrot leaves Manandin, flies out of the gorge, and meets a farmer at the edge.

Scene 11:

As a means to help Manandin out of the gorge, the parrot persuades the farmer to plant a magic palm tree at the edge.

gurindam XII:

The parrot flies away, and the farmer goes to plant the tree. Time passes and the tree's roots grow into the gorge; finally Manandin climbs out along the roots. He meets some strangers on his way and talks to them.

Scene 12:

Manandin asks the strangers where they are going, and they explain that they are on the way to a tournament held to celebrate the upcoming wedding between Subang (Manandin's ex-fiancée) and King Twelve. Not revealing his identity, he asks them about his family and learns that they are still mourning the loss of their son Magek Manandin.

gurindam XIII:

Manandin is sad. He disguises himself as a betel[3] peddler and starts the long journey home. Tired and dirty, he finally reaches a bathing place close by the house of his fiancée. They meet, and, not recognizing him, she is offended by his unkempt appearance and bad smell, and scolds him for trespassing.

Scene 13:

Subang scolds Manandin for entering her private bathing place and orders him to leave. He apologizes, and pretends to be a friend of Manandin. Immediately, Subang becomes friendly and reveals her continuing grief over the loss of her lover. She gives him a poem to deliver to Manandin, if he should ever see him again. Manandin (as the betel peddler) in return claims that he was given a poem for her by Manandin and recites it for her. He tells her not to despair and to wait for her lover, who will come back soon. They part.

gurindam XIV:

Manandin is on his way to his parent's house. He wants to see his sister. She is sitting in front of the house, and he approaches her in disguise.

Scene 14:

Manandin asks his sister about herself and her parents. She answers that they are all still grieving over the loss of Manandin.

gurindam XV:

Manandin leaves his sister and is on the way to the wedding festivities. In the meantime, his ex-fiancée is sleepless and anxious, while the new bridegroom, King Twelve, is happy and excited about the imminent wedding. A wedding parade is heading for Subang's house. Manandin arrives there too, but being dirty and smelly, his appearance is offensive to the other guests.

Scene 15:
King Mighty orders his guards to arrest the filthy stranger who has intruded on his festivities. His daughter calls her maid and prepares to secretly visit the stranger.

gurindam XVI:
Manandin is unlucky again—from the frying pan into the fire. Subang feels ill at ease and goes to see the stranger.

Scene 16:
Subang meets Manandin who has been thrown into a mud pit. She begs him to tell her more about his friend Manandin, because she is ill from longing for him. Manandin reveals his true identity. She rescues him from the pit with the help of the maid. They discuss how they can sabotage her wedding with King Twelve. She decides that he should go to the tournament and gamble for her against his opponent, and that he should take her magic kris, in case King Twelve tries to cheat or hurt him. He agrees and she gives him a rooster, gold, and the kris.

gurindam XVII:
Both agree and their secret meeting is not seen by anybody. They proceed to carry out the plan. The time has come.

Scene 17:
Manandin enters the tournament. He wins, but King Twelve refuses to pay and starts insulting and attacking Manandin. They fight, and Manandin kills him with the magic dagger.

gurindam XVIII:
King Twelve is dead, killed by Manandin. All people are happy to finally learn the truth. King Mighty is ashamed of mistreating his nephew and flees. Manandin's parents and sister are happy, and so is he, because he can finally marry his beloved, and then he is crowned king of his *nagari* (district).

closing gurindam:

We wish to give blessings and thanks to our honored audience.
Please forgive us any mistakes we might have made, after all we
are just children. We promise to tell more, the next time around.

The central topics relating to Minangkabau adat are arranged marriages, marriage between cousins, and the strong role of the uncle.

Magek Manandin and Subang Bagelang are cousins, Subang's
father (King Mighty) being Manandin's uncle. Marriage between
cousins is common among the Minangkabau, and an accepted custom. A nephew was traditionally considered the ideal bridegroom
for one's daughter. Uncles as central decision makers were often
matchmakers. Marriages were commonly arranged by the older
generation—not only by uncles, but also by the mothers, grand-
mothers, and fathers of those youngsters of the right age. While
marriage between cousins is an accepted custom, arranged marriage and the powerful role of the uncle are often criticized in
randai plays and portrayed as the cause of much suffering. This
can clearly be seen in the above example, where King Mighty effectively decides the future of his nephew Manandin by canceling
the wedding between Manandin and his own daughter Subang
after accusations that Manandin is a thief. Although this is certainly
a grave accusation by itself and would bring shame to the family,
King Mighty's personal stakes are higher because he was publicly
shamed by these accusations. In reaction, he overrides the opinion of
Manandin's parents and goes so far as to expel Manandin from the
family. This abuse of power is clearly criticized in the play and the
uncle receives no sympathy for his actions. The fact that he then
rushes to marry his daughter off to King Twelve, the very man by
whom he was shamed, also indicates that he has no scruples. This
negative uncle figure is a common character in randai plays and
one of his stereotypical evil actions is frequently the arrangement
of a marriage against the wishes of everyone involved.

Other standard features that recur in many randai plays are the
dangers of gambling, the use of magic, and a happy ending. Gam-

bling had been an old and persistent tradition of the Minangkabau. Despite the opposition to gambling, first by Islam and then by the Indonesian government, it is still a common pastime for Minangkabau men.[4] Randai groups over the years have been nudged by religious leaders and government officials to try to change the general attitude toward cockfighting and gambling, but without much success. Although the dangers of gambling are clearly depicted in the plays, randai has maintained a somewhat ambivalent standpoint. On the one hand randai stories clearly condemn gambling as a source of misfortune and suffering, but on the other hand they also point out that participation in gambling tournaments was traditionally an obligation that could not be turned down without losing face and that this obligation often continues unspoken today. Also, considering that randai was traditionally an all-male art performed by young Minangkabau men, it is not surprising that those same young men would often participate in gambling events themselves and therefore not really embrace the government messages about the evils of this sport. Besides, randai scenes involving gambling are always a source of great humor, a fact which is exploited by the performers and which softens the criticism.

The use of magic in form of the speaking parrot and the fast-growing tree that save Manandin is another staple of the randai play, as is the magic dagger that Manandin receives from his fiancée to defeat King Twelve.

These aspects of Minangkabau culture will recur in the following examples of plays, but let's now turn to an analysis of the structure of the script. Several structural characteristics become clear from the above example of *Magek Manandin.* The scenes consist of short units that happen in one location, at one time, and include only one or two major actions (the summoning of the guards and the giving of orders, the meeting of family members to discuss the absence of their son, the quarrel and conversation between Subang and Manandin in disguise, etc.). The songs function as bridges between scenes; they reiterate what has just happened in the previous scene, change the focus to a different location, person, or time, and generally hint at what is about to happen next. Often the gurindam songs contain additional crucial information that is not played out in the scenes themselves.

The presented script in its full length (with all seventeen scenes and nineteen songs) would typically stretch over two nights, with a three hour performance on each night. However, if the play is being performed in a single three- or four-hour performance, several of the scenes and songs will be cut, depending on the preference of the group or host.[5] Anything other than the core scenes can be condensed into sung narrative. Different groups give different emphasis to what the core scenes are, but generally the following scenes are considered central: Manandin's asking permission from his father to go to the tournament; his farewell with his fiancée; the robber scene; Manandin's bad luck at the tournament and his arrest; his uncle's order to punish him and his parent's objection to this; his encounter with his fiancée in disguise; his rescue and final fight with his opponent. Most other scenes are secondary to the plot and can be condensed into a few verses of the appropriately located gurindam. This structure allows for very flexible performances. Depending on the skill of the singers, they can adjust to changes in the play and immediately integrate whatever was left out in the previous scene.[6]

The redundancy of the information given through the song lyrics and the dialogue also underscores the fact that the tradition of folk singing (saluang jo dendang) is actually a much older form of storytelling than randai. Acting out what is described in the lyrics is a very recent addition to the Minangkabau performing arts, and the singing is generally still more popular with the audience than the acting (excluding the fighting scenes). Performers are popular and well known for their singing or martial arts skills, but rarely for their acting. Another, more practical reason for the ongoing repetition throughout a play might be found in the sociocultural setting. Audiences tend to wander in and out, talk, sleep, and eat while watching a performance. The performance structure takes this behavior into account. Through continuous repetition the audience can keep track of what is happening in the play.

Language

The Minang language has four different levels of speech: *kato mendata* ("horizontal speech," used between people of similar social status); *kato menurun* ("descending speech," used by a person of high status toward a person of lower status); *kato mendaki* ("ascending speech," used by a person of low status toward a person of higher status); *kato malereang* ("elaborate, metaphorical speech," used in proverbs, ceremonial speeches, song lyrics, etc.). All four levels of speech are present in randai; in fact, they are followed more strictly in the theater dialogue than in standard Minang conversations today.[7] According to the social status and the relationship between characters, an appropriate level has to be chosen; a servant has to address a king or queen with kato mendaki, including long and elaborate titles and praise of the king's or queen's virtues; the king or queen will respond with kato menurun, including shorter addresses and delivered with a more commanding tone. A character who does not choose the right level is instantaneously recognized as one ignorant of Minangkabau adat, and is therefore ridiculed. Evil characters are frequently portrayed using the wrong language level (using kato menurun to everybody, even people of the same or higher social status). The last category, kato malereang, is very prominent and accounts for the richness and depth of randai texts. A character's frequent use of this fourth level of speech shows his or her refinement, good education, and knowledge of adat.

Although the Minang used in randai is very similar to standard Minang in terms of levels of speech, vocabulary, and grammar, some differences exist. Minang used in randai tends to be more literary and poetic, is often metered and rhymed, and more wordy with longer and more complex sentences than everyday Minang speech.[8] With the exception of clowns and robbers, characters have relatively fixed dialogues and generally improvise only occasionally.

Randai texts have numerous stock phrases, idioms, expressions, and proverbs that appear frequently. Standard expressions are used for the opening of a conversation, such as the following one between an uncle and his niece:[9]

Uncle: Alas, where is my dearest niece Siti Nursila?
Flower of the high *anjuang* room,[10]
ornament of the house.
Please come closer to me,
there is something in my heart
I have to tell you.

Niece: Oh my dearest uncle Angku Lareh Mudo,
part of my blood,
hearing you calling me, makes me tremble
and my bones feel weak,
the blood in my veins is racing.
What is it that you have to tell me?
Please explain it to me quickly,
so that I can be happy in my heart
and calm in my mind.

Or like the following exchange between a king and his servant:

King: Where is my guard Salamaik,
the one with the fast hands and quick feet?
The wise man that knows
when to whisper and when to scream,
knows when to face the truth and when to dream.
Bright and smart one, come here,
I have something in my heart to tell you.

Servant: I beg your forgiveness, your highness.
A thousand forgivenesses are begged
for one wrongdoing.
Then ten fingers are folded together,

the head is bent to greet you.
Hearing your call
makes the blood in my body race.[11]
What is it you desire?
Has someone done you wrong?
Has someone disgraced your highness?
Let me punish the wrongdoer at once.
Please explain it quickly, my lord
or I won't be able to be at ease.

These and similar openings in most of the plays consist of polite address, including references to the individual's position, function or personal characteristics. An unmarried girl is praised for her good looks, politeness, and good demeanor; a guard for his good silek skills and effective strategies; a clan elder for his kindness and wisdom. In the course of a conversation several stock phrases recur. Responses are often preceded by an affirmation before an opposing opinion is presented (for example: "If that is what you say, your words are true. But actually it is like this: . . .").

Proverbs *(pantun)* are plentiful in each randai text. They often convey important messages about Minangkabau adat, and are especially used in advising the younger generation about proper decorum and behavior in the community.

Respect the elders,
love the younger ones,
seek consensus with your peers.
The rich ones have to share,
the smart ones have to give advice,
the wise ones have to teach.
Don't search for a fight,
but if there is trouble, don't run away.[12]

Or: There are three pillars of society:
adat, religion, and government.
With any one missing,
nothing good will come of it.
. . .

> If one pillar (of the traditional fire place) is broken,
> the rice will not cook right.
> If one strand is broken,
> the rope will not be strong.[13]

Often, proverbs are used to elaborate on a preceding statement with similar meaning or are used to foreshadow the coming statement.[14] In the above example the last four lines are a proverb dealing with traditional Minangkabau household objects, which are used as metaphors for the unification of the three main elements of Minangkabau society (customs, religion, and government). In a second example, the proverb in the last four lines is an elaboration of the preceding proverb.

> I have listened to your advice.
> Your words are true words.
> I will not forget one word,
> and will not miss a single line.
> During the day I will use it
> as my walking stick,
> and during the night it will
> become my pillow.[15]

Notice that eight lines are used to convey the simple message that one will follow the advice offered. This is typical of randai texts. Two things become clear in the above example. First, the proverb (lines 5–8) reinforces what has been said in plain words before (lines 1–4). Second, the plain statement itself already includes a parallel pair of lines (3 and 4) that basically state the same thing. Thus, the same idea is stated several times.

Repetition also occurs on a larger scale, not just within a single paragraph. Often one character reiterates closely what another character has just mentioned, either in affirmation or in negation:

> A: Why are you so late?
>   We have been expecting you for days.
>   We became tired waiting for you.
>   Did the invitation letter

	not arrive at your house?
	Did the messenger not
	bring you the betel nut?
	What happened?
	Tell me quickly,
	to make my heart happy.
B:	No, it is not because
	the invitation letter did
	not arrive at my house,
	or the messenger did not
	bring the betel nut.
	Actually, it is because
	I was attacked by robbers
	That is why I am late,
	and you got tired waiting for me.[16]

The first character repeats two parts of the statement of the first in negation (the assumed reasons for the delay) and proceeds to give the real reason. The second then closes with a repetition of the fact that the first got tired waiting. Generally, important events that happened earlier in the play will be referred to again and again throughout the performance. Every time a new character enters the scene, a statement will be repeated completely or in abbreviated form, in order to explain past events to the newcomer.

Just as lyrics and scenes employ repetition on the macro level throughout a randai play, individual monologues or dialogues utilize a parallel structure on the micro level. Again, this might further illustrate a tendency of the performers to adjust to the attitude of their audiences, which can be described as selective inattentiveness.

An aesthetic reason for the redundancy on the micro level is that it is considered a desired embellishment of the message that gives the performers an opportunity to display their mastery of the elaborate old Minang language. This love for verbal elaboration and embellishment in randai is not surprising, considering that the Minangkabau people have cultivated the act of giving ceremonial speeches *(pidato)* into a highly complex art form. Each formal social gathering is framed by highly formalized speeches delivered by the elders and leaders of the community. These dignitaries are expected to have an excellent command of Minangkabau language, proverbs, and decorum.[17] This is also reflected in randai where elevated characters display a similar proficiency and frequently use metaphors, allegories, proverbs, and poetic language.

Story Material

Unlike most other dramatic genres throughout Southeast Asia, randai does not draw on the major Indian epics, Ramayana and Mahabharata, which have had considerable influence on the development of dramatic literature in Burma, Thailand, Cambodia, Laos, Malaysia, and many areas of Indonesia (especially Java and Bali). Randai scripts draw their story material almost exclusively from Minangkabau *kaba* (stories),[18] a traditional literary genre that narrates local legends, historical, and mythological stories. Kaba are divided into two categories: classical and new (Junus 1985, 184–85). Randai scripts follow this division and can similarly be divided into classical or "old" stories and new ones.

Traditionally, kaba were considered part of Minangkabau heritage and were passed down orally *(tradisi lisan)* from generation to generation in two main traditions: poetic storytelling (bakaba and sijobang) and folk songs (saluang jo dendang). Randai constitutes the most recent addition to these traditions of telling kaba. In bakaba and sijobang, the *tukang kaba* (storyteller) recites memorized local folk tales, rearranging them as he sees fit to please and educate his respective audiences. In saluang jo dendang the singers do the same. In randai, the telling of the story is shared among the actors, who provide dialogues, and the singers. Traditionally, storytelling and singing were very much a part of communal life and aided in the education of the younger generation. However, it was not only storytellers and singers who retained this cultural heritage. Additionally, all *ninik-mamak* (elders) were expected to know the main local tales and tell them to the children on a regular basis in the evenings after the day's work was done. Therefore, the main stories were well known in most villages and generally the need for written forms of tales and songs did not exist.[19] Elders throughout the community state that when television became common throughout West Sumatra in the late seventies, there was a marked decline in the frequency of communal storytelling events. Gatherings in front of television sets started to replace the traditional gatherings around the storytellers, singers, or village elders, thereby diminishing their roles as entertainers and educators. This shift in preference also brought in a flood of modern stories to compete with the old tales and legends. Although the younger generation generally still knows the principal characters and plot lines of the main Minangkabau stories, the loss of in-depth knowledge is bemoaned by the elders.

Following the division into classical and new kaba, randai text material is divided into two broad categories: old *(tuo)* stories and new *(baru)*. The old stories are based on historical or legendary Minangkabau events and have typically been around in the form of oral tales or song lyrics much longer than randai itself. They deal with Minangkabau characters in traditional Minangkabau familial relations and they focus strongly on adat (customs). The new stories are generally newly written texts or adaptations of new Minangkabau literature, mainly novels. They deal predominantly with modern characters (government officials, soldiers, religious figures, school children) and focus on contemporary topics. Adat, Islam, and government issues are dealt with in a modern social setting.[20] However, many of the randai stories fall between the two poles of classical and modern. A clear separation often cannot be drawn; rather we should conceive of a continuum stretching from old to new stories. For instance, many of the old stories are rewritten and undergo changes to incorporate contemporary topics such as messages from the government. The most popular government messages in recent times center around family planning and population control. This topic is incorporated into revised scripts by giving the main character new lines extolling the virtues of the two-child family. Typically starting with an old Minangkabau proverb about an indigenous forest bird that always has two off-spring—one female, one male—the character then outlines the standard position of the Indonesian government that two children are enough *(dua cukup)*. In randai this government policy is often elaborated on by describing how a family with too many children will remain poor and unable to pay for all the children's schooling, while a family with just two children will prosper because they can be properly educated. The policy is also integrated into the scripts by adjusting the number of children a protagonist has. Characters with more than two children are often ridiculed in the plays. The "modernization" of old scripts often goes no further than such minor changes—for example, the inclusion of a few lines about programs such as family planning or remarks about the need to support community projects through *gotong royong* (mutual assistance). In most of these cases, the main plot remains basically unchanged. On the other end of the continuum, most of the "new" stories still contain traditional Minangkabau characters along with the modern ones, and adat is still the underlying cultural fabric.

OLD STORIES

The old or classical stories can be subdivided into those based on longer, pan-Minang epics (popular throughout West Sumatra), and those based on shorter, local folktales (restricted to a small area or district). The three main Minangkabau epics are *Anggun Nan Tongga, Cindua Mato,* and *Sutan Pangaduan* (the first will be discussed in detail below). These epics are rather long; a complete sijobang performance of *Anggun Nan Tongga,* for instance, may last over fifty hours.[21] Consequently, only segments of the epics are selected for the performance of any given individual troupe. Many different subplots and spin-offs from the main epics also exist, typically dealing with different phases in the hero's life or with adventures of close relatives.

There are several hundred local folk tales, many of which have been adapted for randai in various versions. We have already encountered the story of *Magek Manandin,* a good example of such regional folktales. Others are *Rambun Pamenan,* the story of an abducted queen and her adventurous rescue though her son; and *Sabai Nan Aluih,* about a daughter's revenge for her father's murder (the latter will be dealt with in detail below, when we look at different randai versions of the same basic story).

All epics and folk tales are said to be based on actual historical events, although external proof is not available to confirm such statements. All three main epics and most of the local tales have no original author, and only later and newer versions carry the name of a writer and are dated.[22]

The main topics that recur in most of the stories are key elements of Minangkabau adat: clan relations, family obligations, arranged marriages, wedding ceremonies, child rearing, merantau, silek apprenticeships, gambling, and so on. Other, more universal topics include romance, rivalry, jealousy, power struggles, intrigue, adventure, and revenge. Some of these topics have already been encountered in *Magek Manandin.* The following examples will give a representative sampling of classical kaba and outline how they are transformed into randai scripts.

One of the oldest, longest, and most complex Minangkabau kaba recapitulates the adventures of Anggun Nan Tongga. Although the legendary home of its hero is Tiku, a harbor town in the southern coastal Pariaman area of West Sumatra, this story is popular all over West Sumatra and plays based on this story have been performed by many randai groups from the coast to the most remote hinterland. Since the epic story of the adventures of Anggun involves over one hundred characters and stretches over several decades, only episodes from this long legend are selected for as randai performances.[23] What follows is a summary of the core events.

One day, when still a young boy, Prince Anggun discovers a fact that had been concealed from him by his mother, Contoh Pamai. Fearing that her young son would leave her, she has not told him that his five uncles have not returned home from their rantau travels for many years and are feared to be in serious trouble. When Anggun finds out, he feels obligated to search for them, just as his mother feared he would, and he immediately takes leave of his village and his fiancée, Gondoriah. Upon parting, Gondoriah requests that Anggun obtain for her 121 *syarat kawin* (precious and rare dowry items) on this journey and return within seven months or she will retreat to the top of Mount Ledang as a hermit, never to return. Anggun promises to obey her wish and leaves with his guards, servants, and large army by ship. While he sails the vast oceans in search for his five uncles and the 121 dowry objects, he encounters the pirate Nan Kodo Baha, who has captured the princess Intan Korong. They fight a fierce battle, in which Anggun is victorious. He frees Intan Korong, who in turn repays him by becoming his guide on the unknown seas. After many more adventures and battles in which he is aided by his loyal retainer, Abang Salamat, the spiritual powers of his two teachers, and by various other spirits of the ocean and the wind, he finds three of the uncles and obtains all the desired dowry objects except for one, a speaking parrot. The seven months have almost passed when he comes to the shore of Ruhun, where the two remaining uncles are rumored to live.

Anggun is first welcomed by one of his uncles and his daughter, Santan Batapih, who tries to persuade Anggun to come ashore with her (i.e., get engaged). He refuses but she lures him to her house by pretending she possesses the desired speaking parrot. Once in the village, he discovers that the parrot is not in her possession, but in that of her cousin, Dandomi Sutan. He goes there in search of the parrot. Dandomi promises to give him the bird, but has one request: he has to marry her first. Anggun is unable to persuade her otherwise and eventually gives in to her wish. To find out why Anggun wants the bird so desperately, Dandomi sends the parrot on an expedition to Tiku. The speaking bird finds out that Anggun is engaged to Gondoriah and it is she that draws Anggun there so strongly. Cunningly the bird discloses to Gondoriah that her lover has married Dandomi and has a son with her. Hearing all this, Gondoriah is desperate and fulfills her vow to retreat to Mount Ledang. After receiving the information about Gondoriah, Dandomi constantly invents new excuses why she cannot give Anggun the parrot. Anggun is forced to stay on and more time passes.

After three years Anggun is finally able to trick Dandomi into allowing him to return home for two weeks, with the parrot. Upon arriving in Tiku he finds out that Gondoriah had retreated to the mountaintop, and he goes to search for her. He finally finds her in a cave. From outside the cave, Anggun tries to convince her to come out and return with him to be married, but she refuses. After a long argument, she finally agrees, but they realize that the cave opening has mysteriously shrunk so that Gondoriah is trapped inside. Anggun summons the spirits who break the cave open and the two lovers are reunited. As they climb down the mountain side, Gondoriah gets tired and thirsty, so Anggun walks off to fetch some water for his love. Unlucky again, he gets lost. While Gondoriah is waiting on the road pondering her fate, she grows more and more impatient and suspects Anggun has abandoned her again.

Just then the handsome prince of Indojati, Katik Alam Tansudin, comes by, kidnaps her, and sets out to marry her in Indojati.[24] In the meantime, poor Anggun stumbles through the wilderness for months. When he finally reaches the house of the young maiden Andam Bariah, he is dirty, scratched, and covered with moss and ferns, and looks very unlike a prince. Andam fears he is an evil forest spirit and treats him with contempt. Her father, though, is kind to Anggun. After he receives food, drink, and a bath, Anggun is recognized as the prince he is and learns that Katik Alam Tansudin is about to marry his Gondoriah. He hastens to Indojati to rescue her. There, he enters several gambling tournaments against Tansudin and they play for higher and higher stakes. Finally, both bet all their possessions and lands, and Tansudin places Gondoriah as his last bet. He loses, but refuses to pay his debts, claiming that

Anggun has been cheating.[25] They start fighting and, because they are an even match, the fight goes on for a long time until Tuanku Soru Alam, the venerable teacher of both Anggun and Tansudin, descends from the heavens and ends the fight. He decrees that Anggun and Gondoriah belong together, and that Tansudin should marry Andam, to fulfill a pledge that had been made long ago and forgotten by Tansudin after casting eyes on Gondoriah.

Anggun and Gondoriah return to Tiku and a big celebration and tournament is held to open the wedding ceremonies, but in the middle of the tournament, Anggun's son appears and Gondoriah is again upset and retreats to the top of Mount Bensen. One more time Anggun is able to persuade her to return, but then Dandomi comes to Tiku in search of her son and husband. Seeing this, Gondoriah's retreat is final. When Anggun follows her again, she ultimately refuses to go back with him and turns into a goddess.[26] In desperation, Anggun plunges into the sea and turns into a white dolphin, never to return to his people in Tiku.

One can see how this epic story could easily be extended over several days or even weeks of storytelling. The main characters and events of this epic mark it as a prime example of a classical kaba. The cast of characters, especially the hero and most other main characters are of noble descent, members of a royal family. Familial relations and obligations are stressed and function to propel the story forward, as when Anggun is obligated by adat to search for his lost uncles. The main theme is the thwarted marriage between Anggun and Gondoriah. Although they have been engaged for a long time and this relationship has been sanctioned by adat conventions and the consent of their elders, the fulfillment of the vow is endangered by a series of events and circumstances. First Anggun exposes himself to considerable danger on the quest to find his uncles, to whom he is obligated. Being a true hero, this of course is no real threat for him. The more precarious aspect is that, once he finds them, all his uncles have daughters that they want to marry to Anggun. (As their nephew and a wealthy prince he is considered a highly desired son-in-law.) He escapes the first few of these temptations and obligations as well, although he has to resort to many instances of cunning and trickery. It is somewhat ironic however, that his marriage to Gondoriah is finally thwarted indirectly by Gondoriah herself. Although her demand for the 121 dowry items is perfectly legitimate according to adat, it is also what keeps Anggun from returning home earlier. Eventually, it forces him to marry someone else to obtain the last item and puts him in a highly precarious situation since he also develops ties with Dandomi and has a son with her.

Gondoriah's behavior also brings a somewhat more controversial issue into the play. According to Islam, a Muslim man has the right to marry up to four wives, a behavior not allowed under adat law. Gondoriah is very much in line with adat law and not with Islam by objecting to her fiancé's marriage to another woman. According to Islam, she should gracefully accept her husband's decision and be content and obedient. However, she does the opposite and runs away three times, a reaction that is presented sympathetically in the kaba and the randai plays. In the end she even turns into a goddess, a fact that clearly condones her behavior and portrays her as a positive character. A reinterpretation according to Islamic principles would possibly paint her as a negative character who brings about her own downfall by demanding too much of her husband-to-be and criticizing her for not accepting another woman as her husband's second wife. However, such a version of a randai play does not exist to my knowledge. Minangkabau adat is the dominant and ever-present underlying fabric throughout this kaba. The entire setup of the arranged marriage between Anggun and Gondoriah is based on adat, as is his obligation to find his uncles. The prominent role of merantau is also a cornerstone of adat; all of Anggun's uncles went to the rantau and Anggun himself has to go rantau before the wedding with Gondoriah can be carried out. Another incident that illustrates the strong underlying power of adat is the fact that the spirit of the silek teacher of Anggun and Tansudin interferes with their fight and mediates peace between the warring parties. This reinforces the powerful decision-making roles of teachers and elders, who can interfere and mediate in the lives of others even from the spirit world. The connection to the spirit world points to another element characteristic of old stories, the abundance of mystical and magic events. From the very beginning of the story, Anggun is accompanied by the spirits of his teachers who advise him and by nature spirits (the wind and the sea) who manipulate the elements in his favor. A speaking, intelligent parrot is also part of the story just as in *Magek Manandin,* where the parrot finds and rescues the captive protagonist. In *Anggun* the parrot plays an important role as Dandomi's spy and initiates Gondoriah's retreat to her mountain hermitage. Another key magic event lies in the conclusion of the story, where Gondoriah turns into a goddess and Anggun turns into a dolphin. Throughout the story, magic weapons play a prominent role in the many battles and skirmishes in which the characters are involved. By including all these magic events the kaba is closer in spirit to animism than to orthodox Islam, which prescribes belief in the One God and shuns spirit worship and belief in magic as blasphemous.

Besides its didactic function of perpetuating adat, the kaba is an uplifting and entertaining adventure story with a substantial amount of comic, magic, and highly improbable incidents, full of cunning and trickery, and with an abundance of fighting scenes, both verbal and physical. Thus the kaba fulfills its main two social purposes, to educate and to entertain. These are the two main functions of randai as well.

The most popular segments from this epic that are typically selected for randai performances are: Intan Korong's kidnapping by the pirate Kodo Nan Baha, her rescue by Anggun, and her return to her mother; the encounter of Anggun and Santan Batapih; the marriage and bargaining for the parrot between Anggun and Dandomi; Anggun's search for Gondoriah on Mount Ledang; his encounter with Andam Bariah as an "evil jungle spirit"; Gondoriah's kidnapping and her rescue; as well as several other spin-off stories of Anggun's adventures while searching for his uncles, like his victory over the evil ruler of Tanau, Tombi Bosa, who had captured and enslaved two of Anggun's uncles. The last part of the kaba, Gondoriah's final retreat and Anggun's disappearance into the seas, is rarely performed in randai. Each of the fragments selected for a randai performance can fill a three- to four-hour performance with a structure similar to that of the story of *Magek Manandin* described previously. The story material is distributed evenly between songs and scenes with a considerable amount of overlap and redundancy.

While *Anggun Nan Tongga* is a pan-Minangkabau story well known and frequently performed throughout West Sumatra, the following story is an example of a local tale found only in few locations in the darek region.[27] This kaba is called *Si Umbuik Mudo* and centers around people of humbler origin than those in *Anggun Nan Tongga,* which were legendary, noble characters. Not a prince like Anggun, but merely a poor village boy, the hero, Umbuik Mudo, is involved in a quest to find the murderers of his father. *Si Umbuik Mudo* is a coming-of-age story with a revenge motive, coupled with a sad romance. In it, the young boy Umbuik Mudo (Young Bamboo Shoot) finds his father mortally wounded by a gang of robbers and grows up with a desire for vengeance. As he grows older, having learned as much as he can from his teachers in the village, he decides to go to the rantau, to seek more knowledge and experience and also learn more silek. He spends several years with various teachers in the rantau. Upon his return home, he is invited to join the Qur'an recital of one of his former teachers, in which he excels.[28] The teacher's niece, Puti Galang Banyak (Maiden of Many Ornaments), hears Umbuik's beautiful voice and is enchanted. She comes down from her room and asks Umbuik to repeat his performance. Embarrassed and dumbfounded by the beauty of Puti, he cannot utter a word and is ridiculed by her in front of everyone. Ashamed, he retreats to his mother's house where he falls into a deep depression, lovesick and embarrassed. His mother worries greatly about his health, and when she inquires what he desires, he asks her to go to Puti's house and propose to her in his name. Twice his mother does so, but each time Puti, being proud and spoiled, rejects the proposal with harsh words. Umbuik is desperate. He pleads with his mother to find him a special kind of bamboo from a sacred waterfall, from which he can carve a magic flute. After a long discussion in which she reminds him that he should think instead of his other duty (to avenge his father's death), his mother finally gives in and gets the desired bamboo. Umbuik carves the flute and then lies in wait at the communal bathing place where Puti is about to take her bath. He plays the flute, and instantly she is enchanted and falls helplessly in love with him. But, a change of mood has overcome him; he suddenly feels angry toward Puti for making him suffer so much, and now rejects her love.

He remembers his duty to his father and leaves. She falls sick and no *dukun* (traditional healer) can cure her. When asked what she desires, she can only whisper: *umbuik mudo*. So her father goes to the forest to find it (*umbuik mudo* in the literal sense is a young bamboo shoot) and when he returns with the plant, his daughter becomes even more upset. She finally dies of a broken heart, but Umbuik does not hear about it for a long time, because he is in the rantau again. When he finally gets the news, he is heartbroken and returns immediately to his village. He seeks out a dukun to help him bring Puti back to life. With powerful magic this is accomplished, and they enjoy a brief moment of happiness before she falls ill again and dies, this time forever. Umbuik returns to silek practice. After a long training period, his new silek teacher gives him the final three quests: to live for a hundred days in the dark forest, defeating the wild beasts; to spend a hundred days by the wild streams; and to endure another hundred days in the hills where the fierce robbers roam. After accomplishing the first two quests successfully, Umbuik finally encounters three robbers whom he recognizes as the murderers of his father. They engage in a long and hard battle until Umbuik subdues all three of them. They beg for pardon and Umbuik, hearing his teachers voice that instructs him to have mercy, does not kill them. Instead, he urges them to repent, to renounce their evil ways, and to follow the true path of Allah and the Qur'an. Receiving their pledge, he releases them and helps them to become farmers.[29]

This story is complex and stretches over a long period of time. The main topic laid out in the very beginning of the play, the revenge, is ever-present, but its fulfillment is suspended until the end of the play. The second topic, the unhappy romance, seems like an interlude but actually takes up considerable space and focus in the play.[30] Magic events are again prominently featured and hint at underlying animistic beliefs, as when Umbuik plays a magic flute to win Puti's love, or when a powerful dukun brings Puti back to life.

Like *Anggun Nan Tongga* this story educates about adat and portrays it as the underlying social fabric. Several events in the play underscore the importance of adat: The main character goes to the rantau for various reasons; the first time he leaves his village to seek further education and learn silek skills, a standard reason to go to the rantau. The second time he leaves to get away from Puti's insult and to find the murderers of his father, and the third time to console himself over Puti's death and learn more silek. The combination of reasons for merantau illustrate that it is an integral part of the Minangkabau culture and an accepted and common behavior for young men.

In contrast to *Anggun Nan Tongga* however, the story of Umbuik also illustrates the importance of Islam in Minangkabau society. Anggun goes rantau not only to learn more about adat and silek, but also to improve his knowledge of the Qur'an, and upon his return home he excels at a Qur'an recital held at his teacher's home. This Qur'an recital lasts for a rather long time in the play and shows off the skills of the character as well as those of the actor. The recital is a central scene in the play and leads to the encounter between Umbuik and Puti. Another indication that Islam is important alongside adat can be seen in family relations and obligations. The story is set up so that Umbuik has to avenge his father's (not his uncle's!) death. Compared to the plot of *Anggun Nan Tongga,* we can clearly see a different focus on family obligations.

In *Anggun,* it is the nephew (Anggun) who goes to check on his uncles, and not their sons. In *Umbuik Mudo* it is the son (Umbuik)
who has to avenge the death of his father, not his nephews. This
points to a more patrilineal-Islamic framework of *Umbuik Mudo,*
in which obligations of son toward father are more important than
those of the matrilineal-adat framework of *Anggun,* in which the
obligations of nephew toward uncle are more important. However, it could be argued that the primary obligations in both plays
are those of the sons toward their mothers, in finding *her* brothers
(in *Anggun*) or avenging *her* husband's death (in *Umbuik Mudo*),
thereby staying within the matrilineal-adat framework, a fact al-
luded to in both plays.

Another event in the play points to the importance of Islam in
this story. After Umbuik finds and confronts the robbers, he lectures them on proper behavior according to the Qur'an, with the
result that they repent and vow to become good Muslims. *Umbuik
Mudo* combines adat and Islam and addresses concerns of both in
its plot. It emphasizes that education about both adat and Islam are
essential for young Minangkabau people. The final word, however, is the teaching of Islam.

Sabai Nan Aluih (The genteel Sabai) is an altogether different
play about revenge. With this example I will illustrate how the
same story material is composed into two quite distinct randai
scripts, highlighting the different perceptions of women's roles in
society as prescribed by adat and Islam.

In the first version of the story, the heroine, Sabai, has spent all
day weaving at home, as befits an obedient Minangkabau girl. The
story begins when she is sent out by her mother to look for her
brother, a good-for-nothing little rascal who only lazes about and
flies his kites. On her way, Rajo Nan Panjang (The Tall King), the
powerful and evil ruler from the neighboring nagari (district) and
a notorious Casanova, catches sight of her and instantly lusts after
her. He sends his underling to press his suit with her father, Rajo
Babandiang, who rejects the proposal politely with the excuse that
he considers Sabai too young to marry (actually he dislikes Rajo

Nan Panjang). That night, Sabai has a bad dream and in the morning warns her father not to go to the festivities (cock fighting and gambling) in the neighboring village because she fears for his safety. He does not listen to her and leaves with his servant, Bujang Salamaik. On the way there, he is attacked by Rajo Nan Panjang for rejecting the marriage proposal. They engage in a long verbal dispute and finally start fighting. When Rajo Babandiang is about to win, he is shot in the back by one of the underlings of Rajo Nan Panjang, and they leave him to die. A shepherd finds the dying man and runs to inform his family. Sabai is shocked and follows the shepherd to the scene of the crime, where her father lies, breathing his last breath. Delirious, he calls for his son, not for her, and Sabai feels bitter and sad. When her father expires, she vows revenge. She returns home to inform her mother, asks her permission to avenge her father's death (since her brother is a good-for-nothing coward), takes the rifle that her mother tearfully hands her, and sets out to search for the evil assassin. Eventually she finds Rajo Nan Panjang and, pretending to be willing to marry him, asks him about her father. When he lies about the incident, she challenges him and they begin to fight. After several minutes of combat, Sabai thinks of a trick. She offers to become his bride if he is able to shoot off her ear ornament. If he misses, it is her turn. If she can shoot off the tip of his hat, he has to vow to retreat forever. He agrees to the deal, takes the first shot and misses. Now it is Sabai's turn to shoot and, having no intention to only shoot off his hat, she kills him.[31]

In this version, revenge is clearly the dominant motif, and the heroine is depicted as active and assertive. Important elements of Minangkabau culture are again present: Sabai's mother lectures her about proper etiquette for an unmarried girl according to adat. A lecture that is by extension aimed at all unmarried girls in the audience. Her brother functions as the bad example of improper behavior, he is rude, disobedient, and neglects his duties. In addition, he is a coward.

Another topic already familiar from other randai plays is

gambling. Although it is not featured as prominently as in *Magek Manandin,* gambling nonetheless is described as a social event to which Sabai's father is invited, and, since he is obligated by adat to attend, leads to the encounter between him and his opponent. As in *Umbuik Mudo* it is the father who gets killed, and not an uncle, and his child takes on the revenge. This play is special in that it features a woman in the role of the active hero. Because her brother is incapable of fulfilling the family's obligation to avenge the father's murder, she sees the only solution is taking action herself. According to both adat and Islam, it is generally considered improper for a female to behave as Sabai does and actively take revenge in her own hands.[32] This version nonetheless portrays her sympathetically as a virtuous daughter who is driven to extreme behavior by unfortunate circumstances. Of outstanding character, Sabai is a proper Minangkabau girl, acting to defend her own and her family's honor.

Compared to the first version, the following one—although based of the same historical event—puts more emphasis on Islamic teachings. It demonstrates the broad range within which the same topic can be adapted into quite different randai scripts. This second version of *Sabai Nan Aluih* weaves a different tapestry of events and focuses far more on the male characters than on the female ones. Sabai is portrayed as less active and courageous than in the first version.

The second version of the play begins in the house of the evil and greedy Rajo Nan Panjang, Sabai's adversary. He summons his guards for some illegal undertaking and displays socially unacceptable behavior. In the meantime, Sabai's father, the good-natured and fair ruler Rajo Babandiang, prepares to organize a collective pig hunt to protect the harvest of the entire community. After the pig hunt, the fact that many dogs were injured or lost is discussed extensively and creates chaos among the participants as to how to solve the problem and share the responsibilities. Rajo Nan Panjang has also lost his hunting dog and comes to Sabai's house to blame her father and to claim compensation. This is the first time Sabai actually appears in person in this version of the play (she is mentioned only briefly in the opening song). She sits in the house weaving cloth for her fiancé, Sutan Barido, when Rajo Nan Panjang sees her and demands the beautiful cloth. Through this demand, he symbolically asks her to become his wife.[33] When she politely turns him down, he leaves enraged.

Sabai's father returns home and lectures her about the correct behavior for a girl growing up to become a woman. They also talk about her brother, who only gambles, flies kites, and never attends prayer sessions at the mosque. They both worry about him and when he comes home from another gambling event (at which he lost again), Sabai tries to talk to him and instruct him about how he should change, but he only laughs derisively at her and leaves the house in anger. A few days later, Sabai meets her fiancé. They exchange polite phrases and decide to wait a little longer before she gives him the cloth (i.e., marries him). In the meantime her father receives a letter asking him to join a pig hunt in Rajo Nan Panjang's district and is obliged to accept the invitation. Sabai has a bad dream and warns him not to go to the hunt, but he leaves anyway, accompanied by her fiancé, Sutan Barido. Both die at the hands of Rajo Nan Panjang. Sabai, alerted by a shepherd, finds both dead and encounters the murderer at the scene of the crime. She challenges him to a shooting competition. He gets so nervous that he drops his rifle accidentally and is killed when the gun discharges as it hits the ground.

This second version focuses more on the male characters and introduces and elaborates on an exclusively male activity (the pig hunt),[34] through which the conflict between the two district rulers is ignited and which indirectly leads to the meeting of Sabai and Rajo Nan Panjang. In the first version Sabai is rather active and outgoing. She leaves the house to look for her brother, she goes to take care of her dying father, and she actively deceives and kills her adversary. In the second version she is portrayed as fundamentally passive. She stays inside the house and is met there by the evil king instead of walking outside to search for her brother. Another difference is that she is not engaged in the first version but has a fiancé in the second version. The activities she displays in the second version in general are clearly more domestic in nature. Most importantly, although indirectly responsible for the murderer's death, she does not intentionally kill him as in the first version of this play. Although the ending does not change in the outcome, it does change in form. Sabai in the second version is lucky, and does not need to kill her adversary deliberately. Another interpretation might be that this ending indicates that Allah has taken Sabai's side and avenges her father's murder.

All these major changes make the Sabai of the second version more domestic, passive, and nonaggressive.[35] In general, these characterizations of a female heroine are more acceptable according to Muslim standards. The second version was incidentally performed by a troupe under the leadership of an elder who was also the *alim-ulama* (religious leader) of his community. In this light it might be understandable that Sabai becomes a more subdued figure and that the emphasis shifts to male characters.

This comparison illustrates that randai scripts are rather flexible and that different performers tend to interpret the same basic story material differently. This is true for most stories that are performed by more than one troupe; each troupe has its own version, and the various versions might differ considerably.[36] The same is true for a story performed by the same troupe on different occasions. In that case the variations won't normally be as drastic as the ones between the two versions of *Sabai* discussed above. Nonetheless, depending on the audience and sponsor, a troupe might add advice according to adat, Islam, the government, or all of the above.

NEW STORIES

Contrary to the previously discussed plays—which are based on old Minangkabau tales and legends and deal with traditional topics like adat, family obligations, merantau, and Islam in a traditional Minangkabau setting—the following example, *Sutan Sari Alam,* is a newly written play that deals with similar topics, but this time in a more modern context. Besides addressing traditional themes centering around adat and dealing with general topics like fate, intrigue, and rivalry, this play also includes topics like government programs, land use disputes, alcohol abuse, and sexual assault—problems of special concern for the younger generation.

The parents of the play's hero, Sutan Sari Alam, died when he was very young. A hard-working, obedient, pious, and kind young man, he is taken care of by his relatives, the family of his aunt Mariani. The real son of aunt Mariani, Sutan Pamenan, hates the adopted rival and plots to get rid of him. He tells his mother that Sutan Sari Alam secretly plans to sell their *harto pusako* (sacred heritage, family land) to impress a girl. The mother is enraged and decides to immediately expel the adopted son from the family. Their grandfather Sutan Palito tries to negotiate, but to no avail. Sadly, Sutan Sari Alam leaves the house. In the meantime, Sari Alam's uncle, Sutan Maruhun, has just returned from rantau in Jakarta with his daughter, Rosani. Young Rosani was born in Jakarta and only speaks Indonesian, not Minang. Sari Alam had previously stayed with her family in Jakarta and they are close friends; now he pays them a visit to ask his uncle for advice before he goes rantau himself. (Throughout the play, all conversations that involve Rosani are in Indonesian, and her inability to understand Minang is the source of several humorous incidents.) When Sari Alam arrives at the house, his uncle is still at the mosque and only Rosani is home. The two chat and it is clear that both youngsters like each other, but since Sutan Sari Alam has just been expelled from his adoptive family, he is in a gloomy mood and wants to go rantau. When the uncle returns from his prayers, the three start a conversation about a government project in the village that revolves around the building of a new school. Some of the richer families will be asked to donate land for its construction. Having lived in the capital, Jakarta, the uncle is considered rich and is debating the donation of land, but decides to discuss it with the other village elders first to reach a consensus. Next, Sutan Sari Alam announces his wish to go rantau and asks permission from his uncle, as well as advice on the proper behavior in the rantau. Being interrupted by the arrival of his step-brother, Sutan Pamenan, Sari Alam leaves abruptly without any explanation. Alone with the uncle, Sutan Pamenan again spreads rumors that his rival has sold sacred family land and the uncle is shocked. When Rosani joins them, Sutan Pamenan is attracted to her and tries to flatter her. She responds coolly and evades him by talking about the importance of education and how government programs help rural families prosper. Later that evening, Sutan Sari Alam returns and meets Rosani again while the uncle is sleeping. Sari Alam's determination to go rantau has become stronger, but according to adat he must first obtain permission from his uncle. While he is explaining to Rosani why he is leaving, they are interrupted by the uncle, who, believing the gossip, kicks Sari Alam out of the house. Sari Alam leaves with a sad heart, although Rosani pleads with him to stay. She reminds him that he has a duty to cast his vote in the upcoming election, so that they can improve the living conditions in this village. In the meantime, the grandfather, Sutan Palimo, summons all the family members to discuss the land donation issue. He is surprised that Sari Alam is absent, and when they tell him that his grandson went rantau, he is upset because his permission was not asked. They discuss the land matter further, but no conclusion is reached because the grandfather is too upset about the disappearance of his beloved grandson, and he leaves to search for him.

In the meantime, Sutan Pamenan gangs up with his friend Pandeka Regok, and both go to visit Rosani with the intention of luring her away from home. She agrees to come for a walk, but as soon as they are in the fields, Sutan Pamenan starts harassing her, offering her alcohol, touching her with the intent to rape her, and claiming that she as a city girl must like that. She defends herself, first verbally, then physically. She successfully blocks and parries the first few attacks, but then she is struck and falls to the ground. At that moment, Sari Alam appears and fights with Sutan Pamenan. The grandfather also comes to the scene and tries to stop the fight, but is accidentally stabbed by Sutan Pamenan. Seeing this, Sutan Sari Alam wants to kill Sutan Pamanan for fatally injuring the grandfather. Rosani stops him, saying that this matter is now in the hand of the court. The old man is dying, and while he discloses his last wish (to donate some of the land to the community) he also reveals that Pamenan was adopted just like Sari Alam. Pamenan comes to his senses, repents, and both young men reconcile.

Although this is a recently written play, it illustrates that traditional principles from adat are still important in modern-day Minangkabau. Some of these elements of adat are directly addressed in the play, others are inferred. The ones that are addressed openly are concerned with family and clan relations, land possession, etiquette between the generations, and merantau. According to adat it is customary to adopt the children of deceased relatives as one's own, and Sutan Sari Alam is adopted in that manner by his aunt. Family land *(harto pusako)* owned and inherited along the female descending line cannot be sold, therefore it is a grave accusation by Sutan Pamenan to say that Sutan Sari Alam intends to sell pusako land to impress a girl. Merantau is a common practice prescribed by adat; it emerges in the play on several occasions. Sutan Maruhun and his daughter have just returned from their merantau in Jakarta; Sutan Sari Alam intends to go rantau because he has been expelled from his adoptive family. Another important aspect connected with merantau is that a young person intending to go to the rantau has to obtain permission and advice from the elders beforehand. Sutan Sari Alam therefore acts properly according to adat when he tries to get permission twice from his uncle Sutan Maruhun. However, both times he is interrupted and leaves without it. Unable to obtain permission from his grandfather, Sari Alam disappears and his grandfather is clearly upset that his permission hasn't been asked.

In addition to these openly discussed aspects of local customs, several of the conversations hint at additional underlying cornerstones of Minangkabau adat. The unity of the family is important, which can be seen when the grandfather tries to bring all others to their senses and not break the family apart. The unity of the community is just as important and any matter concerning the larger community has to be discussed by the village elders. In the play, a consensus has to be found before any action can be taken about the land donation for the school.

Despite all these traditional elements, the play is set in a contemporary context. The uncle has gone to the rantau as far as Jakarta, and his daughter was even born there, something unheard of in traditional plays. Rosani has been educated in the big city and brings that knowledge back to her Minangkabau home village. Throughout the play, she is the spokesperson for modern-day Indonesian issues, such as the importance of education and elections, family planning, and several other government programs. Besides elaborating on government issues, she also stresses the importance of adat and religion, thereby reinforcing the image of the three important pillars that hold up society: adat, Islam, and the government. Rosani is outspoken, but at the same time obedient to her father and kind to guests; in short, she is a model contemporary Indonesian girl.

Two things in the story lead to the tragic events toward the end of the story: the obviously evil intentions of Sutan Pamenan and the fact that Rosani is too trusting and agrees to go for a walk with him. Although the play clearly portrays Pamanan as the evildoer and Rosani as a positive role model, there is some underlying criticism of Rosani's behavior. It is improper in the traditional context, and especially according to Islam, for an unmarried girl to go out without family supervision. Her "trespassing" leads to near disaster; she is almost raped, and in the course of the ensuing fight the grandfather is accidentally killed. Although Rosani is never blamed directly, and the play actually ends with the reconciliation of all involved, the message to young women in the audience is clear: the world is dangerous for girls, especially without family protection.

Conflict and Resolution as Themes

Standard themes in randai involve two different kinds of conflict constellations: conflicts of interest that are typically character driven, and conflicts of obligation or loyalty that are created by the larger context of societal circumstances.

Conflicts of the first kind, conflicts of interest, normally culminate in a physical confrontation and are resolved in a silek fighting scene. Such a conflict tends to revolve around a central constellation of distinctly good and evil characters. The evil character's goal is generally to deceive, steal, kidnap, rape, or kill. The protagonist's goal is to prevent that from happening, or, if it has happened already, to execute some kind of damage control or take revenge (or both).

Consequently, negative characters are generally presented as malicious, greedy, rude, brutal, lusty, amoral, corrupt, and uneducated in matters of adat and religion. Examples of evil characters from the previous stories are: the evil ruler Kodo Nan Baha who kidnaps Intan Korong; the robbers who attack and kill Umbuik Mudo's father; King Rajo Nan Panjang, who kills Sabai's father; and the rapist who lures Rosani into the fields.

Positive characters, on the other hand, are typically portrayed as virtuous, kind, pious, obedient to elders, and knowledgeable in matters of adat and religion. Exemplary positive figures from the previous stories are: Umbuik Mudo, who studies hard, goes out to avenge his father's murder, and in the end forgives the assassins; Sutan Sari Alam, who is an obedient son to his adoptive family and rescues Rosani from the rapist; and the virtuous Sabai Nan Aluih, who kills her father's murderer.

However, positive characters, although generally virtuous, often possess traits that would not be considered positive. They are at times boisterous, flirtatious, forgetful, clumsy, or arrogant. In most cases however, these subordinate character traits either diminish in the course of the play as the characters mature, or else the flaws are so insignificant that they do not interfere with the general good-ness of the character. These additional traits make the characters less stereotypical and let them appear as real three-dimensional people who develop throughout the play. Many characters, al-though positive, use trickery and lies to achieve their goals, and as long as the goals are motivated by good intentions, the cunning is perceived as justified, even valuable. The End Justifies the Means is an accepted rule for character behavior. In fact, the audiences de-light in the artistry of the verbal cunning. For example, Anggun Nan Tongga, a truly positive character, repeatedly uses lies and tricks to obtain some of the dowry items for Gondoriah. Further-more, by his cunning he evades two of the women who try to lure him into marriage.[37] And Umbuik Mudo, a generally virtuous character, feels revengeful against Puti, toys with her emotions and indirectly causes her death. He repents and tries to save her, but in vain. Since this all happens in a subplot fairly early in the play, one can conclude that this experience aids in the maturing of Umbuik's character, a development that in the end enables him to show kindness toward the murderers of his father.

Different options for positive behavior become clear in the com-parison of two different stories dealing with the same conflict set-ting. Both *Umbuik Mudo* and *Sabai Nan Aluih* share the same basic plot, revenge for a father's murder. While Umbuik pardons his en-emies and makes them repent, Sabai kills her adversary, Rajo Nan Panjang. However, both endings are perceived as good and just, although one play ends with forgiveness and the other with the cold-blooded termination of the enemy. The difference that allows for this might be that Umbuik's father is killed by poor robbers who, for lack of education and guidance, do not know how to live a virtuous life, while Sabai's father is killed by a powerful, lustful, and intentionally malicious king who is considered beyond re-demption by Sabai (and the audience) and continues to be a threat to her. For the robbers there is the possibility of salvation through Islam; for the evil king there is none, and his execution is therefore a just solution. In character-driven conflicts of interest, truly evil characters are killed, while the others are reformed.

Other conflicts of interest between good characters normally deal with love interests, romance, and marriage. Typically one character wants to marry another who is not interested. The subplot of Umbuik Mudo is a good example. He falls in love with Puti Galang Banyak and proposes to her. Puti, being proud and of a wealthy family rebuffs him, a poor villager. Umbuik resorts to trickery and magic to win her heart, but is overcome by revenge and rebuffs her in return. Ultimately the two can never be united because of their changing emotions and the resulting ill fortune. Their conflict of interest is never resolved. In the end Puti dies of a broken heart and Umbuik goes on with his life, fulfilling other duties.

In the second thematic category, conflicts of obligation or loyalty, the configuration is more complex. Instead of the rather simple constellation of an evil versus a virtuous character, we find conflicts that are created through societal circumstances. Conflicts arise from customs like arranged marriage or family obligations. These conflicts typically do not lead to a physical confrontation in a silek fighting scene, but instead are either solved though diplomacy, trickery, or compromise, or else remain unsolved. The prime example is the story of Anggun Nan Tongga. He is obligated to find his lost uncles, to gather 121 dowry items for his fiancée Gondoriah, and to return within seven months. The conflict is already inherent in this setup. Gondoriah's desire for specific dowry items is a wish based on engagement customs prescribed in adat and therefore perfectly legitimate; however, it leads to the delay of Anggun and the ultimate separation of the lovers. No malicious character or intention is involved in the setup of this central conflict. Nonetheless, the mission cannot be accomplished because it takes Anggun too long to get the last item, and even more important, because he has to marry another woman to obtain the parrot his fiancée desires. Although as a wealthy Minangkabau man

Anggun could legally marry as many as four women, and Gondoriah would be obligated as a Muslim woman to accept that fact graciously, she follows her heart and goes into exile. Her reaction is portrayed sympathetically, although she acts against her obligation to obey the Islamic customs. The conflict remains unsolved and leads to the permanent separation of the two lovers.

Another variation of conflict scenarios deals with bad luck or bad fate. The primary scenario here is set in the context of gambling, a traditional Minangkabau pastime deeply ingrained in the culture.[38] In the days of the Minangkabau kingdom, royal gambling tournaments were held and participation was mandatory for those invited. Today gambling is still prevalent, but is now officially deemed immoral and inappropriate. Randai texts depict endless variations of how gambling leads to misfortune and disaster. It either affects the characters who gamble directly, their relatives, or both, as in the play *Magek Manandin.* Having received an official invitation, the main character is obligated to participate in the tournament, and he loses everything. This triggers a chain of unfortunate events for him, his family, and his fiancée. Less devastating, but nonetheless undesirable, effects are displayed in many other randai texts: loss of possessions and respect, unnecessary fights and quarrels, and addiction to the games, resulting in neglect of family and community duties.

Since female characters are generally virtuous, they become involved in conflicts by forced marriage, by emotional manipulation, or by reacting to assault. Furthermore, they frequently do not act for themselves but rather are rescued or aided by a male relative or friend. Male virtuous characters typically respond directly to evil-doings by their opponent and they fight for themselves. During a fight, both female and male virtuous characters alike take the defensive role.

Conflicts of obligation typically do not emerge between an evil and a virtuous character, as do conflicts of interest, but between two or more good characters. These conflicts are rarely resolved through combat; instead, a solution is reached through negotiation or trickery, or not at all. In plays where the central conflict does not culminate in combat, silek fighting scenes are nonetheless part of the story. Typically they involve robbers or other secondary characters who attack the protagonist and are defeated.

Randai Texts as a Mirror of Minangkabau Culture

Randai scripts, whether drawn from classical kaba or newly written plays, reflect and express aspects of the Minangkabau culture. The flexibility with which stories are played out and reinterpreted illustrates how they adjust to changing social circumstances.

Scripts based on old kaba use an antiquated and more elaborate language enhanced with proverbs, metaphors, and polite addresses; require larger casts that include legendary characters such as kings, spirits, and animals; and feature magical objects and events. Conflicts are more monumental and often involve many characters. Thus, these old plays satisfy the need of the audience to experience a link to their own historical or legendary past and see their customs and religion validated in a larger context. Performances of the these plays educate and entertain the audiences and pass on knowledge and appreciation of the Minangkabau past, thereby instilling pride of their culture in the performers and audiences alike.

Newly written plays also function to uphold customs and religious beliefs. In addition, they address modern issues of concern for modern-day Minangkabau and reflect societal changes more directly than old plays. In order to reflect current issues, these new plays employ more plain and direct language, smaller casts that include modern characters, and little or no magic. Conflicts here tend to be on a smaller scale between individuals. These new plays reflect the struggle of contemporary Minangs to consolidate traditional customs and beliefs with problems of the modern society, which is influenced by strong outside forces. Of major concern are the ramifications of modernization, such as consumerism, drug and alcohol abuse, and loss of contact with traditional values. Randai scripts also reflect the position of West Sumatra within the Republic of Indonesia. Government messages such as family planning, health care, or gotong royong (mutual assistance) are integrated into the scripts in order to employ randai's power to reach and educate villagers.[39]

CHAPTER 6

PERFORMANCE SPACE
AND COSTUMING

RANDAI STAGING and costuming are basically simple and easily recognizable. The majority of performances are still held in an open circular space with male performers dressed in silek-derived outfits and females in ceremonial Minangkabau gowns. Regional differences and preferences exist, however, and specific local dress styles or ornamentation details have made their way into randai costuming.

Randai performances also constantly adapt to sociocultural changes and this is reflected in modifications in the costuming and staging. Over the past twenty years, the use of electric lighting and microphones has increased dramatically and along with the use of raised stages has changed the overall character and appearance of randai from a rather intimate community event to a larger-scale entertainment form that can play to much bigger audiences.

Newly written plays introduce modern characters and their costumes reflect clothing worn by contemporary Minangkabau people. As a result, some performances have rather eclectic mixtures of costumes. Female characters might wear the traditional gown, while males wear modern-day costumes such as military uniforms, jeans, and baseball caps.[1] However, the traditional costuming is still prevalent and according to local artists will be retained because the vast majority of plays deal with characters from old Minangkabau legends and tales.

The fact that female performers today act the female roles as well as participate in the circular martial arts dance galombang has resulted in two different costumes for women, often within the same group. The standard ceremonial gown is worn by actresses and singers, whereas the standard silek outfit is worn by all galombang performers, regardless of their gender.

Staging

Traditionally, performances are given in the open, without any constructed stage. The preferred location is in front of the village's main gathering house, the *rumah gadang* (big house). Depending on the occasion, the performance space may also be in front of the house of the family that has commissioned a performance, in front of a mosque, in the marketplace, or in the schoolyard. Randai artists are highly flexible; they can perform almost anyplace where they find a level space with a minimum diameter of about eight meters. Randai staging is simple. A circular area is roped off and the audience surrounds this space. This bare, circular, open-air configuration is considered the most traditional, appropriate, and effective performance location. Other variations of staging are nevertheless found throughout the region. Sometimes a traditional silek practice space will be used for randai, in which case the area will be demarcated by a knee-high bamboo fence with a simple roof overhead. Other types of roofs are sometimes improvised with poles and tarps, leaving the sides open and protecting only the immediate performance area. Raised stages are becoming more and more popular. On several occasions I have witnessed randai on raised, roofed stages with audiences on one, two, or three sides. According to local artists however, this is a recent innovation and is not appropriate to the circular form of randai. Raised stages are mainly used when the performance is organized or commissioned by government officials, religious leaders, or wealthy individuals who frequently insist on supplying a more modern setting for the performance. Often in these cases, the audience can be seated only on one side, and the actors must adjust to the new circumstances by abandoning the traditional circular movement pattern of randai.

Lighting is only provided as general illumination and continues to be supplied by a few open flame torches stuck in the ground or gas pressure-lamps suspended from poles around the performance space. Sometimes lightbulbs are hung over the center of the stage, often powered by generators. Almost all troupes use hand-held microphones. However, the microphone cables are often rather short, and limit the movement range of the actors to the length of the cables. In case a group possesses only one microphone, the actors have to hand it back and forth among themselves which tends to be cumbersome and interferes with the smooth flow of the line delivery.

Costumes and Props

Costumes for female and male roles are very distinct. Male actors wear outfits derived from silek clothing, whereas the costume for female roles traditionally consists of authentic ceremonial gowns that are worn for processions, weddings, inaugurations of village chiefs, and other similar festivities.

The basic female costume includes a sarong (floor-length, wrapped skirt), a *baju kuruang* (knee-long blouse worn over the skirt), and a *salempang* (shoulder drape or sash). In addition to these basic pieces there are three predominant types of head dresses. An unmarried girl of high standing wears a *suntiang* (tall, highly elaborate golden tower-shaped headdress with a multitude of little pieces of tinsel, tassels, mirrors, bells, and ornaments attached to its basic semicircular structure).[2] This crown also has regional variations, but never fails to dazzle the audience with its rich ornamentation. An actress portraying a married woman wears a *tangkuluak tanduak* (traditional Minangkabau horn-shaped hat).[3] There are numerous regional variations of this hat, but the basic shape is the same and it is always red with gold and black embroidery. Sometimes a piece of fabric is attached to it and draped over the back. Lesser female characters, mainly servants, siblings, or those in other

Randai actress in full costume, heavily embroidered in gold and complete with an elaborate headdress

Randai actress in red costume embroidered with gold, and traditional Minangkabau horn-shaped hat

supporting female roles wear a variety of simple headdresses and ornaments. The older characters wear headdresses created by wrapping a piece of cloth tightly around the head so that the hair is entirely hidden. Younger ones typically wear no headdresses, but instead use various small golden ornamented hairpins as decoration.[4]

Additional character differentiation is accomplished through ornamentation and jewelry. A young well-to-do heroine, for instance, wears more elaborate costuming than a servant. The female singers who do not take part in the acting are dressed in the standard Minangkabau ceremonial outfit, consisting of the three main pieces (sarong, blouse, and sash) and the horn-shaped hat. The predominant colors of the female costumes are black, red, and gold, which are also the colors of the Minangkabau flag. Other less frequently worn colors for female costumes are green and blue.

The central costume piece for male roles is the *sarawa galembong*. These are long, wide pants with an extremely low crotch that often reaches almost to the floor. Traditionally they are black with some gold embroidery at the hems, but contemporary versions also appear in red or gold, and less frequently in blue, green, white, pink, orange, or violet. The prototype of these pants is derived from the pants worn in silek practice. However, for randai some changes are made in the embroidery or color, and, most important, in the shape.

Silek   Randai

Design of silek and randai pants

Costume of a male randai performer with shirt, pants, sash, and headcloth. Notice how the pants are used for the tapuak slapping technique, which produces drumlike sounds.

To enhance the sound the dancers make by slapping the fabric, the center section between the legs has been enlarged and now reaches almost all the way to the bottom hem of the legs. This allows the performers to get an optimum sound when the pants are "popped" open at an approximately 80-degree angle.

The male performers also wear a *taluak balango* (long-sleeved shirt), and various kinds of hats. These can either match the color of the pants, or not, depending on whether a coordinated color scheme or added variety and extra color is desired.

Some groups dress all their male actors in a simple black outfit, with no differentiation between characters. In these groups all actors are participants of the galombang circle. Other groups vary the costume according to the different role types. Elaborate costumes may be worn by actors who do not participate in the galombang circular dance, and only act in the scenes. Most groups, however, are balanced somewhere between these two extremes. Typically, all male actors participate in the galombang and wear the same basic outfit.

Minor character differentiation is accomplished through variations in the color and degree of embroidery and ornamentation of shirts, sashes, and hats. Robber-clowns always wear a *deta* (a soft cloth, wrapped around the head), while other young males wear a *saluak* (stiff, triangular pointed hat); older males sometimes wear a traditional *deta datuak* (somewhat stiffer version of the regular deta, prewrapped and fixed in place to form a hat). All male characters normally wear a hip sash *(kabek pinggang)* and a shoulder sash *(salempang)* along with the hat. Except for the hip sash and the deta, which are made from batik fabric, all other colored fabrics used for pants, shirts and sashes are monochrome, shiny, and bright. Sashes are often embroidered with gold or silver threads.

An interesting combination of male and female costume is employed by exceptional female characters who have to fight at some point in the play. They wear the standard female combination of sarong and long blouse, but concealed under the sarong they wear silek pants (sarawa galembong). Before they engage in fighting, they lift their sarong, tuck the corners under the belt and reveal the silek pants in which they now enjoy a greater freedom of movement. Women who participate in the martial arts dance galombang wear the same outfit as the male performers. Female impersonators wear the traditional female costume.

Normally actresses cannot participate in the galombang as do the actors because their movement is restricted by their tight costumes. Some groups, however, have recently incorporated the actresses into the galombang to add novelty and excitement. In these cases, the actresses will only engage in the movement sequences that are possible in their costumes, and then simply stand or walk when the regular galombang members perform the more dynamic and martial movements. This again shows that modification and innovation is an integral part of randai theater.

Traditionally neither makeup nor artificial hair pieces were used. However, some groups incorporate simple wigs and beards for ghost or spirit characters. Villainous characters occasionally sport exaggerated beards, made-up eyebrows, and mustaches. A few groups use animal costumes, consisting of full-body suits with large three-dimensional face masks of tigers, water buffaloes, and monkeys. Other groups use two-dimensional masks drawn on cardboard to represent the faces of evil characters.[5]

Modern dress has started to be incorporated into randai performances, but is still rare and employed almost exclusively by male characters. Modern plays incorporate contemporary characters like government officials, police officers, and gangsters, and depending on the roles, the male actors may wear suits, military uniforms, jeans, T-shirts, baseball hats, sunglasses, and other nontraditional costumes. Women typically wear traditional costumes.

Props are all handheld and normally consist of simple household objects like letters, handkerchiefs, prayer mats, umbrellas, farming tools, binoculars, cards, dice, and musical instruments. They are either carried to indicate simply a character's occupation or social standing, or else take on dramatic function in the form of a lost treasure, a magic heirloom, and the like. Weapons like knives, swords, and daggers are also employed, most frequently in fighting scenes.

Chapter 7

MUSIC

Three main distinct types of music are used in randai: instrumental music by an orchestra of talempong, flutes, and drums; songs accompanied by a flute; and percussion performed by the dancers. Instrumental music is played during the entrance and exit parades at the beginning and end of the performance that feature the entire orchestra and thus musically frame the actual theater performance. During scenes with dialogue, the musicians often provide an underlying and unobtrusive musical background to establish the overall mood of the scene, emphasize the acting, and provide sound effects for fighting scenes.

The songs and flute music are performed during the galombang dance along with the percussion performed by the dancers. Two singers and a flute player move to the center of the circle, where they perform, accompanied by exciting rhythmic clapping and shouting from the dancers. These two musical elements, songs and percussion, are woven together and complement each other during the dance.

The Instruments and Their Function

The orchestra for a randai performance can include up to twelve different instruments. However, the minimum instrumentation consists of the three: a large bamboo flute called saluang;[1] a five-piece set of bronze kettles struck with sticks, called talempong; and the *gandang katindik*, a medium-size horizontal drum with two heads of different sizes, that can be played with bare hands or sticks.

For a richer sound, the saluang and the drum are often doubled and other instruments are added. Additional wind instruments consist of two kinds of smaller bamboo flutes called *sarunai* and *bansi,* and a very thick, somewhat shorter bamboo flute called *sampelong.* Two other wind instruments often complement the flutes: one is made from the horn of the water buffalo *(pupuik tanduak),* and one consists of a tightly rolled banana leaf *(pupuik gadang).*

The other drums that can be added are: a slim, oblong, two-headed drum *(gandang sarunai),* a standing drum *(doll* or *tambua),* a large drum with equal-sized heads suspended from a shoulder strap *(gandang tasa),* and small, medium, and large frame drums *(rapa'i, rabana,* and *adok).* All drums can be played with either the hands or sticks, or both. String instruments are rare. Only the Arab-influenced two- and four-string fiddles *(rabab darek* and *rabab pasisir)* are used occasionally.

The horns, with their very loud and piercing sound, mainly function to alert the audience to the imminent beginning of a performance. This prelude with horns and other instruments (talempong and drums) might play for up to half an hour before the performance is ready to start.

The talempong has three functions. First, it is the leading instrument in the songs played for the entrance and exit parades; second, it creates mood music for emotionally charged scenes; and third, it adds excitement to fighting scenes through lively tunes. It is typically not played during the galombang dance.

Once the performers are ready to enter the stage area, the musicians follow the entrance procession while playing a specific opening tune called *dendang pasambahan* (greeting song). During this procession the talempong is played by three people in a formation called *talempong pacik*. In this, the first player holds the lowest-tuned kettle in one hand and beats it with a small stick, maintaining an even beat. The second player holds two higher-pitched kettles in his left hand and beats them with a stick, playing the skeletal melody. The third player also holds two kettles and plays variations of the melody.

Once the musicians reach the performance space and the randai has started, the talempong players either remain in the talempong pacik formation or switch to a different configuration, for which they place their kettles in a wooden frame. In that case it is called *talempong duduak* (seated talempong) and is played by just one musician. The other two are freed to play other instruments like flutes, gongs, or drums during the performance.[2] Most frequently however, the talempong is played the same way in the procession and within the performance, as talempong pacik: held in the hands of three players.

Mood music and fighting tunes are numerous and normally reflect the respective regional musical styles of the company. There are about twenty different talempong tunes used for fighting scenes, and several others to accompany wedding processions, wedding receptions, funeral processions, and the like. For sound effects the musicians have no standard tunes, but create on the spot what they deem necessary to highlight the scenes, such as percussive accents for the entrance of a major character.

The drums accompany the talempong during entrance and exit parades, as well as during fighting scenes. They can also supply additional sound effects. Some groups also use drums during the galombang, where they reinforce the percussive sounds made by the dancers as they slap their pants. This practice is a fairly new innovation and highly disputed among randai artists. Purists feel that the sound from the pants slapping is strong enough by itself and does not require drum enhancement, which can sometimes overpower the slapping. Others argue that since audiences are growing larger and thus noisier, the need for clear and audible sound effects justifies the use of the drums during the galombang.

The saluang flute, considered the most important instrument within randai, also has three functions. Its main purpose is to provide accompaniment for the songs performed between scenes. Within scenes it has two additional functions: to provide general mood music as background for the acting and to accompany sad songs that are part of the scenes. The location of the saluang player changes according to the function of his music. When he accompanies the two singers, he will normally move to the center of the circle with them, where all three can enjoy the full attention of the audience. When he plays mood music while the scene is in progress, he will remain outside the circle so as to not interfere with the acting. When songs are sung within a scene, the saluang player might enter the circle and sit down next to the actor or actress singing the song, providing a more intimate atmosphere.[3] In the latter case, the flute has a dramatic as well as a musical function.

Flutes can be integrated even further into the play and assume a more dramatic function. In the play *Umbuik Mudo* for instance, the protagonist desires a magic flute to win the love of the young girl Puti Galang Banyak. He plays it when he sees her at the bathing place and she instantly falls in love with him. The search for and the playing of this magic flute are pivotal moments in the play. In other plays the hero is often portrayed as an accomplished flute player. The display of his skills can offer relief from dramatic tension, as when he simply plays for the entertainment of his friends, or create tension, as when he plays by himself in the wilderness and is thus exposed to the danger of being discovered by robbers or wild animals.

All instruments can be prominently featured in scenes within scenes. In cases where the plot calls for musical entertainment during a wedding celebration, parade, or gambling tournament, the members of the orchestra have an opportunity to display their skills and play for two audiences simultaneously, the audience portrayed by the actors, and the audience watching the randai. Instruments featured as part of the entertainment within the play include talempong, flutes, drums, and sometimes string instruments as well.

The Songs and Their Function

Most of the songs featured in randai are derived from the folksinging tradition saluang jo dendang (flute and song) mentioned earlier. They are performed by two singers, the *tukang dendang* (lead singer) and the *tukang jajak* (supporting singer). Both alternate in singing the verses using a specific overlap technique. In this, the second singer (B) joins the first singer (A) in the last one or two lines of the first verse and then continues to the second verse, while the first singer fades out slowly. The same system is repeated, with roles reversed, for the subsequent verse, and so on (see illustration page 104). This practice blends the voices and creates a seamless transition from one singer to the other, which is considered aesthetically pleasing by the performers and audiences.

Most importantly, this practice gives each singer a break from singing during which he or she can make up new lyrics for the next verse. This allows for improvisation on the spot by changing interpretations of the story. It also gives the singers an opportunity to incorporate commentary on current events, add humorous lines, and otherwise entertain the audience with their quick wit.

The galombang dancers sometimes join in singing the last two or four lines of a verse, called *nyani basamo* (singing together). This also helps to blend the transition from one singer to the next and adds variation and volume to the sound. This practice also facilitates the synchronization between the galombang dance movements and the song.[4]

Depending on the preferences of a group, the importance and function of the songs vary greatly. Some groups focus on the acting, and therefore the songs function primarily as bridges between

  singer

verse 1   _____   A

             _____   A

             _____   A

             _____   A

             _____   A

             _____   A

             _____   A (B fading in)

             _____   A and B

verse 2   _____   B (A fading out)

             _____   B

             _____   B

             _____   B

             _____   B

             _____   B

             _____   B (A fading in)

             _____   B and A

verse 3   _____   A (B fading out)

             _____   A

             (the pattern continues)

Alternation of singers for saluang jo dendang

scenes by simply indicating changes of time, place, mood, and circumstances. This is often accomplished in as few as two or three verses. Other groups rely on the songs to convey central parts of the story, and therefore the songs are considerably longer and more elaborate, while the acting is used merely to illustrate certain moments in the song. The latter groups rely on strong singers who can spontaneously add verses as they go along and are able to improvise depending on the audience responses and the given time frame.[5]

Approximately thirty-five standard song melodies are used in randai, plus a large number of adaptations from local folk songs. Once the individual melodies are chosen, the lyrics are created to fit the story being performed. For entrance, opening, and closing songs almost all groups today use the same standard melodies (Dendang Pasambahan, Dayang Daini, Simarantang Rendah, Simarantang Tinggi, etc.) and then add their own lyrics. This custom is fairly new though, and some groups still use their own regional tunes for their opening and closing melodies.[6]

The songs are divided into two categories, *bagurau* or *gembira* (happy, joyous) and *ratok* (sad). The happy songs are more numerous and can further be divided into subcategories by lyric content; they might describe a journey, marriage preparations, the meeting of lovers, activities at a gambling tournament, and the like.

Almost all songs sung between scenes are performed by two singers, but occasionally an actor or actress might sing a sad song within the scene itself, most frequently as a lament after a loved one has died or a lover has left. Sadly, these beautiful scene-songs are found less and less frequently. Groups today choose a more realistic acting style to express sadness and replace these songs with "real" weeping and crying. However, in my opinion the scene-songs possess a much stronger theatricality and are also more effective in conveying the sadness or desperation of the character. I have never seen an audience laugh or joke during one of these songs, but they regularly break into laughter and mocking when an actor or actress cries real tears.

Percussion Performed by the Dancers

The percussive sounds performed by the dancers are referred to as *tapuak* and are typically performed between the verses of each song.[7] Two types of tapuak exist: *tapuak galembong* (slapping the pants) and *tapuak tangan* (clapping the hands).[8] The tapuak galembong can be considered the signature technique of randai; when performed correctly and by all performers simultaneously, it produces the magnificent drumlike sounds that are responsible for much of the excitement randai creates.

The tapuak galembong is a technique derived from two kinds of slapping techniques used in silek. In the first variation, the practitioner slaps his thigh, hip, or torso with one hand while stepping forward or backward. This is intended as a signal to alert the partner in practice, or to fool and distract an opponent in a tournament. A second variation within silek is a high frontal kick, which stretches the fabric of the pants. The fabric is hit with both hands simultaneously as the kick is executed and the leg is in the highest position. This variation can most frequently be observed when silek is performed as entertainment or demonstration, and is intended to draw the audience's attention to the attack.

From these simple slapping techniques used in silek, randai performers have developed an impressive percussive repertoire. In addition to the simple frontal kick with the slap, similar slaps are now executed while the leg is raised to one side, in the process of stepping forward or backward, and even while turning, spinning, or jumping. With each step the leg swings up high, to an approximately 90-degree angle. Since the creation of a strong slapping sound is crucial, it is important that the leg swings out and up in time to reach the highest point at the precise moment the slap has to be performed. In the instant of the hit, the hands do not actually contact each other like in a hand clap, but pass each other closely, thereby stretching the fabric between them to produce the sound. It is the fabric being hit and stretched that creates the sound, not the hands actually touching each other through the fabric.

Performers of the circular galombang dance in randai slap their pants in unison to create sound effects. (Photo by Edy Utama.)

Another main tapuak technique consists of the following constellation. Both feet are on the ground, the torso is slightly bent forward, and both hands hit the front of the stretched fabric between the legs. In the instant of the hitting, both knees are jerked apart slightly to give the fabric the extra bounce, thus producing a loud and sharp thudding sound (model A in the illustration page 108). Experts can time this so well that the pitch of the sound actually changes from low to high in the process of stretching the fabric.[9] Sounds can also be altered by spreading or closing the fingers and by the intensity with which the hits are executed.

Patterns of individual slaps and claps are composed into simple or complex sequences, depending on the skills of the performers and the preferences of the galombang leader. Several dozens of different rhythms exist. Within a single song, the percussive sequences between verses will generally be the same and are cued and led by leader of the circle through vocal sounds like *hep* and *ta*. These vocal cues become an integral part of the percussive pattern and also serve to coordinate and synthesize the movements and sounds of the performers.

Two tapuak pants-slapping techniques

A

A: The fabric is slapped in front, with the right and left hands alternating. Both feet remain on the ground at all times.

B

B: The fabric is slapped from the back and the front at once, both hands pass each other. One leg is raised to stretch the fabric.

The following notation, based on the TUBS (Time Unit Box System),[10] will illustrate some of the basic percussion patterns as performed in the galombang sequences of randai. Each box stands for an equal duration of time. For the various ways the sounds are produced, I have created specific symbols. Hand claps are indicated by a simple dot, while fabric slaps are indicated by symbols drawn from the leg positions and shape of the pants during the production of the sound.

Symbols for various tapuak

     Clapping with both hands in the air.

Slapping of the pants as shown in model A in the previous illustration. The fabric is stretched between the legs thereby forming a triangle of cloth that creates a distinct sound when hit. The letters *r* and *l* indicate slaps with the right or left hand.

Slapping of the pants as shown in model B in the previous illustration. This gives a slightly higher pitched sound because the leg swings up and forcefully stretches the fabric right before the hit. Both hands hit the fabric simultaneously.

The arrow indicates that the performers turn 180 degrees during a tapuak, thereby changing from facing the inside of the circle to facing outward, or vice versa.

Besides the standard sounds of hand clapping and slaps on the stretched fabric, there are several other percussive sounds, like finger snapping and the slapping of body parts other than the hands and thighs. These are secondary, however, and are not included in the following examples. The first example shows a simple and standard tapuak sequence used by most groups at least once during their performance. It is performed by all members of the galombang simultaneously.

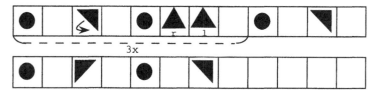

Standard version of a single tapuak pattern

The first part is repeated three times, and each time the performers execute a 180-degree body turn on the second tapuak (indicated by the arrow). They start the first part facing into the center of the circle; on the second repetition they face toward the audience; on the third they face toward the center of the circle again. Then they pivot 90 degrees to the left, so that the last three hand claps and slaps are executed while the performers walk clockwise in the circle. This is a standard ending of a tapuak sequence. However, some groups will only do two or even just one clap-slap combination, while others add double hand claps or slaps. What all the endings have in common is that they are initiated by a vocal cue from the galombang leader to indicate the end of the sequence and the transition into the next sequence. This transition, typically a short walking section, is followed by the next verse, accompanied by a silek or dance sequence. This in turn ends with a new tapuak sequence, and so on, all through the play.

The following example shows a different tapuak pattern with the same elements as the first, but in a different order and tempo. The second example has a short ending consisting of only one clap-slap combination. This second pattern is normally faster in tempo than the previous one.

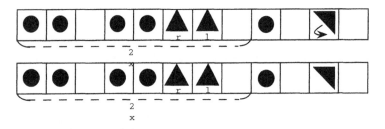

Variation of a tapuak pattern with a short ending

On the fast double hand claps the performers tend to extend their arms to the upper left side, reaching high with both hands during the clapping. From there they rapidly bring the hands down to slap the fabric, thereby creating not only an interesting percussion pattern, but also a visually exciting sequence.

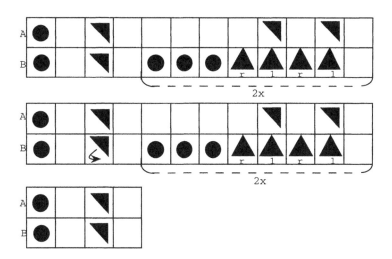

Ensemble arrangement of a tapuaʔ sequence

In the third example above two different interlocking patterns are played simultaneously. Typically the members split into two groups for this choral arrangement.

Circular formation for a tapuaʔ choral sequence

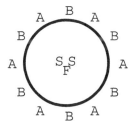

For tapuaʔ choral sequences the galombang members split into two groups (here indicated by A and B). The two singers (S) and the flute player (F) stand in the center.

An interesting variation of this arrangement is performed when only the two galombang leaders play pattern A and the rest of the group play pattern B. In this variation, the two leaders leave the circular formation and enter the center of the circle for the tapuak sequence. That way, the sound differentiation is made visible by the spatial separation of the two groups. In this variation, the singers and flute player will stay outside the circle and perform there in order to allow the two leaders to use the space inside the circle.

As mentioned before, some groups choose to enhance the percussive sounds further with one or two drums. Some drummers even take the liberty to improvise on top of the percussion patterns performed by the galombang dancers. In the traditional and more pure style however, the percussion is created solely by the dancers' slapping of the fabric and clapping of the hands.

There is a clear gender differentiation for the musicians. Most singers are female, whereas instruments are predominantly played by male musicians. A few groups feature female talempong ensembles, and individual female singers occasionally play the drums, but these are exceptions.[11]

Randai music has undergone some changes over the past twenty years, although these are not yet as dramatic as those that have affected the troupe composition, staging, or acting styles. However, modern tunes from Indonesian and Malaysian pop music have become more and more accessible through cassette tapes and are widespread in all of Sumatra.[12] Their infiltration into randai has become so widespread over the past years that the organizers of the West Sumatra Randai Festival in 1994 deemed it necessary to limit the number of pop tunes to a maximum of three per performance in order to maintain a higher level of the traditional Minangkabau tunes within randai. The popularity of pop tunes has also effected the dance style. Generally groups that use pop tunes (referred to as *dangdut* melodies) also use less of the traditional movements; instead, the galombang dancers borrow movements from popular modern Malaysian and Indonesian dances like *joget*. Consequently, silek-derived dance movements are on the decline in these groups.

CHAPTER 8

ACTING

RANDAI'S UNIQUE character is created by various specific acting conventions: the metered and melodious speeches, the positioning and movement of the actors, the fighting scenes, and the interplay between songs and acting. Generally speaking, acting is a more flexible element than the songs or the galombang movements; and it has changed more significantly than the other elements, possibly because it is the newest addition to the composite art form of randai. Performers seem to take more liberties with improvisation and innovation in the area of acting than in the songs or galombang dance, which are more strictly preserved in their traditional forms.

Acting takes place within the circle formed by the seated galombang members. In this empty open space, without scenery, and with a minimum of props, the actors rely on the singers to establish location, time, and general mood in the song preceding each individual scene. The scenes are enacted in a form of storytelling in dialogue form with elaborate vocal stylization. In contrast to the vocal style, most actors and actresses today simply stand in place while they deliver their lines. Except for choreographed fighting scenes, their movement is limited to a few steps and gestures. The focus is clearly on the content of the words where there are words, and on silek where there is movement.

Role Types

As we have seen in chapter 5, there is a wider range and larger number of male role types in a randai play; female roles are often limited to just two per play. The major male role types include young heroes, older fathers or uncles, kings, religious leaders, silek teachers, traditional healers (pawang or dukun), villains, robbers, clowns, guards, and servants. Female role types are typically defined primarily by their relationship to men: young unmarried daughters, wives, mothers, and servants. The large amount and variety of male roles is clearly reminiscent of the fact that randai was initially an all-male theater form centered around male-male relationships and conflicts.[1] On the average, the male roles outnumber the females by four to one. Often plays have only one female character, although the standard is two females (often mother and daughter) and six to eight males. The play *Umbuik Mudo*, for instance, has seven principal male roles: the young hero, Umbuik; his teacher, who is also the uncle of the maiden Puti Galang Banyak; her father; a second silek teacher in the rantau; and three robbers. Secondary male roles are Umbuik's father, who dies in the first scene; several male villagers who find the dying man, and who later double as guests at the teacher's house; and a third teacher in the rantau. The two principal female roles are Puti Galang Banyak and Umbuik's mother. Secondary female roles are Umbuik's sister, and Puti's mother. In the much longer play *Anggun Nan Tongga,* the female-male ratio is similarly unequal. Although the entire epic has five main female characters, each segment that is typically performed as an individual randai play has only one or two principal female roles, typically a young unmarried girl and her mother. Male roles again are far more numerous and include, besides the young hero, Anggun: his friend, guard, and advisor Bujang Sala-maik; his five uncles, whom he finds in different parts of the world; his countless adversaries; his teachers; and various healers and magicians, fishermen, peddlers, and peasants.

The same ratio can also be found in newer plays written after women began to act in randai. *Sutan Sari Alam* offers only one principal female role, the girl Rosani, who returned from the rantau in Jakarta with her father. The only secondary female role is an aunt. The principal male roles include the young hero, Sari Alam, his uncle, his grandfather, the would-be rapist Sutan Pamenan, and Pamenan's friend. Clearly, new plays have a cast distribution similar to that of older plays.[2] Male characters are the principal carriers of the plot, and consequently they have by far the greater share of lines and action.

The comparison of acting styles according to role types shows various stereotypical behavioral patterns. Male roles generally use a larger kinesphere than female roles;[3] villains, clowns, and robbers in turn use a larger kinesphere than other more refined male characters. Unrefined roles also speak in harsher voices and show more uncontrolled emotions like anger, fear, or contempt. The more refined and educated a character is, the more he or she will control emotional outbreaks, speak a high-level language embellished with metaphors and proverbs, and move in a controlled and slow manner.

The least refined characters are the robbers, obvious stock characters who always appear in groups of three or four. They have a large repertoire of standard sets of antics, jests, and pranks. A prominent example of their clowning is their frequent mistaking of members of their gang for enemies, upon which they start fighting with each other before they recognize each other as friends. A robber gang normally consists of an older leader and two or three younger, cowardly underlings. Once they face an opponent, they boast of their strength and meanness, but as soon as the fighting is about to start, the younger ones get frightened and push each other forward to take on the enemy. Clown-robbers are depicted as malicious, ill-tempered, simple-minded, gullible, uneducated, clumsy, and boisterous. Nevertheless, they are typically not entirely evil, and upon encountering a superior hero they can be reformed to follow the right path.

Another type of unrefined character is the stereotypical villain. For example, Rajo Nan Panjang, the murderer of Sabai's father, is a thoroughly vicious despot. He struts around commandeering everybody and demanding everything at once. He is bad-tempered, either speaking in a loud voice and with unrefined expressions, or else using cunning and a falsely sweet language to manipulate others. Malicious, powerful, arrogant, and vengeful, he shows no respect for the rules of adat and religion, and laughs at people who do.

A refined male hero, on the contrary, behaves according to adat and religion, obeys his elders and teachers, and fulfills his familial obligations. Rambun Pamenan, the young male hero of a play by the same name, for instance, goes to rescue his mother, who has been imprisoned by an evil and lecherous king. A dutiful son, he is also courteous and respectful toward those he meets on the way. He is kind, even to the two watchmen who guard his mother. He convinces them to turn against their malicious boss, always speaking in a kind, refined, and eloquent voice. Rambun's speeches and body language indicate that he is in control of his emotions and therefore of the situation. When he finally has to face his mighty opponent, he is brave, skilled, and fair in his fighting.

The female impersonator, bujang gadih (boy girl), acts similarly to female actresses portraying female characters. Neither an exaggerated high voice, nor extremely softened movements are observed.[4] The actor portrays the character primarily through the content of the lines and the female costume, and only secondarily though his voice and body language. Unfortunately, because there are so few female impersonators left in randai theater today, it is impossible to determine if and how female performers have been influenced by the performance style of their predecessors.[5]

Female characters are differentiated by age and social status. Older females appear in the function of mother or aunt, where they normally enjoy the respect of the younger generation. Young females are unmarried girls, often portrayed as naive, uneducated, and foolish in their behavior, which justifies their patronage by elders. Exceptions like Sabai are rare. She is wise, although young, has good judgment, and acts with determination. The more standard young female is like Puti Galang Banyak: naive, a little spoiled, and without initiative; or like Siti Nurina, an obedient, dutiful daughter and trusting fiancée. There are no female equivalents to the male evil kings or robbers. Female characters can be mischievous or use trickery at times, like Dandomi, who lures Anggun into marriage, but they are neither overtly evil nor powerful. Accordingly, their body language and vocalization is that of a refined character, with small gestures, restrained flow of movements, and a moderate voice.

Animals and spirits are a special class of role types and are portrayed in various ways. Several plays have a speaking parrot (nuri) as a major character, while others feature tigers, monkeys, or buffaloes. The latter three are portrayed by actors in full body suits with face masks, and they don't speak. The nuri, however, can be portrayed in two distinct ways, either by an actress or actor wearing the standard female or male randai costume and speaking the bird's lines face-to-face with the other characters, or else by a fake bird in a cage with an actor offstage providing the voice of the bird. The first type of impersonation is closer to the storytelling tradition in which the narrator lends his voice to the character. Here the need to change the outward appearance does not arise. The second type attempts a more realistic enactment, using a bird in a cage and an offstage voice.

A similar distinction can be made for the portrayal of spirits and ghosts. One type of enactment of spirits has an actor with a veil or wig concealing his face speaking to other characters in the center of the circle. The second type uses only an offstage voice as the voice of the supernatural entity. In this case, the acting partner will wander around, staring into space, trying to locate the source of the voice (unsuccessfully, of course). The impression of the presence of the spirit is created indirectly by a voice out of nowhere and the re-action of other characters to the voice.[6] Here, it is actually hard to determine which of the two types of enactment is the more "realis-tic" depiction of a ghost; the invisible one, or the one with the wig or veil. According to Minangkabau beliefs, ghosts and spirits can appear in various human and animal shapes, and as disembodied voices. However, the concurrent existence of different approaches to the depiction of animals and spirits raises the possibility of the recent development of a more realistic acting style. If the recollec-tions of older randai artists are correct, randai has indeed become more realistic over the past twenty-five years. The use of an actual bird, for instance, is not remembered as an element of randai in the past, nor are the use of wigs or veils for ghosts. The emergence of greater realism could be explained through the growing exposure to the realism of Western media such as television and film.

Vocalization

Most of the speeches in randai are delivered in a melodious, fairly regular meter, filled with rhymed proverbs and stock phrases. Depending on the skill and experience of the performers, contem-porary comments and ad-libs are integrated to fit the meter, so that the melodious flow of a speech is sustained. Traditionally, this melodious and metered vocalization is sustained even when emo-tions like anger, sadness, surprise, or fear are expressed. Emotions are normally conveyed through the content of the words rather than though emotional outbursts and graphic enactment. Excep-tions are the utterances of clowns and villains, who curse, laugh, use Indonesian and foreign languages (English and Dutch), and make nonsensical sounds for comic effect.

Increasingly, more and more groups add "realistic" enactment of emotions in high points of a scene. Crying and sobbing are added to scenes of grief. Puti Linduang Bulan (the mother of Ram-bun Pamenan) for instance, is kidnapped by the evil king Rajo

Angek after her husband dies. During her initial confrontation with the lusty despot, she retains her composure and speaks in eloquent phrases reminding him of adat rules and propriety. He reacts with derisive laughter and threatens her with his knife. She goes to her knees, requesting extra time to mourn properly for her husband, all still with customary metered and melodious speeches. However, as soon as she is alone with her maidservant, they both cry and lament over the forthcoming misery. Puti Linduang Bulan crouches on the floor, while her servant embraces and comforts her. Their sobbing lasts for several minutes until the end of the scene. A song then describes Puti's suffering in the lyrics.[7]

Movement Conventions

The circular formation of a randai performance and the fact that audiences are traditionally on all sides of the circle has led to unique acting conventions. Actors position themselves on opposing sides within the circle, and this artificially enlarged distance

Two male actors of the randai group Palito Nyalo. Notice the galombang dancers seated around them. (Photo by Edy Utama)

between characters gives the dialogue a larger-than-life quality. This distance is generally maintained even if characters have conversations with rather intimate content.

In addition to this positioning, the basic movement patterns within the circle are also remarkable. After the exchange of several lines, the actors interrupt the talking, walk a few steps clockwise or counterclockwise in the circle to a new position and resume the dialogue. This is intended to give all audience members equal opportunity to see and hear clearly. It also adds an almost Brechtian *Verfremdungseffekt,* since the scenes are interrupted repeatedly and the spectators are constantly reminded that the actors change places to give all of them a better view. This convention is only altered when the performance is given on a raised stage with the audience on only one side. In that case the actors face front at all times and they also tend to stand closer together.

Another movement convention is the *langkah duo,* a two-step pattern derived from silek. First, an actor takes one step forward, placing the rear foot close to the front foot; he pauses and then

A male and female actor of the group Sago Sejati perform a scene from the play Umbuik Mudo.

takes one step backward, placing the front foot close to the rear foot. The knees are slightly bent at all times. This movement convention echoes a basic silek practice wherein participants try to blend their movements and achieve a harmonious flow. Both combatants continuously adjust their movements and body positions to each other, typically keeping an equal distance while exchanging strikes and blocks.

Traditionally, this stepping technique in randai was also accompanied by arm movements and hand gestures derived from silek blocks and strikes, but today these are only infrequently used. One step is typically taken per spoken line, timed to the tempo of the speech. There are many variations of this technique. Although traditionally used only by male actors, it is nowadays also used for female roles. Some groups use it only for the character that is speaking while the other characters remain still. Other groups coordinate this stepping pattern so that all actors step in unison on all lines spoken. While facing each other, actor A moves backward and actor B moves forward and vice versa, so that the distance between them remains the same. The langkah duo is employed to different degrees by various groups or various actors within a group. Some actors move exclusively in this fashion, while others use it only occasionally to emphasize important lines.

Another characteristic movement convention is a silek-derived stepping sequence mainly used for the first entrance of servant characters and prior to fighting scenes. Called *langkah tigo* (three steps) or *langkah ampek* (four steps), depending on the silek style, it is a formal greeting consisting of three or four steps and a final pose. If the actor plays a servant role, he enters with the silek steps and assumes a crouching position, folding his hands above his head in what is called a *sambah* (greeting). A servant character addresses a higher-standing character in this fashion to show respect and deference. This pose is typically used by the first character who enters the circle at the beginning of the play, in order to show respect toward the audience and to honor the ancestors of both community and performers.

A more elaborate variation of this entrance is used by male characters who are not servants. As an indication that they will be involved in a fighting scene at some point in the play, their first entrance opens with a sequence that also includes the three or four silek steps. The pose, however, is different. The actor crouches and extends both arms diagonally down toward the floor, palms facing up, fingertips touching the ground. From here, he raises both his hands to his head, touching his temples lightly with the fingers. He momentarily holds both poses. He might then turn his body to face a different direction and repeat the greeting up to four times.[8]

During scenes the amount and quality of movement of a character is determined by the role type and circumstances. A refined character like an older mother, a young maiden, or a respected village chief generally uses small gestures and a restrained movement flow, while unrefined characters like clowns or villains use larger gestures and a less restrained flow of movement. The basic gestures are the same: pointing with the index finger, making a fist, holding the right hand to the heart, covering the eyes, putting one hand on the hip, pushing out the palm to stop someone, and other standard randai gestures. Intensity, duration, and range of these movements, however, vary according to the type of character.

There are no strict rules, and different groups use different movement types. A few groups incorporate silek steps for each movement in space as well as hand gestures with each step, both timed to the spoken lines. Other groups incorporate virtually no movement, and the actors merely stand in place and deliver their lines as storytellers.[9]

Interaction between Characters

Generally, scenes in randai have a single focus. In most cases only one action or exchange of speeches happens between two or three characters at a time. Occasionally, multifocus scenes are created when additional characters act outside the circle, indicating a different location than the main one inside. A prime example can be found in the performance of the play *Umbuik Mudo*. While Umbuik is engaged in the competitive Qur'an recitation in his teacher's house, the teacher's niece, Puti Galang Banyak, walks back and forth outside the circle, indicating that she is in the an-juang,[10] the room from which she listens intently to Umbuik's beautiful and captivating voice. Another example in which the space outside the circle is incorporated into the scene is when rob-bers sneak up on lone travelers or other unsuspecting victims. In this spatial constellation speeches can occur simultaneously in the two different locations and overlap considerably, something that is strictly avoided in regular single-focus scenes. Eventually, parallel scenes will merge into one; Puti descends from the anjuang to re-quest that Umbuik repeat his recitation, or robbers catch up with the victim and attack, thereby converging the two imaginary loca-tions into one.

Physical contact between characters is rare. Handshakes be-tween male characters or comforting embraces between female characters occur, but they are brief. In scenes where someone is sick, injured, or dying, he or she typically lies on the ground, while other actors kneel close by. In moments of intimacy or sadness, ac-tors also tend to kneel close to each other. Ultimate intimacy is ex-pressed in scenes where two lovers vow to either marry each other or die, and even this highly emotional exchange is typically sealed with a mere handshake and a longing glance. No other contact oc-curs.[11] Again, closeness is expressed through lyrical proverbs and metaphors rather than through body language. The most unre-strained physical contact is displayed in fighting scenes and during interactions among characters like robbers who teasingly push, drag, and carry each other around, stumble over each other, and engage in mock battles.

Scenes of Conflict

In almost every randai performance, a conflict escalates and then culminates in a physical fighting scene. Often, the actual physical fighting is preceded by a lengthy verbal exchange. This verbal fight or *silek lida* (silek of the tongue) can be a kind of competition of verbal fighting skills during which both opponents ad-lib insults and threats intended to proclaim their strength and to intimidate each other. This strategy is often used among robbers. In other scenarios, the silek lida can be used by a virtuous character to verbally defeat the aggressor and preempt a physical attack. This strategy, however, is rarely successful in randai, and typically the hero will have to engage in a physical fight to defeat his opponent. Once it is apparent that a physical confrontation can no longer be prevented verbally, a standard phrase will be exclaimed by one of the fighters: "Open your step!" or "Let's compare our steps!" (both referring to silek steps). Both performers then circle each other in low crouching steps, and exchange the first attacks and defenses. Often a second or third attacker will join and the excitement builds further when one of them draws a weapon.[12]

During a fighting scene the actors stay in character. A boisterous robber for instance will strut around showing off his muscles between attacks, while a refined character will simply stand composed and look at his opponent with contempt. A cowardly fighter will try to hide behind his companions and fight only when they push him toward their opponent. Fights are frequently interrupted by the participants to shout more insults at the opponents and comment on the other fighters' lack of good silek techniques. When several robbers are engaged in combat, they frequently ad-lib advice or encouragement to their companions and insults at their common enemy.

The outcome of fights varies according to the plot and the characters involved. Fights in which robbers attack an innocent hero tend to end in a standard manner. After the robbers are defeated, they give up and beg for mercy in an exaggerated and comic fashion. They tremble and stutter, shriek and cry. The hero will then normally spare their lives after he makes them promise to give up their criminal ways and follow the true and righteous path of Islam. Rarely are robbers killed for their crimes.

In more serious combat between two equally strong opponents, either one can be defeated. If the evil character wins, it is frequently through the use of trickery or black magic. The antagonist might shoot his opponent in the back like Rajo Nan Panjang, who shoots Sabai Nan Aluih's father, or he might call several underlings, who then overwhelm the good character. The villain will triumph without remorse. On the contrary, if a good character kills an evil one, he or she will typically express compassion and sorrow for the adversary. Sabai Nan Aluih, for instance, grieves for both her murdered father and his murderer after she has taken revenge and killed him.

Other confrontations are solved through the interference of a higher entity, often a village chief, uncle, or teacher. A prominent example is the combat between Anggun Nan Tongga and Katik Alam Tansudin. Katik loses in a gambling tournament that is intended to determine who can claim Gondoriah as his fiancée. Katik maintains that Anggun has been cheating and attacks him. Since they are of equal strength, the winner cannot be determined and they fight for a long time. Finally, the spirit of their old teacher descends from the heavens, stops the fighting, and decrees that Gondoriah belongs to Anggun.

CHAPTER 9

MARTIAL ARTS AND DANCE

As I ARGUED in chapter 2, randai most probably developed out of silek. Two of the evolutionary steps can still be seen as part of randai performances today: the silek fighting scenes and the galombang circular martial arts dance. Movements in the fighting scenes are simply called *main silek* (play silek), indicating that they are perceived as pure silek moves, since the term *main silek* is also used for regular silek practice. Silek movements in the galombang, on the other hand, have undergone changes and have become more dancelike.[1]

Fighting Scenes

The previous chapters on scripts and acting described how conflicts arise and culminate in fighting scenes. In this chapter, the composition and choreography of these combats shall be examined. Fighting scenes are of great variety, ranging from short encounters of only three or four exchanges of attacks and defenses, to long scenes with multiple encounters between several characters. These scenes can consist of pure silek sequences, or of silek interspersed with theatrical elements like acrobatics, clowning, and physical and verbal jokes. Weapons are a vital part of combat and feature prominently in randai.

A frequent, almost stereotypical fighting scene involves the protagonist and a gang of three or four villains. Typically, they will engage in a heated verbal encounter (silek lida) consisting of stock phrases before the actual physical attacks start. One of the robbers attacks first, often being shoved into that role by his partners, who are too afraid to attack the hero themselves. After successfully defending himself against each of the attackers individually, the protagonist is faced with a new level of attack in which the robbers then team up and attack as a group. The scene will, therefore, feature one-on-one fighting sequences as well as sequences with multiple attackers, a constellation that is also practiced by more advanced students in silek training sessions. Frequently, all attackers are subdued and pinned to the ground with a pin called *kunci mati* (death lock). This technique is applied to their wrists or ankles in such a way that escape is impossible. On rare occasions the hero is overwhelmed and taken prisoner by the robbers.

The robber scene is the most frequently played scene in randai for four reasons. First, since most of the plays contain a travel scene, it can be built into almost any play. Outdoors, attackers can find an easy target in someone, typically the male hero, who is going rantau, or in someone, typically the female heroine, who is going to the market or to an outdoor bathing place by a river. Second, the robber scene is highly popular with the audience because it mixes serious fighting with clowning and joking. Third, it has pedagogic implications, instructing the audience that living as a robber is immoral and will normally end in defeat and disgrace. Fourth, it incorporates long sequences with multiple attackers and thereby allows for the display of a large repertoire of silek techniques.

Although it might seem that robber scenes are often inserted

The final technique in a fighting scene in randai, the kunci mati, or "death lock." This technique, here applied to the arms, traps the opponent and leaves him no way to escape.

Another "death lock" technique, here simultaneously applied to the ankles of three attackers

into a play only for these reasons, they are in fact often integral to the story line. In many stories a female character is attacked by robbers while on the road, and a stranger comes to her rescue. Predictably, the woman then falls in love with the stranger and desires to marry him. This, in turn, often creates the story's main conflict, especially if her family has already chosen a husband for her. This is the case in the such popular stories as *Siti Nurina* and *Siti Ramalan*. A slightly different conflict arises from a similar rescue scene in *Anggun Nan Tongga*. When the protagonist saves Intan Korong from the evil pirate Kodo Nan Baha, she also falls in love and wants to marry her rescuer. However, this time the male hero is already promised to someone else and has to refuse the offer.[2]

The following examples describe in detail silek techniques that are used in different kinds of fighting scenes. I will compare and contrast fighting scenes with one-on-one fighting and multiple attackers; then I will address those that display serious combat (which ends in the death of one opponent) and those which are more humorous (in which silek is mainly used for entertainment). In addition, I will look at several special and unusual features like long-distance techniques, magic weapons, and female characters in combat.

The final scene from the play *Maelo rambuik dalam tapuang*[3] will illustrate the structure of a typical fighting scene with only two opponents involved. The story leading up to the fight is fairly simple and shall briefly be recounted here. The young maiden Anggun Bainai is ordered by her father to marry Sutan Lembang Alam, an arrangement that has been agreed on by both families in years past. However, Lembang is an immature hothead, prone to gambling, and without manners. Anggun Bainai dislikes him for good reason. Besides, she already has a sweetheart, Sutan Nagari, and when she resists the match her father curses and abandons her. She is ready to kill herself when her uncle, Datuak Rajo Mudo, takes pity and helps arrange for the wedding between the two lovers. The disgruntled ex-fiancé, publicly disgraced and ridiculed, is enraged and driven only by thoughts of revenge. He confronts

Anggun Bainai and Nagari with the intention to murder them both. The physical fighting scene is preceded by a verbal challenge uttered by Lembang in which he brags about his fighting skills. He also states boldly that he will take revenge and kill them both. To no avail Nagari attempts to calm him and bring him to reason, and so the battle begins. Three other characters are present during this scene: Anggun Bainai, who basically stays at the fringes of the action, and two friends of Lembang. The latter two initially enjoy the intensifying confrontation and make comments and jokes, much to the amusement of the audience. However, as the fighting becomes more serious, one of them eventually tries to stop it. This typical combat scene is accompanied by a lively tune played by the talempong orchestra. The music starts quietly under the verbal confrontation and becomes increasingly louder as the fighting intensifies.[4]

The following will give a detailed description of the four silek movement sequences used in this theatrical combat. The reader might find the long description a little overwhelming and might want to skip ahead. However, the following examples are excellent representatives of silek fighting scenes and it will be helpful in highlighting the important attributes of randai combat in general.

At the beginning of the combat the opponents take their position on opposite sides of the circle. Both move in unison and assume a low kudo-kudo stance; they freeze in this position for a moment, then execute a fast gelek turn.[5] They then take three slow steps forward counterclockwise along the perimeter of the circle, keeping an equal distance between them. Again the last step ends with a gelek turn and a pose in the low kudo-kudo stance. This sequence is repeated once more, this time clockwise. This opening sequence indicates to the audience that the fighting is imminent and the excitement rises. The two performers then use gelek and three forward steps toward the middle of the circle to approach one another. A total of four set attack and defense sequences (jurusan) are then performed; the first three empty-handed, the last one with a dagger. Between the individual sequences, the opponents retreat to their positions on the perimeter of the circle again and repeat steps similar to the opening sequence.

The first jurusan sequence consists of five kicking attacks and various defensive responses. It begins from the neutral starting position, sikap pasang. From there, opponent A (the attacker, Sutan Lembang Alam) starts with an outside swinging kick with the left leg, aimed at the head of D (the defender, Sutan Nagari).[6] This attack is intercepted by D with a fast 360-degree body turn before the kick can reach his head. The full turn ends with D's left-handed block of A's right leg and is rapidly followed by an ankle hold. While holding A's ankle in the bend of his left arm, D thrusts his free right hand toward A's neck and executes a *sapik kalo,*[7] a strike to the throat with the inner blade of the hand (the part that spans between the extended thumb and index finger). They pose in this kunci mati[8] position for a moment before D releases A's leg and both quickly bounce back into a kudo-kudo stance. From here, D executes a straight front-snap kick *(antam)* with his right foot to A's head (while simultaneously slapping the stretched fabric of his pants with both hands). A evades this kick by rapidly ducking into a very low crouch and coming back up into a kudo-kudo stance. D attacks again with the right leg, this time with a side kick, which is countered by a front-snap kick by A to D's head. Neither kick hits its target. D continues to attack by spinning 360 degrees and launching another front-snap kick at A's head. He then continues spinning another 180 degrees until his back is turned toward A and then executes a straight back kick *(palantin-gan)* with his body stooped and both hands touching the ground for support. A dodges both these kicks, which are executed in rapid succession. This ends the first jurusan; A and D separate and retreat to the perimeter of the circle, as the audience yells support to both performers. The following jurusan are increasingly more exciting and spectacular.

The second jurusan starts with A's side kick toward the knee of D, which is evaded by D through a retreating step. A kicks again and simultaneously extends both his arms forward to hit D on both temples. D blocks the strikes by raising both his arms to head level and pushing the arms of his opponent outward. A's leg is still raised for a kick, but D drops both arms, sidesteps the kick, and pushes his opponent's foot to the side with both hands. D follows this defense with a counterattack, a straight punch *(dorong)* to A's midsection. A blocks this punch with one hand. D continues to attack with an elbow strike *(antak siku)* also aimed at A's midsection. A catches the elbow and pushes D back. D takes a step backward to regain his balance, then immediately continues attacking with a back kick. A dodges the kick. Both reassume a kudo-kudo stance. D executes a straight front kick; A dodges again, this time very close to D, and catches D's extended right leg and pulls it over his shoulder. This move forces D to fall over A's shoulder. D extends his hands forward and transforms his fall into a forward roll. Both opponents immediately assume a kudo-kudo stance and retreat to the circle perimeter. After these first two encounters, the combat is still indecisive, and the spectators again yell encouragements, primarily toward the actor playing Sutan Nagari (D), who has shown more daring techniques than Lembang Alam (A).

After catching their breath, the performers start the third jurusan. It begins with a straight front kick by A, which is parried by D through sidestepping, a swift body turn (gelek), and a push with the left hand to A's leg at knee level. Through this defense, A's foot drops back to the ground into a kudo-kudo stance. D counters with a fake front kick, rapidly followed with an outside crescent kick with the same (left) foot. A catches the ascending leg in midair. He intentionally drops to the ground with the leg caught under his left arm and thereby takes D down with him. The ensuing ground combat constitutes a new and increasingly exciting stage of the fight.

Both opponents are poised in semi-squatting positions from which either one could execute a kick. D starts by swinging his left leg over A's head; A bends backward to avoid being hit and counters with the same kick. D evades the kick by rolling backward onto his back, bringing his legs up until his feet touch the ground behind his head. From there he propels himself up by flinging his legs forcefully front again, landing on his feet, knees bent. He continues the forward motion with another forward flip onto his hands and onto his feet again, and ends by snapping into a kudo-kudo stance. This acrobatic element earns him spontaneous applause from the spectators. His opponent pursues him with a forward roll and also assumes a kudo-kudo upon arrival on the circle perimeter.

The fourth jurusan is even more exciting and begins with A picking up a knife.[9] Both opponents continue circling clockwise while A brandishes the knife in his hand, twirling it around and up and down, not unlike a *pistolero* in a movie Western. Both partners keep a wider distance between themselves than in the previous empty-handed jurusan. After circling three times, A takes several fast forward steps and lunges with the knife held in his right hand straight at D, trying to stab him in the torso. This attack is repeated three times; each time D reacts with a different defense. As A lunges the third time, D evades to the outside with a side step

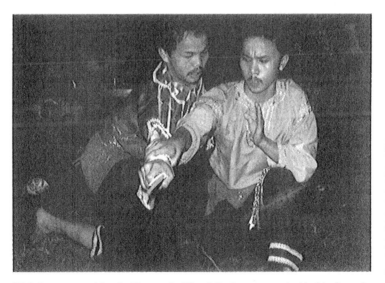

Fighting scene with a knife attack. The defender uses an inside block to the arm of the attacker, thereby gaining control of the hand holding the knife.

and full-body spin. He pushes A in the forward direction of the attack. Through this technique A loses his balance and stumbles closer to the ground. D grabs the hand with the knife and the elbow of A's right arm, drops him even lower, and presses A's shoulder down to the ground by kneeling on it with his left knee. He twists A's hand and is about to take away the weapon. In this situation D is clearly at a major advantage and could kill A.

Seeing his friend in danger of losing the fight, one of the onlookers jumps into the action trying to rescue A (Sutan Lembang Alam). However, in the following short dialogue Lembang Alam makes it clear that he does not appreciate the interference by his friend and claims that he was not at all in danger of losing. He accuses his friend of treachery and attacks him. The ensuing fight consists of two jurusan similar to the previous ones.[10]

The above example illustrates several basic characteristics of randai combat. There is a progression of difficulty and excitement in the sense that the techniques used in the first jurusan are simpler and easier than the following ones. The fighting advances from standing techniques to ground techniques and then to weapons. Each jurusan has a specific focus; the first consists mainly of kicking techniques, while the second jurusan focuses on hand techniques. Furthermore, the second also includes a takedown technique and a recovery in the form of a front roll. The third jurusan starts with kicking techniques followed by a takedown and subsequent ground-kicking techniques and some acrobatics. The fourth and last sequence features a dangerous knife combat with a sharp weapon. This progression reflects on one hand the various levels of silek training from the simple standing techniques to the more complicated ground fighting and more dangerous weapon techniques.[11] On the other hand it serves as a dramatic device to increase tension and build excitement in the course of the fighting scene. This fighting scene also illustrates how actual silek jurusan are used and modified in the theatrical context. All four jurusan are basically authentic practice jurusan selected from the silek pauh style of the Padang Pariaman region.[12] However, they are slightly modified for added theatrical effect. For instance, they include kicks to the head level instead of to the customary torso level; the former is perceived as more exciting and difficult. The acrobatic finish (forward flips) of the third jurusan is also not a part of the traditional form, but is added for theatrical effect as well. In addition, the execution of the techniques is typically faster in randai than in a practice session in silek. In silek training the practitioner's intent is to learn the moves and improve details. Therefore a movement sequence will often be repeated slowly several times, until both partners can execute it rapidly and precisely. In performance however the preset sequences are typically highly rehearsed and faster, which is obviously also more exciting for the audience. To give a well-received performance, fighting scenes have to look "real"; therefore the movements have to be executed with considerable speed and the attacks and defenses have to come as close as possible to the target without actually inflicting injury.[13]

The next example illuminates how a fighting scene is choreographed to add excitement by involving more than one attacker.[14] As in many randai plays, the central plot revolves around the struggle of two men over a young woman, Reno Nilam. The conflict arises between the hero, Bujang Baganto, and his opponent, Palimo Gagah. Although Palimo has won Bujang's fiancée, Reno Nilam, by gambling with her uncle, she refuses to marry Palimo because she is in love with her fiancé. Palimo decides to kill Bujang to get Reno Nilam and sends two guards out to murder his rival. Bujang, however, defends himself successfully against the two guards, and finally Palimo personally attacks his adversary and after a fierce fight kills him.

The fight starts with A1 and A2 (the two guards who are attacking) on one side of the circle and D (the defender, Bujang Baganto) on the other. They execute a similar opening sequence as described above. After a fast gelek both attackers quickly charge forward with a straight right-hand punch toward D's midsection. D quickly steps forward, positioning himself between his two attackers, and executes a fast gelek turn so that he now faces one attacker and has the other one behind his back. He kicks with a straight back kick to the midsection of A1 behind him, while at the same time he executes a palm heel strike with his right hand to the chest of A2 in front and pushes both of them away. Through this simultaneous technique, both attackers are propelled away from D and fall to the ground.

They get back up, resume the same starting position as before the first jurusan, and move around on the circle with langkah and gelek moves while their chief, Palimo Gagah, yells encouragement at them. Then the attackers simultaneously charge toward D and kick with a straight front kick to his midsection. D has anticipated this attack, and as before, steps forward one step. He then bends his knees and swings his extended arms under the attackers' legs, locking them in his bent arms. Both attackers are caught with their kicking legs trapped in D's hold. A1 loses his balance first and falls backward onto the ground. A2 struggles to keep his balance and briefly hops around on one leg, while D pushes and twists his leg, until A2 finally falls backward. Both attackers recover and assume their ready positions on the circle.

The attacks that open the third jurusan are again straight punches to D's midsection. This time, however, D does not move in between his attackers, but evades to one side and engages them in succession. First, he parries A2's punch, as he is closer to him, by blocking the outside arm and sweeping A2's leg in a circular motion out from under him. A2 looses his support and falls to the ground between D and A1, where he becomes an involuntary obstacle for A1's attack. A1 has to move around A2's fallen body on the ground to attack D. He launches a circular kick, which is intercepted by D in a fashion similar to that in the second jurusan. He catches the leg from underneath and A1 loses his balance and falls to the ground. A2 is still stretched out on the ground and D kicks him out of the way. Defeated, A2 moans theatrically and rolls to the side of the circle, where he remains. By this time A1 is once again back on his feet and attacks D with a straight punch to the face. Again D defends himself successfully and after several more exchanges he finally ends the fight with a takedown and a final punch to A1's face. After the fight Palimo mockingly congratulates the defender, Bujang, on his good silek skills and then challenges him to a "real" fight.

In this fighting scene with two attackers we find that the individual jurusan are extremely short. The first two consist only of one attack and one defensive move each. The third one is slightly longer, with three attacks, but again only the first attack is executed by both opponents at the same time. A two-on-one situation is difficult to choreograph and execute properly because, if it were a realistic fighting scene, the defender could not spend an excessive amount of time with one attacker without being stabbed in the back by the second. The defender must control the position of both his attackers at all times. He does this effectively in the above example by keeping the sequences short and on one occasion by using the nearest of the opponents as an obstacle for the other by throwing the first in between himself and the second.[15]

The following (and last) example will illustrate what can happen if the control of both opponents is not maintained. The (theatrically) tragic result is brilliantly demonstrated in the play *Siti Baheram*. The heroine is one of the few female characters who engages in fighting. She is attacked while she is on her way home from the market. Two robbers want to steal her jewelry. Although she defends herself successfully for several minutes, she eventually makes the crucial mistake of turning her back on one attacker for too long.

At the first encounter with the attackers, Siti Baheram is wearing a woman's costume with a long sarong under her overskirt, and must prepare her outfit for the fight. She grabs the ends of her sarong, hitches them up, and tucks them into her belt, revealing galembong pants underneath. This move frees her feet for wider and quicker steps. It also draws considerable roaring and laughter from the audience, mainly because female fighters are rather rare in randai. The two robbers joke about a woman assuming silek stances. Seeing that she knows the techniques, however, they quickly quiet down and attack her in earnest. The first attacker (A1) grabs a knife while A2 looks on. The following jurusan sequence is performed with no break and in rapid succession. Almost all attack and defense moves are executed in time to the accompanying talempong music. This fight starts when A1 stabs straight to the midsection of D (Siti Baheram). D evades to the outside of A1's arm and pushes him so that he spins a full 360 degrees around his vertical axis. D also does a full-body turn and they end up facing each other again. A1 tries to slash D with a circular knife attack from the outside. D evades to the inside of the arm and executes a palm heel strike to A1's chest, which pushes A1 back one step. A1 takes one step forward again and stabs straight with the knife, but D evades to the outside, parrying the arm at the elbow and pushes A1's arm away. Six similar attacks and defenses follow. So far, D has responded only with blocks, parries, or evasions. Finally she responds with a different technique. As A1 stabs at her, she holds on to the arm of her attacker and forces him down on the ground by applying pressure on his elbow. At that moment her back is turned toward A2, who jumps at her with a side kick. She spins half around and parries with her right hand extended backward. A2 follows with a straight punch; D spins the other way and parries with her left hand extended backward. A2 executes another punch with the other hand and she spins one more time, evading the punch and now facing her second opponent. The first attacker is still on the ground, but behind her back. A2 keeps attacking with strikes, which D blocks and evades without pinning. After eight more attack-defense combinations similar to the ones between A1 and D, she finally brings A2 to the ground and pins his arm. At that moment her back is still turned toward A1, who now sneaks up and stabs her in the back twice. She screams, holds her wound, and falls to the ground. The two robbers then steal her jewelry and leave her to die.

The way the scene is choreographed, there is no simultaneous attack by two attackers, as in the previously described scene from *Palimo Gagah*. However, Siti Baheram is involved in a two-on-one

A female character (Siti Baheram) engages in a fighting scene. She disarms her opponent, who has at-tacked her with a knife.

fighting scene, but each attacker has a rather long sequence, with ten and twelve attacks respectively. Most defensive techniques here involve only parries and blocks and evasive moves, as opposed to previously seen styles where counterstrikes, punches, and kicks as well as locks, pins, and holds are frequent. This might be explained by the fact that the silek style *(silek luncua)* from which this randai troupe draws its techniques is focused more on purely defensive techniques without counterstrikes. A more compelling reason might be that for a woman in combat it is considered appropriate to move defensively, but not suitable to launch too strong and effective counterattacks. Therefore the heroine evades and dodges all attacks. The entire scene is accompanied by a lively talempong tune, and despite the fact that all silek moves are executed rapidly and precisely, the even rhythm of attack-defense sequences establishes an almost dancelike quality.

According to the story, Siti Baheram is killed and consequently the performers have to find a combat choreography in which she is defeated according to the logic of silek strategies and knowledge. This is accomplished when she turns her back on the second attacker for too long, thereby creating an opportunity for him to come in for the kill. Since the story is well known to the spectators, they (especially the children) anticipate the imminent murder of the heroine and frequently yell out warnings to her, which, of course, are ignored by the actress.

Knife wounds do not necessarily mean one's death or even injury, however. Many silek styles pride themselves on the ability to make the practitioner invincible to ordinary weapons. This is often demonstrated in an exaggerated way in randai fighting scenes. A prominent example is the fighting scene in the play *Siti Nursila*. Three robbers attack the young woman Siti Nursila, who is on her way to the bathing place, but luckily Sutan Alam (Prince of Nature) comes to her defense. He fights the three robbers one at a time until finally one pins him while the other two grab his arms and hold him tight. One of them then grabs a knife and attempts to kill Sutan Alam by stabbing him repeatedly in the stomach.[16]

Sutan Alam, however, possesses powerful inner strength *(kebati-nan dalam)* and no weapon can harm him. Even when one robber tries to slash Alam's throat, he is unsuccessful. Finally, Sutan Alam frees himself, subdues the three robbers, and bestows forgiveness on his attackers.

Another way in which magic plays an important role in randai fighting scenes is in the form of magic weapons. One such example can be seen in a second version of the play *Palimo Gagah,* as performed by the group Sutan Budiman.[17] In it Bujang is attacked by two of Palimo's guards (not simultaneously, as in the version discussed above), and then by Palimo himself. Palimo carries a magic kris (traditional Malay dagger), and grabs it after he is defeated in the first empty-handed encounter.[18] The magic power of the dagger is demonstrated by the fact that the hand that holds the weapon trembles and twitches, seemingly pulled by the jumps and spins that the magic kris performs by itself.

The fighting scene here consists of three sections. Although each section starts like a jurusan of the sungai patai style, the performers quickly move into a freestyle exchange of kicks and strikes. The first section consists of hand-to-hand combat. The second starts with Palimo pulling the dagger and attacking Bujang, who disarms him as the weapon is hurled to the ground. Bujang picks up the dagger and the third section starts with him momentarily attacking and wounding Palimo, only to have Palimo retrieve his dagger and kill Bujang.

As a prelude to the first encounter, the opponents are on opposite sides of the circle and move back and forth on the perimeter in a long sequence of langkah and gelek moves in which they stay low to the ground. They move toward each other in the center of the circle, but instead of exchanging strikes, they pivot past each other closely without touching, thus increasing the tension in the audience. The first attack is executed by Palimo with a front snap kick with the left leg, during which Palimo also slaps the fabric of his pants. This pants slapping is very prominent in the sungai patai style.[19] What follows is a fast exchange of kicks and blocks, mixed with a few punches and a leg sweep by Bujang, which brings Palimo to the ground. Sitting on his behind, Palimo continues to defend himself against Bujang's double-handed slaps to the face and kicks to the groin. After a few blows, he manages to escape and get back to his feet. More kicks and punches follow and then Palimo retreats to the other side of the circle, where he pulls the dagger.

When the dagger is out of its sheath, the pace of the fight quickens. During the actual attack-defense sequences the kris is clearly controlled by its bearer, and no antics such as trembling or shaking are displayed. After several stabbing attempts, thrusts, and slashes, Palimo is disarmed by Bujang through a wrist lock, and the knife is flung to the ground.

In the next round Bujang grabs the knife and attacks Palimo. After a series of several attacks and defenses similar to the ones in the second round, Bujang executes a fast body turn, swings the dagger overhead and plunges it downward toward Palimo's chest. Palimo can only partially block it and is slightly wounded. However, he quickly wrenches the dagger from Bujang's hand through an outside wrist twist and stabs him in the stomach. Bujang is mortally wounded and falls to the ground, dying. His fiancée, Reno Nilam, rushes onto the scene and starts her lament.

A magic weapon wounding its bearer is a somewhat unusual feature in randai, since such a weapon cannot normally be turned against its owner. This exception can be explained only by the fact that Bujang might possess magic that temporarily subdued the power of the dagger, or else that the weapon was stolen and is now unwilling and capricious in serving its new owner.[20]

Most major heroes in randai possess one or more magic weapons, although they are not necessarily actively used in combat. Their mere presence gives added power to their owners. Magic weapons can be used by good and evil characters. If they are used by good characters, their strength is generally praised because they are used to fight evil.[21] On the other hand, evil characters use magic and magic weapons which are feared because they inflict harm and misery on innocent victims.

The peak of silek expertise is another type of magic that does not involve weapons. Called *gayueng angin* (carried by the wind—i.e., long-distance techniques), it enables one to defeat an opponent with no physical contact. In the performance of *Intan Pangirian,* for instance, this is theatrically displayed when the hero gathers all his strength in a low kudo-kudo stance, closes his eyes, trembles, pushes his hands forward slowly with restrained force, slowly brings them back, and then thrusts them rapidly forward again. At that moment his opponent, who is standing at the opposite side of the circle, screams as he is swept off his feet and falls to the ground. Of course, real gayueng angin is not used; instead the actors dramatically mime its legendary power. Gayueng angin would never be displayed in public and is considered one of the best-guarded secret techniques, one that only few have mastered.[22]

In the creation of the fighting scenes, the *guru-tuo silek* (silek master) typically draws mainly on the specific silek style(s) of the region or district in which the randai group is in residence; however, elements from other styles are often integrated as well, mainly through the custom of merantau.[23] Besides this exchange of new techniques through the migration of the practitioners, there are two other factors that contribute to the frequent modifications of silek elements within randai: festivals and touring.[24] Randai festivals draw many groups from different regions together at one time and location where they can watch each other perform; there also is a strong sense of competition, especially in terms of the quality of the silek employed. Touring has always been part of Minangkabau performances. Many private hosts frequently invite troupes from other regions. These outside groups might feature ex-members of the local village that went rantau and still have strong family ties at home, or otherwise might be groups with outstanding reputations that attracted the interest of a host. Either way, the exposure to other variations of silek in randai through migration, festivals, or touring alone does not seem to constitute a sufficient reason for the actual borrowing and integration of these new elements. Generally, randai integrates new silek elements more freely than silek itself as a martial art form, probably because the very nature of randai was from the beginning that of a composite art form drawn together from preexisting arts, always open to innovation and change. Also, it is mainly intended for entertainment; therefore new elements that satisfy the need for novelty and spectacle will be embraced as long as they are approved of by the leaders. Nevertheless, specific and unique features of the dominant regional silek styles remain preserved and visible in their respective adaptations into the local randai movement styles.

The Martial Arts Dance Galombang

Silek movements from fighting scenes reappear regularly in the galombang in the form of basic steps and partner jurusan. Each galombang dance consists of several parts: an opening bridge, several basic silek moves and one jurusan performed during each song verse, percussive tapuak sequences between verses, and a closing bridge.

The opening bridge begins immediately after a scene is finished, while the actors remain standing in the center of the circle. The galombang members get up from their seated position and move with silek steps toward the actors in the center. Upon meeting, the male characters from the scene become galombang members and execute the same movements when the circle moves outward again. The male characters seemingly disappear into the galombang. At the same time, female characters leave the circle and change places with the singers, who then move to the center of the circle and start the song. The opening bridge therefore facilitates a smooth transition between the end of a scene and the beginning of a song and is aptly called *garak panghubung ka gurindam* (movement connecting to the song). The closing bridge does the same in reverse and is called *garak panghubung ka curito* (movement connecting to the story). Both bridges consist strictly of silek moves and tapuak patterns.

Galombang dancers surround two dendang singers and a flute player. Note the low stances and the uniform costuming.

A galombang dancer displays a low stance and hand gestures derived from the silek bungo style.

Female galombang dancers in the same costume as the male dancers

Each song consists of several verses during which the dancers perform a series of silek moves. These often include short jurusan that are executed in pairs; therefore an even number of circle members is mandatory. The same movement sequence is repeated for each new verse of the song and also ended by the same percussive tapuak pattern. After the tapuak, the performers often walk a few steps until the singer begins the next verse. As soon as the singers have finished the song, the dancers conclude the galombang by a closing bridge that has a similar function as the opening bridge. It allows a smooth transition and exchange of singers and actors in the center of the circle. Again, some of the galombang members "reappear" as characters in the scene.

For each new song a new galombang with different subunits is performed. The jurusan are usually built into the main body of the galombang; some groups do prefer to integrate them into the opening or closing bridge, but these are exceptions. Most groups favor the display of their jurusan several times within one galombang, once in each verse, rather than only once within one single opening or closing bridge. This may be because jurusan sequences are generally considered some of the highlights within the galombang. When executed quickly and precisely, jurusan never fail to delight the spectators, who evaluate the performers' silek skills by how well they execute these drills. Most groups include them in at least half of their galombang circles. Jurusan in the circular dance are typically shorter than the ones used in fighting scenes and consist of only two to four attacks and defenses. Since these moves are performed in time to the song melody and have to be executed simultaneously by all members of the circle, they are also generally done at a somewhat more even pace than in a combat scene.

There are also differences in regard to the focus of the performers, their spatial orientation, and the repertoire of movements used. The performers strive to move in unison by following the movements and vocal cues of the *pambalok galombang* (circle leader) closely. Therefore they have to focus on the leader and, at the same time, on their partner so as to not accidentally hit or kick him or her. They execute their movements in the same constellation in each verse and repeat them as often as the singer sings a new verse. At all times their movement direction is in relation to the circular formation and in relation to the other circle members. They move clockwise in unison for the main part of the circular galombang sequences.[25]

The combination of all these elements, the even pace, the simultaneity, the circular orientation, the focus on the leader, and the repetitiveness gives the silek moves in the galombang a more dancelike quality than the execution of "pure" silek moves practiced by combatants in a fighting scene.[26] This dancelike quality of the silek within the galombang is also the reason why local performers often call their performance *tari randai* (randai dance). This name is old and stems from the time when randai was still a nondramatic form. It does not reflect the recent development of incorporating other Minangkabau dances into the repertoire.

Jurusan (partner drills), here displaying kicking techniques, are part of the galombang dance. Two singers stand in the center of the circle.

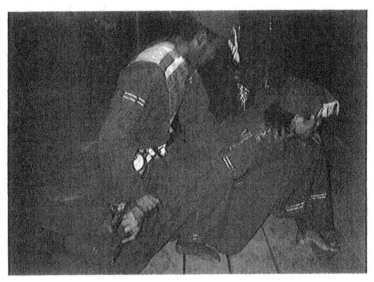

Another jurusan within the galombang dance, here consisting of a knife attack and a defensive arm twist and takedown

Dance

Although traditionally only silek-derived movements were used in the galombang, two new developments can be seen.[27] First, regional traditional Minangkabau dances are becoming increasingly popular and widespread within randai, and second, popular culture is also gaining a foothold: dance within the galombang is being influenced by joget, originally a modern Malay welcoming and socializing dance, and dangdut, modern Indonesian pop music and dance.[28]

Traditional Minangkabau dances have always been part of randai performances as intermission entertainment.[29] In a new development, they are incorporated directly into the galombang. The most relevant addition is the *tari piriang* (plate dance).[30] It is popular all over West Sumatra and is probably the most characteristic and exciting dance of the region. The performers balance a fairly large porcelain plate on the palm of each hand, and on each index finger they have fixed a nutshell with which they rhythmically hit the plates while swinging them around in astonishingly fast acrobatic moves. In a galombang version of this dance, some of the galombang members hold plates and dance in the center in a smaller circle (the singers and flute player stay outside in such cases). The remaining galombang members without plates execute the same or similar movements as the plate dancers, with both circles often moving in opposite directions.[31]

Significantly, the modern galombang versions that rely on popular dance elements are not based on silek-derived movement. Instead they consist of high stances with the feet much closer together, and a stepping technique that consists of a step-tap combination in which one foot steps diagonally forward and the second foot is placed lightly next to the first, touching the ground only with the toes, before it in return takes the next forward step and the other foot does the tapping. The legs are almost straight and the torso is upright, a striking difference from the low crouches and slightly inclined torso of most silek styles. Together with these movements of the legs, the arms are very relaxed and swing freely from side to side to about shoulder level; there the hands execute the *jantiak* (finger snapping) before the arms swing back to the other side.

There is also a basic rhythmic difference between the more traditional galombang and the joget or dangdut. In the traditional galombang, often there is no strict metered beat. Although the dancers move in time to the song, they are not moving on the beat, because the song often has no regular meter. Instead, the dancers follow the undulating rhythm of the singers and the vocal cues of the galombang leader and his movements. In the case of a song with a 4/4 meter, the emphasis is on the second downbeat. In joget and dangdut on the other hand, there is always a basic even beat in a 4/4 meter, and the emphasis is stronger and more regular on the first and third downbeat.

This obviously influences the way the dancers move. In the modern version, they simply follow the basic straight beat, and this often makes the members look mechanical and isolated from each other. In the traditional version without a strong basic beat, all performers have to cue into the movement and vocal exclamations with which the galombang leader initiates the dance sequences. As a result, the dancers seem to perform on a higher concentration level and with a tighter group feeling. A more intense concentration is also needed because the traditional galombang still consists of silek moves, and silek demands concentration and precision to execute generally difficult techniques, whereas joget as a purely recreational activity demands less concentration and precision to execute generally simple techniques.

Summary

Silek undergoes changes in each of the two contexts in which it is used. In the fighting scenes it is rendered theatrically. Various combat constellations exist: one-on-one fights, fights with multiple attackers, serious and humorous kinds, as well as those that employ magic weapons or magic techniques. The majority of fights occur between male opponents, but female characters occasionally engage in combat as well.

The great variety of techniques used and the many different styles of choreography and composition might at first seem confusing and overwhelming. However, certain key features are always present. Each randai fighting scene relies on techniques from the prevalent local silek style. Basic stances and footwork are identical to the dominant silek style, and so are most of the individual jurusan. Several other factors, however, make the display of these silek techniques theatrical. First, to achieve a sense of mounting dramatic tension, the selected jurusan are typically displayed in an order of increasing difficulty. They might move from simple hand-to-hand combat to kicks to ground techniques to acrobatics to weapons. Also, the increase might be in relation to the speed and complexity of the techniques used. Second, fighting scenes are accompanied by music that becomes increasingly louder and faster and thus supports the mounting excitement of the fight. The combatants do not adapt their movements to the tempo of the music; rather, the musicians typically pick up the tempo of the moves and adjust their playing to suit the actors.[32] Third, the breaks between individual jurusan and the circling of the opponents are also used dramatically as moments of suspense. The fighters have a chance to catch their breath and reevaluate their opponent(s). Also, since the spectators are familiar with this standard silek practice, they do not perceive the breaks as interruptions in the fight but as an integral part of it. During the breaks the fighters move with extreme care and heightened awareness, which communicates the sense of an impending high point in the combat. Fourth, improvisation is also often used. Fighters might initiate a combat sequence with a traditional jurusan, but then move into freestyle fighting. This again is recognized instantly by most spectators, who are generally familiar with the basic jurusan of their regional martial arts style. Freestyle fighting is therefore also used to increase the excitement and spectacle of a scene.[33] Fifth, the fight is often accompanied by verbal exchanges or by clowning. This clowning can include acrobatics, jokes, and other antics. Depending on the composition, these elements can either increase the suspense, or relieve dramatic tension. Either way, they increase the theatricality of the fight.

In the galombang, silek takes on a dancelike quality augmented by percussive patterns and vocal cues. Basic silek steps and partner drills (jurusan) are executed simultaneously by all members in time to the song and the vocal cues of the galombang leader. Within a song each song verse is accompanied by the same sequences of silek steps, partner drills, and percussive patterns. Each new song has new and different sequences.

Traditionally only silek-derived movements are part of the galombang, but in a new development two kinds of dances are integrated as well: traditional Minangkabau folk dances and modern Indonesian dances. However, the more traditional and pure form of the galombang relies solely on silek for its movement repertoire.

CHAPTER 10

CONCLUSION

Significance of Silek in Randai

THIS STUDY has focused on the influence of silek in randai. We have seen how silek played an important role in the emergence and further development of randai, how silek is featured thematically as a topic in the scripts, and how it influences current performance features. It seems virtually certain that randai evolved out of silek via the circular martial arts dance called dampeang, which was customarily employed in silek training, and which was accompanied by music and songs that related simple stories. In the process of the development of randai, movement and songs became more complex. Other elements like storytelling, additional folk songs, and, later, acting were adapted and integrated to create this unique composite performance art of the Minangkabau.

The story material of randai incorporates silek in several principal ways. It is featured thematically when major characters are silek students or masters, or when they go rantau to learn more of the martial arts. Almost all male and several female characters are proficient in silek and it is therefore always present in most of the stories. The quest for good silek training by many male characters in connection with their going rantau illustrates that silek is seen as an indispensable part of the education of young men. Silek masters are generally portrayed as wise, kind, and virtuous, and students seeking knowledge and silek mastery are depicted as maturing, positive role models in the plays.

Even more importantly, silek is central to the resolution of conflicts in almost all performances. Typically, conflicts arise, escalate, and then culminate in a silek confrontation. Basic philosophical concepts of silek are also integral to the plays. A virtuous hero, for instance, is portrayed as obeying the central ethical rule of silek: to use it solely as a means of self-defense. Fighting in randai plays tends to be resolved in a way that propagates proper behavior, and therefore conflict scenarios, fighting scenes, and conflict resolution serve as vehicles of morale instruction. Good characters typically prevail, while evil ones perish or are redeemed.

The current performance features bear witness to the important role of silek in the evolution and development of randai. First, the costumes for male actors and for all galombang dancers regardless of their gender are derived from the standard silek outfit. The pants are altered slightly in shape and sometimes the entire costume is enhanced with additional embroidery, but basically the outfits are virtually identical. Second, the percussive patterns performed by the galombang dancers are derived from specific slapping techniques used in silek that have been developed into a complex and exciting musical feature of randai. Third, the spatial arrangement of the galombang is also directly derived from the circular formation of the dampeang martial arts dance. Fourth, the movement repertoire of the fighting scenes and the galombang in randai is derived from the prevalent local style of silek. In the fighting scenes standard jurusan (attack-defense sequences) are used and slightly modified to render them more theatrical. Also, to enhance the dramatic nature of these fighting scenes, jurusan are often arranged in an order of increasing difficulty, and complemented with acrobatics and acting. The galombang is based on silek movement and often incorporates jurusan. These are modified and arranged into a circular group formation. Due to this formation and to the repetition and synchronization of these movements with the music and vocal cues from the circle leader, the galombang takes on a dancelike quality. Its foundation, however, is silek. Although randai continues to be modified and adapted to evolving sociocultural changes, the martial arts remain at its core, foremost in terms of the movement repertoire.

Change and Continuity

Women have assumed increasingly greater importance as performers. Formerly an all-male tradition, randai has integrated women initially as singers, then as actresses and musicians, and most recently also as members of the galombang dance. Female galombang members are required to be proficient in silek, and, like the male performers, wear identical costumes and perform the same movement repertoire.[1]

Only very few all-male groups remain, and most groups have female performers participating in at least one or two of the four categories (song, acting, music, or martial arts dance). Unfortunately, due to the rapid disappearance of all-male groups, it is difficult to compare their overall performance styles to those of mixed groups, and it is impossible to judge if and how female impersonators influenced the acting style now used by female performers. What can be seen today is that actresses and the few remaining female impersonators perform female roles in a similar manner.

When we compare the performance style of all-male galombang dances to mixed versions with male and female participants, there is also generally no marked difference. Therefore it seems that the form and aesthetics of randai have not changed perceptively with the increased presence of female performers.

The content of randai also remains virtually unchanged by the increased presence of female performers. Male characters in the stories remain generally more powerful in decision making and are therefore generally more active than female ones. Female characters have little decision-making power and considerably less space and time in individual plays. Therefore randai does not reflect the new role of women within the performance art. If and how this will change in the future, when women become more and more established in randai, remains to be seen and should be the focus of another study.

Interestingly, this absence of influential and powerful female figures in randai also does not reflect the traditional Minangkabau matrilineal and matrilocal social structure of the extended family, but rather the more modern patriarchal power structure with the father as leader, enforced by Islam, and the nuclear family structure propagated by Western influences. This dominance and control of male characters in randai may be explained through its origin and early development. As an initially all-male art form based on an all-male martial art, randai logically focuses on male-male relationships, male conflicts, and male decision making. Consequentially, most conflicts are resolved by physical combat between male characters.

The custom of voluntary migration (merantau), the prevalence of touring, and the increased number of festivals, have made the borrowing of song melodies and lyrics, movement repertoire, and acting styles among randai groups both frequent and widespread. Still, groups in remote locations that have not yet participated in festivals typically retain their regional performance style more fully.

Over the past twenty-five years new elements—such as newly written stories, more "realistic" acting styles, modern song melodies, dance styles, and costumes—have been incorporated into randai. Modern staging techniques often impact the performances through raised, proscenium-style stages, brighter lighting, and sound amplification. Almost all groups today rely on microphones.[2]

However, although one of randai's characteristics is openness to innovation and change, the central components have remained the same. Most randai performances still take place in the traditional setting in a level, empty, open-air space, with performers in traditional costumes relating an old Minangkabau tale through songs, martial arts, and acting. Randai performers seem to have found a balance between the preservation of old traditions and innovation.

Traditionally, the three main social functions of randai were entertainment, education, and the perpetuation of Minangkabau customs and heritage. This is still generally true today. Each individual randai component—silek, storytelling, and folk singing—is considered a pusako (sacred heirloom) handed down from preceding generations. Randai, combining the above three elements, is likewise treasured as a pusako. Although randai is relatively new compared to its predecessors, it is considered one of the pillars of Minangkabau culture and one of its most expressive art forms. Furthermore, randai reinforces other aspects of the Minangkabau culture by addressing topics like history, adat, and religion. The continued practice of randai therefore expresses the Minangkabau identity and thereby perpetuates Minangkabau cultural and social values.

Appendix A

Questionnaire and Results

Questionnaire

The following questionnaire, here translated from the original Indonesian, was distributed to the 181 randai troupes that participated in the West Sumatra Randai Festival in 1994.

Name of the troupe:
Story performed:
Address:
Number of members: (Male: Female:)

I. GENERAL INFORMATION

1. When was the troupe founded?
2. When did women become members of the troupe? What are their positions?
3. On an average, how many performances are given in a period of three months?
4. How long is one performance normally?
5. Are there regular rehearsals? How often and when?

II. INFORMATION ABOUT THE STORY PERFORMED

6. Please give a brief summary of the plot.

7. Who are the main characters in the story?
8. What is the theme of the story?

III. INFORMATION ABOUT SILEK

9. Are there conflicts or fights in the story?
   If yes, between which characters and why?
10. Which silek style do the members of the troupe use?
11. Is every performer expected to know silek?
    Does every performer in the troupe practice silek?

IV. INFORMATION ABOUT THE CIRCULAR GALOMBANG DANCE

12. Do the individual galombang have names?
    If so, please state the names.
13. Are there modern dances used in the galombang?
    If so, please give the names.

V. INFORMATION ABOUT THE FUNCTION OF RANDAI IN YOUR COMMUNITY

14. In your opinion, what is the function of randai in your community?
15. What do you think were significant changes in randai within the past thirty years?

VI. INFORMATION ABOUT SUPPORT FOR RANDAI

16. Does your randai group receive support from the government? If so, from which officials or agencies?
17. Is government support vital for your troupe?
    From what other sources do you receive support?
18. How do you feel about randai festivals?
19. Please fell free to include any other comment you would like to make about randai.

Results

The following figures illustrate some of the significant findings from the questionnaire answers.

GRAPH 1

TROUPE COMPOSITION BY GENDER

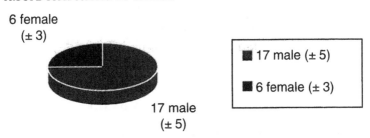

6 female
(± 3)

17 male
(± 5)

| ■ 17 male (± 5) |
| ■ 6 female (± 3) |

Among the randai troupes that responded to the questionnaire, the average troupe was comprised of about 23 performers. Thus, about one-fourth (26%) of these randai performers are female.

GRAPH 2

TROUPE COMPOSITION BY AGE

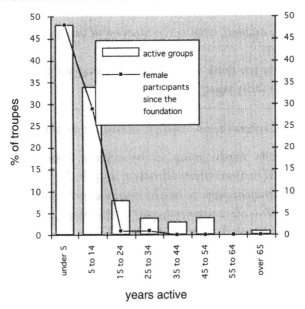

years active

All troupes less than five years old have had female members since the foundation of the troupe. Many older troupes started as all-male groups and included female performers at a later date.

GRAPH 3

FEMALE PERFORMERS IN ACTIVE RANDAI TROUPES

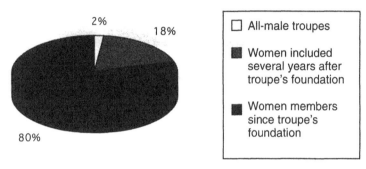

2%

18%

80%

☐ All-male troupes

■ Women included several years after troupe's foundation

■ Women members since troupe's foundation

Of the troupes that have had female performers since their founding, most were founded after 1975.

GRAPH 4

FREQUENCY OF PERFORMANCE

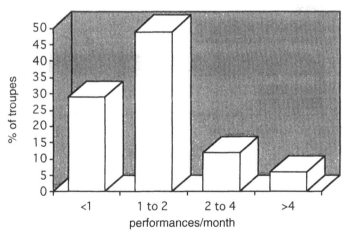

% of troupes

<1   1 to 2   2 to 4   >4
performances/month

Twenty-nine percent of the troupes give less than one performance per month. The largest share (49%) are those who perform once or twice per month. Considerably fewer troupes perform more often than that; 12 percent perform two to four times, and 6 percent more than four times per month.

GRAPH 5

AVERAGE DURATION OF RANDAI PERFORMANCES

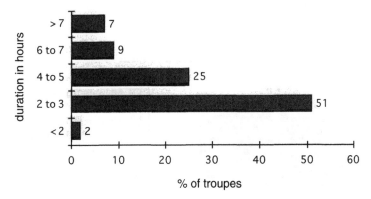

GRAPH 6

NUMBER OF COMBAT SCENES IN RANDAI PERFORMANCES

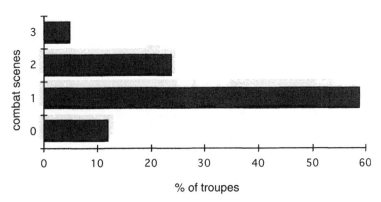

Combat scenes typically come at the climactic moments in the play. Silek as part of the galombang is not included in this figure.

GRAPH 7

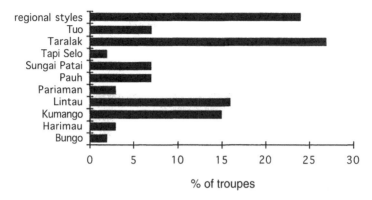

The troupes surveyed identified these styles as the ones employed in their performances. Various regional styles have been grouped together and constitute 24 percent of all silek styles employed by the troupes surveyed.

GRAPH 8

SILEK PROFICIENCY OF RANDAI PERFORMERS

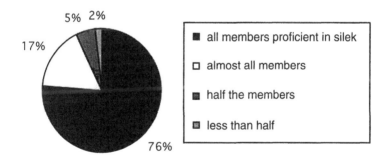

If a troupe states that almost all its members are proficient, it typically means that all the galombang members are proficient, but some actors or musicians might not be. In a few troupes (less than 10%), "only" half or less than half of the members are proficient.

GRAPH 9

GOVERNMENT SUPPORT FOR RANDAI TROUPES

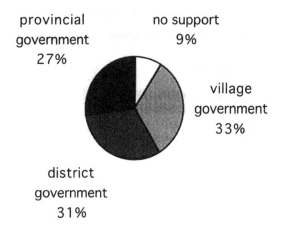

provincial government 27%

no support 9%

village government 33%

district government 31%

Government support normally includes the commissioning of performances and small monetary donations (amounts were not specified).

Appendix B

Sabai Nan Aluih

The Genteel Sabai is a play performed by the group Riak Danau from the village of Koto Tinggi, district of Susun Tanjung Betung, West Sumatra.

Roles

Sabai Nan Aluih — a young, unmarried Minangkabau girl
Mangkutak Alam — Sabai's brother
Sadun Saribai — Sabai's mother
Rajo Babandiang — Sabai's father
Bujang Salamaik — servant of Babandiang
Rajo Nan Panjang — evil ruler of a neighbor district
Palimo Banda Dalam — guard of Rajo Nan Panjang
Lompong Batuah — guard of Rajo Nan Panjang
Siti Narawatu — Rajo Nan Panjang's wife
A shepherd, villagers

Opening

Greetings and apologies to the audience.
The play is *Sabai Nan Aluih*.
We find her in the *anjuang* room
weaving a beautiful cloth.
Her mother comes in,
deep in thoughts.

SADUN SARIBAI:
Dear child, treasure of the morning and the afternoon, cure for our fatigue and fever, the most important part of my body, my daughter, let's sit here. I feel something in my heart, and it is about you.

SABAI NAN ALUIH [*coming to her mother*]:
Forgive me, Mother, my blood is surprised in my heart, what will you tell me? Please tell me quickly to make me happy in my heart and calm in my mind.

SADUN SARIBAI:
Oh, dear Daughter, listen to me and I will tell you something. Our character as women demands that we don't leave the house too often. The one who leaves a lot and talks too much, is the *patandang* girl. If there are guests in the house, beautiful or ugly, good or bad, welcome them with a nice face. Ask them to sit down first and bring the *siriah* and the water for eating and drinking. Only after the *pinang* has been eaten can you ask carefully what they want here. When the conversation is over, it's time for you to say farewell and let them go. This will make everybody happy in their hearts. Just like in our proverbs from the ancestors:

> the red one is *sago*
> the multi-colored one is *gundi*
> the beautiful is *baso*
> the good one is *budi*
> [meaning: be polite to the guests]

If you receive an invitation to go to another village, you have to follow it. Friendship is the main thing. Therefore, even if you go broke and the gold gets used up, the people will still like you. But if you don't behave well, it will be very bad for you.

SABAI:
About your advice, I will tie it strong in my heart. I will keep it for ever and ever. Does that make you happy?

SADUN SARIBAI:
If that is what you say, you make me happy in my heart and calm in my mind. That is all I want to say for now, I have to go to the back, there is a lot of work waiting to be done.
[*short galombang dance; Mangkutak enters*]

MANGKUTAK ALAM:
Dear Sister Sabai Nan Aluih, right here and now, give me permission to go and fly kites at Sawah Bunta. The wind is good, so let's listen to the sound of the kite.

SABAI:
Dear younger Brother Mangkutak Alam, it is Friday and prayer time. When the people come home from the mosque they will see you playing with your kite. It will bring shame onto our father. And one other thing: the day is very hot, if you get ill, you will be the only one to feel this. That is all from me, it's up to you.
[*Short galombang takes Mangkutak Alam to fly his kite; Sadun Saribai enters.*]

SADUN SARIBAI:
Dear child Sabai Nan Aluih, the day is passing, the sun is setting, the shadows are growing longer, but Mangkutak Alam still hasn't come home. Please find him.

SABAI: If that's what you want, let me find him.
[*She goes to the yard.*]

Gurindam
Sabai walks delicately.
If she should step on an ant,
the ant will not be harmed.
But if there should be
a pole blocking her way,
it will break into pieces.

She walks for a long time
and finally arrives.

We cannot escape bad luck,
and we cannot force good luck.
The *murai* bird sings at the door;
it is a greeting from us.

The story changes,
but it is still the same,
and we move to Rajo Nan Panjang.
He has a sudden idea to take a trip,
wants to travel to Ranah Padang Tarok.
He calls his two guards.

SCENE 2

RAJO NAN PANJANG:
Hey, you two guards, come here quickly, [*They enter.*]
Right now and here we will take a trip to Ranah Padang Tarok.

PALIMO BANDA DALAM [*surprised*]:
Oh, it is you my Lombong Batuah, your ugly face got almost broken by my fist.

LOMBONG BATUAH [*laughs loudly*]:
Hey, you son of a bitch, Palimo, your ribs almost got spread out all over because of my feet. [*Both of them laugh loudly.*]

PALIMO:
Hey, when will your fate change? By now, other people are of higher standing than you; other men smoke real cigarettes, but you still smoke *nipah* leaves; other people make a fortune, but you go broke; don't you see: Rajo Nan Panjang, the old womanizer, has become richer and richer and has many wives.

LOMBONG BATUAH:
Eh, you, what are you saying? You can only talk like that in front of me. Trying to speak in front of Rajo Nan Panjang is like trying to stop your fart. [*Laughing, Rajo Nan Panjang enters.*]

RAJO NAN PANJANG:

Hey, you two guards, come here! [*They come closer.*] Right here and now, get ready to depart.

LOMBONG BATUAH:

If that's what you want, let's go soon. You go first, I'll follow. [*They start walking. Suddenly Sabai passes them; Rajo Nan Panjang is surprised and starts talking.*]

RAJO NAN PANJANG:

Oh, dear Lombong Batuah, let me talk to you for a minute. Answer a question, please: Who's daughter is this?

LOMBONG BATUAH:

Dear lord, did you forget this girl? She's the daughter of Rajo Babandiang, from Padang Tarok; her name is Sabai Nan Aluih.

RAJO NAN PANJANG [*thinking*]:

If that's what you say, it's clear now. Let's go back home. [*Quiet galombang leads Rajo Nan Panjang home; Mangkutak Alam enters with Sabai Nan Aluih.*]

SABAI:

Younger Brother, you waste your time with kites, our parents are angry, you have to come home right now.

MANGKUTAK ALAM:

If that's what you say, Older Sister, let's go home. [*Galombang takes them home to the house of Rajo Babandiang.*]

RAJO BABANDIANG:

Dear wife, come here for a moment, I have something to tell you about Mangkutak Alam. His king is his heart, his sutan are his eyes, he only flies the kites all day. Other people know how to untangle the jumbled strings, they know that the tight string will become slack. [meaning: it is hard to educate the son] But I don't.

SADUN SARIBAI:

If that's what you say, it's up to you. Whatever is the best way for him, you decide, and we follow.

All words are spoken between
Sadun Saribai and Rajo Babandiang;
the story changes, but is still the same;
it changes to Rajo Nan Panjang,
he wants to go to Padang Tarok and
get engaged to Sabai Nan Aluih.

SCENE 3

RAJO NAN PANJANG:
Oh, dear Palimo Banda Dalam, right here and now, come closer so
I can talk to you. Please go to Rajo Babandiang's house and ask for
Sabai Nan Aluih's hand for me.

PALIMO:
Dear Rajo Nan Panjang, if that's what you say, I'll spread your
wisdom, I'll wear it as my clothes, I'll follow your order. I'll go before noon.

Gurindam
After a long journey
he arrives and walks up
into the house; there
he is met by Rajo Babandiang.

PALIMO:
Dear Rajo Babandiang, right here and now, I've come a long distance. I came up into your house, ate siriah, and smoked; may I
now start to talk about important things?

BABANDIANG:
If that's what you want, it's time to discuss it.

PALIMO:
Rajo Nan Panjang asked me to come here, he wants to ask for
Sabai Nan Aluih's hand.

BABANDIANG:
If that's what you think, let's see. Although Sabai is actually over twenty years old, she is still younger than seventeen in her mind. We have no intention to marrying her off yet. Tell this to Rajo Nan Panjang.

PALIMO:
If that's what you say, it's clear and I'll return home.

Gurindam
All words have been spoken;
Palimo Banda Dalam goes back
to report to Rajo Nan Panjang.
When he arrives he explains
what he heard from Rajo Babandiang
and Rajo Nan Panjang gets angry.
He writes a letter and asks Palimo
with the fast feet and light hands
to deliver the letter.
Palimo goes directly
after obtaining the permission.

SCENE 4

BABANDIANG:
Oh, dear Sabai Nan Aluih, come, stand close to me, I have something to tell you. Come on, Sabai Nan Aluih, I called you loudly, answer me please, don't you care about me? I really hope you'll come out of your room.

SABAI:
Oh, dear Father, listen to me, let me talk to you. This Saturday, you'd better not go to the market. I had a dream last night: the pole for the siriah plant fell down, and the *rankiang* [rice barn] looked like it had grown roots. Our buffalo was stolen, and our speckled chicken flew away. Then I suddenly awoke. When I looked

behind me, I saw no one. I don't know if it was the devil or a ghost. It made my hair stand on end.

BABANDIANG:
Oh, my dearest child Sabai Nan Aluih, if that was your dream, it was true. Please sit closer to me, let me interpret your dream of last night: The siriah pole falling down means good luck, the rankiang with roots means our harvest will be big; the stolen buffalo means that our livestock will increase; the chicken flying away means that our Mangkutak will be engaged to somebody.

SABAI:
Oh, dear Father, really, the water is flowing straight down, and you still say that it's turning left or right. The *pandan* plant will carry the risk. [meaning: you say my bad dream was good, but I will suffer from it]
Please understand, it's up to you now.

BABANDIANG:
I have spoken, and it's not my style to take back my words, because I am a man. I will go now, my daughter, you stay here.

SABAI:
Dear Father, I try to prevent disaster, and I can't, it feels like I'm up against the tall *sampia* tree, and I can't fell it. The eggs are hatching, and I can't stop them. If I try to stop you, I can't. It seems like trying to stop water from flowing down a hill. So I have to let you go. Listen once more, Father. If you want to take a bath, please do so and brush your body with *jambak* leaves. If you really want to go, Father, have Mangkutak accompany you.

BABANDIANG [*calling the guard*]:
Dear Younger Brother Bujang Salamaik, come here, it has been safe here for a long time, thanks to you. Your feet are very fast, and your hands are quick. Take our black horse, Birau Ucin, and saddle it. It's a beautiful horse; it can run fast and has a nice tail.

BUJANG SALAMAIK: If that's what you want, let me do it right away. Just a moment. [*They leave together.*]

<u>Gurindam</u>
Rajo Babandiang and Bujang Salamaik
leave with the horse,
they travel long and
finally reach Padang Pahunan.
They meet Rajo Nan Panjang and Lombong,
and they start to talk.

SCENE 5

RAJO NAN PANJANG:
We're tired from walking uphill, although we used walking sticks.
I'm tired of waiting. Many cigarette butts are scattered on the
ground and the lord Rajo Babandiang takes his time. It's been too
long a time to be twisting the strings, it's been too long a time since
I sent the letter. What kept you so long?

BABANDIANG:
Even if you hadn't sent me the letter, I would have come here.

RAJO NAN PANJANG:
Oh, my lord, get down from your horse, please.

LOMBONG BATUAH:
My lord Rajo Nan Panjang, listen to me, let me tell you something.
Think carefully before talking. Rajo Babandiang might shoot you.
If he aims at a new shoot on a siriah plant, he will hit each kernel.
Even if he aims wrong, the bullet will hit its target.

RAJO NAN PANJANG:
Dear Lombong Batuah, I never thought before that we would take
a bath at the place of Koto Tuo. The reason for our struggle is you,
my dear Rajo Babandiang, and your arrival at our *sasaran* [silek
training place].

LOMBONG BATUAH:
Let's open our steps [begin silek], so we learn how hot the chili is,
and how salty the salt is.

RAJO NAN PANJANG:

Oh, dear Datuk Rajo Babandiang, listen carefully. We came here for a reason. It concerns our last discussion. It's about the siriah, which is going into the house and coming back out [the engagement was neglected]. What do I lack? Explain it to me. Hurry up.

BABANDIANG:

About Sabai Nan Aluih, don't even mention her, she's not old enough for marriage. Besides, she's no match for you. You'd better find another woman. I can help you with that.

RAJO NAN PANJANG [*angry*]:

Don't speak about another woman; don't give that kind of advice! I've married twenty times, and no one ever dared oppose me, except for you. Remember, I'm not an ordinary man, I'm the king of Situjuah Banda Dalam, if Banda Dalam has a handle, I can carry it, or I can throw it down; I can make Banda Dalam black or white. Its fate depends on me.

RAJO BABANDIANG [*calm*]:

You speak about your status and power, my lord; I already know this. You are the king of your nagari, but I'm the king of my nagari. You show off your strength, but I'm not afraid of anybody. We are men of equal standing. The only way you can take Sabai Nan Aluih is in your dreams.

RAJO NAN PANJANG [*angry*]:

Hey, you son of a bitch, watch your tongue! Don't you love your life?
[*to his guards*] Hey, you two, quickly finish off this ugly old man!
[*Both guards close in on Rajo Babandiang and all three start to fight.*]

BUJANG SALAMAIK:

If one takes the first step, it is no use to take it back. [*They fight one by one, and both guards lose.*]

RAJO NAN PANJANG:

Oh, Datuk Rajo Babandiang, right here and now, let us measure our steps, let us test the value of our gold. Which one has more shine? Let us find out how spicy the chili is and how salty the salt is.

BABANDIANG:
Oh, Datuk Rajo Nan Panjang, if that's what you want, you read my mind. Open your *langkah tigo* [three steps], and I will open my *langkah serong* [diagonal step].
[*They start fighting hand to hand.*]

RAJO NAN PANJANG:
We've been playing for a long time, but we haven't touched yet, let's shorten the distance. [*Rajo Nan Panjang takes his kris out, but he is trapped. He gives a sign to Palimo, who shoots Babandiang in the right shoulder.*]

BABANDIANG:
Aaaaagh! Shot in the back. . . . [*He falls down and Bujang Sala-maik runs away.*]

RAJO NAN PANJANG [*laughs*]:
My lord, you can see our gun; it's a pusako from our ancestors, and we see the blood.

LOMBONG BATUAH [*examines Babandiang*]:
Good job, Palimo, the veins are cut, and I think he'll die.

PALIMO:
We got want we wanted. Looks like the rat is gonna die. Let's go, and leave him to the bugs. Let's ask the night wind to take him away. How's that, eh?

RAJO NAN PANJANG:
It's true. Off we go to Ranah Padang Tarah to pick up our award, Sabai Nan Aluih.

LOMBONG BATUAH:
If that is what you want, my lord, go ahead, we will follow behind, ha ha ha.
[*While they walk, the shepherd enters and looks around in surprise.*]

SHEPHERD:
Oh, oh, my lord Rajo Babandiang, good father of Sabai Nan Aluih! Who killed him? I have to tell them right away! [*Shepherd leaves.*]

Gurindam
The story changes again,
the shepherd goes to Padang Tarok
to look for Sabai Nan Aluih.
He travels a long time and
finally meets some villagers.
They start to talk.

SCENE 6

SHEPHERD:
Oh, dear villagers, please tell me the truth. Where can I find the house of Sabai Nan Aluih? Her father has been shot by Rajo Nan Panjang in the middle of the struggle, in the middle of the meadow. I don't know if he is still alive or not. His blood was all over.

VILLAGERS:
Dear young friend, if you want to know the truth, I will tell you. If you need a clear answer, I will tell you all the details. Walk down this long road, at the crossroads one way leads to Padang Tarok, one to Talang Aliak, follow this one and then you will see a house with flowers in front. That is her house.
[*Galombang takes the shepherd to Sabai Nan Aluih's house.*]

SHEPHERD:
Oh, dear Aunt Sabai Nan Aluih, why do you spend all your time weaving? I have important news for you. I ran a long way, but please don't worry about me. Your father was shot by Rajo Nan Panjang. I don't know if he's still alive.

SABAI:
Oh, Younger Brother, what did you say? It can't be true. Say it again, please.

SHEPHERD:
Dearest Sabai Nan Aluih, if I repeat it, my hair will stand on end. Your father is dead, because Rajo Nan Panjang shot him.

SABAI:
Oh, dear Mother, listen to what I will tell you. Stop your work please, because maybe my father has died.

SADUN SARIBAI:
Oh, Daughter, don't leave full of worries, maybe someone made a joke.

SABAI:
How can we not believe it, when someone comes all the way here to tell me the news? Give me permission to search for Father. I won't come home until I find him. As soon as Mangkutak comes back, ask him to go and find me at Padang Pahuanan. Don't let him rest, but send him directly.

Gurindam
Hearing the news from the Shepherd,
Sabai Nan Aluih feels very shaken.
She asks permission from her mother
to leave and search for her father.
She walks long and finally
arrives at Padang Pahuanan,
where her father lies dying
due to the evil done by Nan Panjang

SCENE 7

SABAI: [*She runs and embraces her father.*]
Father! Can it be true? What happened? Who did this? I told you before, but you didn't care or take it to heart. You ignored my warning, and now your body and spirit suffer the results. Father, you're losing blood. I told you about my bad dream, but you insisted it was a good sign.

BABANDIANG:
Oh, Mangkutak, . . . Mangkutak, . . . where are you, my son?

SABAI [*while crying*]:
Trying to call your son, Father? Mangkutak never did what he was asked to. And still, you always gave all the good food to Mangkutak, and only a little rice was left for Sabai. When you went to the bathing place, Mangkutak was sitting on the horse, and Sabai always walked. When you sliced the chicken, the meat was for Mangkutak, and the bones were for Sabai. And now that is what you get. Call him again, Father, maybe he can take the blemish from your forehead. It is the wrong time to be disappointed right now, and I have an idea now.

BABANDIANG:
Oh, my daughter Sabai Nan Aluih, don't be disappointed now, it is not the right time. You know about my condition. I will die soon; all my blood is leaving my body. I feel very ill and weak. I am really thirsty, please give me some water. And my body feels rather hot, is there no breeze? My head hurts very much. Only the grass is my pillow, and the land is my mattress. Please find me a pillow, my head feels like it will break.

SABAI [*while crying*]:
Oh, dearest Father, where can I get water in the middle of the forest? How can I create a breeze? In this deep valley, where can I find a pillow? We are in the middle of the jungle. Oh, Father, if you really want water now, please drink the tears of Sabai; if you need fresh air, I will fan you with my sleeves; if you need a pillow, I will cut off my arm for you. I hope it will make your heart happy.

BABANDIANG [*fainting*]:
Mangkutak, oh, Mangkutak. . . . where are you Mangkutak? No one can stop Rajo Nan Panjang anymore. [*Babandiang dies; Sabai cries, watching his last breath.*]

SABAI:
Rajo Nan Panjang! He, he killed my father! [*screams*] Where are

Mount Merapi and Mount Singgalang, oh, where are lake Singkarak and lake Maninjau? Even though I am a woman, I know where to take my shame. If we owe gold, we have to pay in gold; if we owe a soul, we have to pay with a soul. Stay here for a moment, I will find Rajo Nan Panjang.

Gurindam
Sabai Nan Aluih is desperate,
the blood in her chest is in turmoil.
She wants to run fast and
look for Rajo Nan Panjang.
After a short while,
she hears something,
the sound of a horse from far.
She looks around and sees him.

SCENE 8

RAJO NAN PANJANG:
My dear younger sister Sabai Nan Aluih, actually you seem to be playing the game here, I have been looking for you everywhere and it has made me tired. Now I am lucky. Finally meeting you makes all the tiredness disappear from my body. All my pains are cured, because now I meet the heart of hearts. How severe my sickness was! And I have had it for a long time. Everywhere I searched for medicine, but only after I meet you I do feel healthy again.

SABAI [*with a little smile*]:
I came here for no one else than you. After looking at you carefully, I think you are the right man. . . . You are the best one to become my husband.

RAJO NAN PANJANG [*satisfied and happy*]:
My love for you has been growing since even before you were born. I cannot stop it, so let's unite our love.

SABAI:
You are the only one I can share the path with, the only one I will trust all my life, you will be my fantasy during the day, and my dreams at night. Come my lord, Rajo Nan Panjang, I am a woman, and you are a man. But first, may I just ask you a tiny question? Did you kill my father? And why?

RAJO NAN PANJANG:
About the death of your father, let me explain. Listen carefully. I can't say yes or no. I was attacked from the back, but because I am a good pandeka [silek master], his weapon got turned against him. But forget this now, my dear sister. Right here and now, it is our luck that we finally meet here. I see your surprised face, I can imagine how beautiful it will look on our wedding. [*He tries to get closer; she backs up.*]

SABAI:
Oh, dear lord, master of sweet words, you were a friend of my father for so long, and now you have killed him.

SITI NARAWATU [*enters and speaks with surprise in her voice*]:
Oh, my lord, and dear Younger Sister Sabai Nan Aluih, if I may ask a question: What really happened here? What befell your father?

SABAI:
Oh, dear Aunt, to make it clear for you, listen please. Rajo Nan Panjang and Rajo Babandiang were friends for a long time. They are of the same age, they used to sleep in the same place. He is not shy with the people in the village; this old man has a sharp taste [he likes his food spicy, i.e., likes young woman].

RAJO NAN PANJANG:
Oh, dear young Sabai Nan Aluih, don't speak like that.

SABAI:
Speak no more! I am here to meet you, Rajo Nan Panjang. I want to clear my father's shame; you can try me. I won't take back one step. To clear the mark from his forehead, I have to go all the way.

SITI NARAWATU:
Dear Rajo Nan Panjang, you'd better retreat. Don't you hear what this girl is saying? She doesn't know how spicy the chili is, or how salty the salt is. She doesn't know adat. If you fight her, the people will bring you down. Let's return home.

RAJO NAN PANJANG:
Dear Siti Narawatu, Sabai Nan Aluih passed over the sky, and I am after her. Please be patient for a moment, I am an adult man. [Proverb: "A very wide grass field. We want to spit it out, because it is bitter." Meaning: the situation is hard for all of us.] I need new clothes. It is written with golden threads, who will wear these clothes? Only me, Rajo Nan Panjang. It's true what they say about me, it is taboo for me to take my words back.

SITI NARAWATU:
Dear husband, the center of the net, leader of the nagari, when the people of Limopuluah Koto find out that my lord fights with a girl, all the trees in the forests will shake. All the fish in the streams will jump out of the water. What will become of Sago mountain?

RAJO NAN PANJANG [angry]:
Young Siti Narawatu, it is obvious what you want, I command you to return home! [Siti Narawatu turns around but doesn't leave. Instead, she hides behind some bushes, and Rajo Nan Panjang shouts.] Hey, you clever Sabai! I'm offended by this proud girl in the middle of the meadow. So here, I give you my best. . . . [He attacks Sabai; she evades his attack.]

SABAI [ridiculing him]:
You're good at quarreling. Who taught you? Let's have a competition. I shall be your bride if you can shoot off my earring. If not, you shall retreat forever, if I can shoot of your deta [head cloth].

RAJO NAN PANJANG [upset]:
You girl from Padang! You want to go to Banu Hampu? Sabai, in the middle of the meadow? Suffer this shot! [He shoots once.]

SABAI:

Hey, you're a good shot! You actually managed to hit my clothes. [*He shoots again.*] You shot twice, but you still haven't hit the ring on my ear. [*He shoots again.*] You shot three times, and you have only loosened my hair bun. Now, listen to me, I'm getting bored. Now it's my turn.

[*Sabai takes her gun from her shoulder and aims at Rajo Nan Panjang. The first shot hits his left shoulder. After realizing the situation, Siti Narawatu runs out from her hiding place; she embraces him and they fall down together. She cries.*]

SITI NARAWATU:

My lord Rajo Nan Panjang, this is my bad fate. When I wanted to stop you, I could not. You only follow your heart. Now, who will you leave me with? My fate has turned foul, I depend on you but you abandon me. [*She looks at Sabai.*] Oh, Sabai Nan Aluih, you're such an evil deceiver; you have no shame; your heart is like the heart of the banana [which has no heart]; you killed the one dearest to me.

SABAI:

Oh, my older sister Siti Narawatu, don't speak like that. Although he was clever, he always scared his friends away. Everything he did was only for his own advantage, just like a fence eating up the plants.

SITI NARAWATU:

Oh, guard your tongue! Who will ever take you? You'll stay a spinster until you die. I always assumed that you were a pleasant fish, but really you're a gigantic crocodile.

SABAI:

Rajo Nan Panjang had a wife in every village; he has children under every stairway. He's been lying to you. He wanted to come home to me too, but I'm not that kind of flower. I can only be wooed for a serious marriage. All I need is enough food to eat, and some gold to be wealthy, but I would never sell my body. Dear

Older Sister Siti Narawatu, even though you're a widow, and I'm just a young girl, we're the same; we're women. Let's stop this argument. All this is our bad fate and unfortunate for everyone of us. It will be a disgrace when the people find out about this. Right here and now, take your lord home, please, and I will take my father home.

[*She sees Mangkutak Alam approach and calls to him.*]

Dear Younger Brother Mangkutak Alam, please come closer. Why are you standing over there? [*Mangkutak Alam comes closer, Sabai starts crying*] Oh, Mangkutak Alam, my younger brother, son without a father. He was shot by Rajo Nan Panjang. If you are really a man, now is the time for revenge. If not now, when?

MANGKUTAK ALAM [*while crying*]:

Dear Older Sister, about Rajo Nan Panjang, we cannot fight him; he's a very strong man. People say he has powerful knowledge.

SABAI:

Oh, young one, you've been spoiled for too long. You always show off, you never work, and now you don't even know how to repay anybody.

MANGKUTAK ALAM:

Don't be angry, my sister, I can't go to war, I really don't know any silek, I can't use weapons. Take me to a teacher first.

SABAI [*angry*]:

You ask for a teacher now? Now you ask to learn silek and weaponry? We're in the middle of the forest; now is not the time to study! Now is not the time to teach. You make me ashamed. A younger brother shouldn't behave like that. You'd better change your clothes; you can wear mine. Punch holes in your ears and wear earrings. Pick up the *parian* [household container to fetch water]. Try to cook some rice and make different kinds of curries. That would be best for you. [*Mangkutak is crying; Sabai feels sorry and comforts him.*]

My younger brother Mangkutak Alam, don't cry any more and

don't be afraid. I have shot Rajo Nan Panjang, that's his corpse over there. [*Mangkutak Alam is afraid to look at the corpse. Sabai embraces her brother, and they cry for the father.*] Oh, Father, Father. Oh, *pipit* birds, who fly over the bushes and land in the rice fields. We can see it [their looming fate] from Bukittinggi. We are two in this family whom you left behind, we have bad luck. [*Sadun Saribai enters and looks at both her children. She is shocked to see her husband's corpse. She bows down by his side and cries.*]

SADUN SARIBAI:
The heartstring has been cut; the place where I can set my foot has broken down, the place I can hold on to has disappeared. [*She caresses her children.*] Dear daughter Sabai Nan Aluih, dear son Mangkutak Alam, the mark of my bones, it is not our will, but it is Allah's will that comes true. Because the day is getting hot, let us take Father home.

SABAI NAN ALUIH [*shouting*]:
Oh, villagers, help us, please. Bring my father home, please.

Gurindam:
Before reaching the *dusun* [district]
there is a valley;
we can see it
from the slopes of the mountain.
The story is finished and
the narration is resting.
Everything is silent.
Next time we'll try it again.

If you go to the forest,
break a stem of the *sudu-sudu* plant
and use it to wrap fish.
Look at the clouds passing overhead,
we can find a sasaran anywhere,
at DepPen, or other places.

Appendix C

Umbuik Mudo

Young Bamboo is a play performed by the group Sago Sejati from the village of Baruh Bukit, district of Sungayang, West Sumatra.

Roles

Umbuik Mudo — the young hero
Sutan Saripado — his father
Mother of Umbuik
Rambun Ameh — his sister
Panjang Jangguik — Umbuik's teacher
Puti Galang Banyak — the niece of Umbuik's teacher
Father of Puti
Mother of Puti
Tuanku Tuo — silek teacher
Pandeka Cingkahak — a robber
Pandeka Langkisau — a robber
Pandeka Garagasi — a robber
Villagers

[*Note:* The first song and scene have been included recently, maybe due to the need for a more realistic and dramatic opening. Traditionally, the play starts with a greeting and introduction song followed by scene two.]

<u>Gurindam</u>
[melody: Simarantang Rendah]
Many people are around,
when someone with a severe injury
lying face down is found.
One person gets close and
touches the body of that man.
It is Sutan Saripado.

SCENE I

VILLAGER 1:
He is still alive!

VILLAGER 2:
Let's try to turn him over. Who is he? [*They turn him over.*]

VILLAGER 1:
Oh, it is Sutan Saripado, the father of Umbuik.

VILLAGER 2:
When did he come back from rantau? [*Many people gather.*]

VILLAGER 1:
Don't get too close! Let some wind get in here!

VILLAGER 2:
He wants to say something, so everyone be quiet. [*All are quiet.*]

SUTAN SARIPADO:
Umbuik, . . . Umbuik, come closer please, my dear son. . . .

VILLAGER 3:
Umbuik has not come yet, please be patient while he is called. Please tell us what happened to you.

SUTAN SARIPADO:
I was robbed in the wild forest. Umbuik, Umbuik. . . .

VILLAGER 1:
Tell us who robbed you. What is their name and title? What did they look like?

SUTAN SARIPADO:
I was robbed by three men; one was Pandeka Langkisau, one Pandeka Garagasi, one Pandeka Cingkahak. Oh, Umbuik, come here, get close to me, please. . . .

UMBUIK MUDO [*arrives*]:
Oh, Father. . . . What happened? Why are you covered with blood? Explain it to me so that I am happy in my heart and calm in my mind.

SUTAN SARIPADO:
Come closer, my son. My fate has come to me. You will be an orphan soon, the devil will get me, and Allah's fate has come to me. My dear and only son, take revenge! Drown the wood in the water. [kill the enemy] There is no God besides Allah.

UMBUIK MUDO [*He cries.*]:
Father, Father. . . . [*Many people speak a prayer for the dying person.*]

Gurindam
[melody: Ratok Ramala Hanyuik]
The children of Silayang Tinggi
are torn apart and tossed down,
when thinking about the father's death.
Their stomachs are cramping and
they get bent over by the pain.
It is cut and measured,
the misery has come to Umbuik.

The sky comes tumbling down,
and the earth cracks open.
A day becomes a month,

a month becomes a year,
and Umbuik has grown up;
his mother is getting older.

SCENE 2

MOTHER OF UMBUIK MUDO:
Oh, my dear one and only son Umbuik, medicine for my tiredness and fever, please come closer, I have something to tell you.

UMBUIK MUDO:
Dear Mother, hearing you calling me makes the blood tremble in my chest and my bones feel weak. What happened that you call me? What is it that you want to tell me? Please explain it to me so that it makes me happy in my heart and calm in my mind.

MOTHER:
Dear child, please listen carefully, pay attention to what I have to say. Don't take it lightly, take it seriously, my dear Umbuik. Listen to my proverb: I am getting older, but you haven't received enough education yet. I think you already know about me. I had to be your mother and your father, and even your uncle. Now you have grown up and it is time for me to know what you want to do with your life. It is time to become the brother-in-law of someone else. Even so, I am worried about something. If I die in this season, the earth will scream receiving my body, and my corpse will be turning in its grave because I left something behind. My son hasn't received enough education yet.

UMBUIK MUDO:
If that is what you ask, teach me please. I will use it as a walking stick during the day, and as my pillow at night. Does that make you happy?

MOTHER:
Since you have been growing up, all you do is play around, joking, flying kites, and playing *sipak rago* [game with a rattan ball]. You

just stroll around. You are an orphan, your father died and you don't have an uncle. You only follow your carefree heart and forget about the mistakes young people make.

UMBUIK MUDO:
Listen to me, Mother, please. What I like most is smoking, eating siriah, and strolling around while I am still alive, before my spirit leaves my body. When we're still alive we carry the world. When we get old, we will be of no use.

MOTHER:
If that is what you ask, you have the wrong ideas. The people will make fun of you left and right. There will be gossip about you everywhere. You don't know who you are. Now, I will educate you. Listen carefully and pay attention. The mistakes of the young come in three versions: *Mudo Parisau* [dreamer], *Mudo Pangasau* [troublemaker], *Mudo Langkisau* [hothead].

UMBUIK MUDO:
Dear Mother, would you please explain that to me? If it's good I will wear it like my clothes; if it's bad, I will throw it away.

MOTHER:
Dear child, listen carefully. A *Mudo Parisau* always has a longing heart, day and night, night and day. In the afternoon he has a bright heart. Before I call, he will hear me. Before we make a joke, he will laugh. His mind is like a flea-ridden goat.

UMBUIK MUDO:
Oh, Mother, so what is a *Mudo Pangasau*?

MOTHER:
He makes trouble and fights everywhere he goes. He wants to get everything he sees. That's a *Mudo Pangasau*. And now listen about the *Mudo Langkisau*. He's like a flash flood—no education, rotten ideas. He doesn't appreciate good things and his heart is full of revenge.

UMBUIK MUDO:
If that's your advice, I'll think about it. Now I want to play sipak rago, please give me your permission to leave and I'll go.

MOTHER:
Oh, young Umbuik, I haven't finished talking yet. I don't appreciate that you want to go already. You haven't listened to my advice yet. You just think it's like wind passing by. It goes in your right ear and comes out your left ear.

UMBUIK MUDO:
My dear mother, don't be angry. Give me permission please, my friends are waiting for me.

MOTHER:
Of course I'm upset and angry. You don't know who you are and how poor you are. Only your style makes you look like a rich man. No, you will not go to play, you'd better start looking for a good job.

UMBUIK MUDO:
What kind of good job can I do? I'm still young; I'm not old enough to work.

MOTHER:
How about becoming a trader?

UMBUIK MUDO:
It's not easy to do. A good trader has to know about loss and gain, and how to count the investments.

MOTHER:
What do you want then? To work in an office?

UMBUIK MUDO:
Dear Mother, it's not easy to be an official; he has to have fast feet and light hands. He has to be awake more than asleep, his blanket for the night is only dew. During the day his only umbrella is the sky. He only walks with short legs [has no vehicle for transportation].

MOTHER:
If that's what you think, you'd better become a guard.

UMBUIK MUDO:
Oh, dear Mother, forgive me. It's not easy to be a guard either. He has to be strong and invincible. He always stands at the door to death. He straightens things that are crooked.

MOTHER:
So you don't want to be a trader, an official, or a guard. What do you like then?

UMBUIK MUDO:
Forgive me, my dear mother, I don't like any of these. Please give me another option.

MOTHER:
If that's what you ask, I have something else. Do you want to study the Qur'an?

UMBUIK MUDO:
Yes, Mother, that is the young shoot. We dig for a spring and the water comes. That is what my heart wants.

MOTHER:
Hurry up, now, get ready. Prepare everything for your journey. Take some gold with you, you will leave tomorrow. You will go to the *surau* of Panjang Jagguik.

Gurindam
[melody: Sijobang]
Umbuik goes on his way,
he goes to study at Ranah Kampuang Auah,
at the surau of Panjang Jangguik,
bringing all his travel gear.
After walking for a long time
he has arrived there.
He has started to study the Qur'an.

After a year, after two years,
he can read the Qur'an.

His heart is getting brighter,
and his thinking is getting clearer.
He can translate the Qur'an well
and read it beautifully.
Now, Umbuik is longing to travel again.
He wants to study with another teacher.
Improve his knowledge,
abilities, and experience.

SCENE 3

UMBUIK MUDO:
Dear teacher, I bow my head and bend my knees before you, I fold
my hands to greet you.

PANJANG JANGGUIK:
Dear student, what is the reason you come here, what is in your
heart? What appeared before your eyes? Explain it to me so that it
makes me happy in my heart and calm in my mind.

UMBUIK MUDO:
Dear master, I have stayed with you for three years now. You have
taught me many things, too much of your knowledge you have be-
stowed onto me, my mind has opened and my soul is enriched.
How can I ever repay you? How can I value your good manners?
But even so, I ask you permission to go study further, at another
surau. Just like the elders say: If we sail far, we can see many
things, if we live long, we can feel many things.

PANJANG JANGGUIK:
My dear son Umbuik, if that is what you ask, it makes my heart
very sad and my mind very worried. Why? Because I don't take
you as my student, you are like my son and my nephew. Why do
you want to leave? What worries you? Explain it to me clearly.

UMBUIK MUDO:
If that is what you ask, you are right. The reason I want to go rantau, is that my heart is not quiet any more. I have studied too close to my village.

PANJANG JANGGUIK:
If that is what you ask, you are right. According to our Prophet, you have to seek knowledge, even if you have to go as far as China. Seek knowledge until you are close to your grave. But even so, I feel something, a debt I haven't paid yet.

UMBUIK MUDO:
Until now, there is nothing you haven't given me. I think I am indebted to you.

PANJANG JANGGUIK:
My debt as your teacher is different than your debt as my student. My debt is that I haven't given you my entire knowledge. You can read the Qur'an, even though you are not too good at it. In silek, I only gave you a few basics. It is not enough to just evade attacks, kicks, or knives. I better pay my debt now. I want to teach you more silek in the few remaining days.

UMBUIK MUDO:
Ever since my father was killed by the robbers, I have had the desire to learn silek, but I was afraid. My feet are heavy and my hands are slow. Besides that, I think silek is forbidden for one who studies the Qur'an.

PANJANG JANGGUIK:
To protect our body and our honor is our duty as Muslims. We don't look for the enemy, but if he comes, we don't run away. That's why a good Minangkabau *ulama* [Muslim wise man] also has good silek skills. But not many people know that. Just like our proverb: the tiger hides his claws. Now, I have an idea, young man. Call all your classmates together in the practice space, let me teach them silek.

UMBUIK MUDO:
If that is what you ask, teacher, I will carry out your order quickly.
[they practice silek]

Gurindam
[melody: Indang Payakumbuah]
Umbuik has started to learn silek
from his teacher, Panjang Janggiuk.
Due to the teacher's love for his student,
there were many things he gave to him.
After Umbuik has mastered silek he leaves.
He goes to the surau of Imam Mudo
in Ranah Pandai Sikek and studies there.
He is very clever and obedient to his teacher.
He can memorize every word.

Now he is longing to go home.
He feels like something is calling him.
He asks his teacher for permission.
After traveling for a long time he gets home.
After a day in the village,
a week in the house,
someone comes to pick him up.
He is invited by his old teacher to come
to Puti Galang Banyak's house for a party.

SCENE 4

MOTHER OF UMBUIK:
Dear child Umbuik, don't stay too long, go there soon, to the house
of Puti Galang Panyak, the niece of Panjang Janggiuk.

UMBUIK MUDO:
Dear Mother, look carefully at what I am wearing now. How does
it look to you?

MOTHER:
If that's what you ask, I have no bad feelings. It's perfect.

UMBUIK MUDO:
My younger sister Rambun Ameh, would you please look at this.
Do I look handsome wearing it?

RAMBUN AMEH:
If that's what you ask, you look very handsome in it. You look like
the son of the king. But I worry about something. What do you
think if another girl cares about you? How will you deal with it?
How will you carry the world? We are orphans and very poor.
Think about this first.

UMBUIK MUDO:
Why do you trouble your heart? I am invited to go to read the
Qur'an with my old teacher at his niece's house. I don't intend to
go to the *galanggang* [gambling hall].

RAMBUN AMEH:
Oh, dear Brother, I'm more dizzy and confused than from falling
down. Why? Because Puti is my friend, and so are her six sisters.
I'm afraid that you'll fall in love with one of them.

UMBUIK MUDO:
Dear Younger Sister Rambun Ameh, I am Umbuik Mudo, well
known in this region to be a good Muslim. I have studied the Qur'an
and *hadith* for five years. I don't want to be accused of something
like that. I don't wink at girls. I'm not confused by sweet words.

RAMBUN AMEH:
Even if you talk like that now, don't let your words jump. Don't
push your mouth, because of the holy sea and the good fortune in
the rantau. There is much magic in this world.

MOTHER OF UMBUIK MUDO:
Dear Son, dizzy people die easily by falling down. Worried people
die easily in the flood. Don't talk too much, better go now before
the day passes.

UMBUIK MUDO:
If that is what you ask, give me permission to go.

Gurindam
[melody: Sijobang]
Umbuik leaves the house on his horse,
the day has almost passed;
he arrives at the house
of his teacher's niece.
His horse makes a loud sound,
so everyone comes out to see him there.

SCENE 5

PANJANG JANGGUIK:
Dear Umbuik Mudo, don't stand there too long, wash your feet and come up into the house.

UMBUIK MUDO:
Forgive me, teacher, I am late.

PANJANG JANGGUIK:
Dear young Umbuik, before you arrived, many words were read, many songs were sung, and now, please show us the songs that you learned in other regions.

UMBUIK MUDO:
If that is what you ask, I will try my best. [*He starts to read the Qur'an.*]

PUTI GALANG BANYAK [*walks around the circle and listens to him reciting. She comes in and speaks to him after he has finished.*]:
Dear lord, many people have read the Qur'an, and many people have already presented their songs. They were all good Muslims, but I didn't care to listen. But when you started to read, my heart started to beat and my mind opened up. My ears could hear very clearly. So I came down. Dear lord, listen to me, please. I request that you repeat your song, so that we can listen to it again.

UMBUIK MUDO:
If someone asks me, I will try my best, even if I cannot do well. I haven't read the Qur'an in a long time.
[*He tries his last song, but after a few words, he cannot continue. He stops, confused.*]

PUTI GALANG BANYAK [*making faces at him*]:
Actually, you forgot your lesson. Actually, you are rather crazy on the prayer mat. You didn't study enough, you are just like a flower that doesn't blossom.

UMBUIK MUDO [*ashamed and embarassed*]:
Oh, my dear master, forgive me, please. Let me go home, I am no use here.
[*He starts to leave, but his teacher stops him.*]

PANJANG JANGGUIK:
Don't leave yet, wait for the party to finish. You have to eat and drink first.

UMBUIK MUDO:
Forgive me many times, master. Don't have a small heart. I want to leave right away.

PANJANG JANGGUIK:
I cannot stop you; it is like trying to stop the river from coming down the hill. So I have to let you go.

Gurindam
[melody: Sutan Pangaduan]
There is no bigger shame than this.
The shame is like a ship crashing into a wall,
like a mark on the forehead.
If the mark was on the body,
he could hide it with clothes,
Umbuik is devastated in his heart.
He is full of disappointment and
remembers the words of his younger sister.

He rides his horse back
to his mother's house;
after a long time,
he arrives at the yard.
Because of his sad heart
and his lost thoughts,
he is very gloomy and sad.
It makes his mother worry.

SCENE 6

MOTHER OF UMBUIK:
My dear son, for a long time you have been sitting around all gloomy, sometimes you almost cry. What is the reason? Did you get sick? Do you have a fever? Did you lose in the competition reading the Qur'an? Did you oppose someone's opinion? Explain it to me please, to make the day bright and my heart feel happy.

UMBUIK MUDO:
If that's what you ask, I didn't lose in reading the Qur'an. I didn't lose because of my words or my clothes. My younger sister was right. I can think of nothing else but Puti Galang Banyak. Something is bothering me about these young maidens. Oh, Mother, if you feel sorry for me, if you have any compassion, if you really love me, please go, if I ask you to go. Fill your bag with all the magic things, with your magic love items, and please go to Kampuang Aur, go to Puti's house and have a careful conversation. Tell them that I got sick, and the only medicine for me is Puti.

MOTHER:
Dear and only son, you have read the Qur'an for a long time, and you were in the rantau for a very long time. You forgot all my advice. You forgot about the mistakes of young people. Do you remember? Think about it. What's the name of what you have done? Do you remember the *Mudo Parisau*? He has a longing heart all day and all night. You will get into big trouble.

UMBUIK MUDO:
Oh, Mother, my mother. Listen to me carefully, if your heart is not a banana's heart [a banana has no heart]. There is no shame bigger than mine. Some magic has happened to me; Puti Galang Banyak has bewitched me. My tongue was tied when I tried to read the Qur'an. My mouth was locked when I tried to sing. And then she made fun of me. She said that I'm crazy because of the prayer mat. If you feel sorry for me, go to her. Ask her to come here to cure the wound in my heart.

MOTHER:
Think about this carefully, my son. What if she refuses? How shameful it will be for us.

UMBUIK MUDO:
It means you don't feel sorry for me. You've come back before you left. What is your heart made of, and what is your soul made of?

MOTHER:
If that's what you ask, let me try. I'd better go quickly before the day passes.

Gurindam
There were seven maidens
in Ranah Kampuang Auah,
the nieces of Umbuik's teacher.
The maidens were seven,
stunningly beautiful,
nice and clever, all of them.
Their true match could only be a king.
It is hard to find a sutan for them.

If we talk about their faces,
they looked like the full moon;
they were yellow, as yellow as yellow is.
Their ears look like small traps,
their lips looked like slices of oranges.

They cut their nails like a moon crescent
[more ad-lib]

If we had to chose
between these maidens,
the most beautiful is Puti.
The beloved of the heart of her father.
The treasure of the people in the village.
The one to whom Umbuik's love fell.

The story changes now.
Even though it changes,
it is still the same.
We change to the mother of Umbuik.
She arrived at the house of Puti
and she calls from the yard.

SCENE 7

MOTHER OF UMBUIK MUDO:
Oh, dear Puti Galang Banyak are you home? Please come out for a
moment.

MOTHER OF PUTI:
Dear daughter of mine, please come to the door for a minute. Who
is it?

PUTI GALANG BANYAK:
It is the mother of Umbuik Mudo. Oi, dear, don't stand outside
any longer, wash your feet and come up into the house.

MOTHER OF PUTI:
Oh, dear Sister, Umbuik's mother. What brings you here? Please
explain it clearly.

MOTHER OF UMBUIK MUDO:
I have come here not just to come. I bring a message from Umbuik
to Galang.

PUTI GALANG BANYAK:
Dear Mother of Umbuik Mudo, what is his message? Did he leave something behind when he came here to read the Qur'an? Did he lose something? Explain it to us, please.

MOTHER OF UMBUIK MUDO:
If that is what you ask, you are right. About his message, yes, he left something, and yes, he lost something.

PUTI GALANG BANYAK:
If I may ask, what was it? If we replace it, how much would it cost?

MOTHER OF UMBUIK MUDO:
If we talk about the form of the thing that was lost, its form is not clear to me. And if you ask about the cost, it cannot be sold or bought. If you ask about replacing it, according to his message, only you yourself can replace it. About Umbuik, he is lying down alone, his body is very tired and weak. His face is very pale; he has lost all the color in his complexion. He feels that even the water he drinks is like thorns in his throat.

PUTI GALANG BANYAK: Dear Mother of Umbuik Mudo, if Umbuik Mudo got sick, why don't you try to find a dukun? Why don't you look for medicine to cure him? Why did you come here? Why don't you tell me?

MOTHER OF UMBUIK MUDO:
If the water is murky in the river, we have to find the source. If the string is jumbled at the end we have to start untangling at the beginning. About the sickness of my son, it has sprung from you. If his attention is weak, it is because of your wink. If his heart got sick, it is because your words touched it.

PUTI GALANG BANYAK:
Don't say that all this is my fault. It is his mistake as well. Just like our elders say: If we don't study enough, if we don't finish our education, we are like flowers without blossoms.

MOTHER OF PUTI:
Oh, dear Mother of Umbuik Mudo, ask Umbuik to go study again, he hasn't achieved the real goal yet. He just sang a song.

PUTI GALANG BANYAK:
About his message, I don't want to be the medicine, I don't want to go to him. Find someone else.

MOTHER OF UMBUIK MUDO:
Oh, Puti Galang Banyak, listen to me carefully. It will get him into even more trouble. Don't keep us hanging any longer.

PUTI GALANG BANYAK:
I said no, but you still say yes. Listen carefully, Mother. Listen to every one of my words. I never thought about Umbuik, and he is never in my dreams at night. There is one more thing, I want to tell you. Tell him the truth clearly. Don't give him any hope. This is the truth from me.

MOTHER OF UMBUIK MUDO:
Dear Puti, I will go home, now. Maybe if I have good luck, I will come back here again.

PUTI GALANG BANYAK:
We didn't invite you here, and we won't escort you home.

Gurindam
Umbuik's mother leaves the house
and walks with a sad heart.
She returns home full of worries
thinking about her son.
After a long walk
she arrives at the yard
and goes directly into the house.

Looking at her son she sees
that he is sitting there,
his pale face all gloomy.

He looks like he has been sick
for a long time.
He had big hopes and big worries.

SCENE 8

UMBUIK MUDO:
Dear Mother, did you meet her? Did you give her my message?
What did she answer? How did the conversation go?

MOTHER OF UMBUIK MUDO:
I fell down before I went; that means bad luck will come.

UMBUIK MUDO:
Tell me the truth, tell me all. What did she say? What did she
want?

MOTHER OF UMBUIK MUDO:
The last word was spoken. I won't tell you more or less than what
she said. Listen to me: "About Umbuik, I never think of him in the
day, he never enters my dreams at night." Galang said: "In the next
year or two I don't want to get married. I don't want a husband
yet. I have no idea of getting a man; I want to stay single. Tell him
the truth. Don't change my words, don't ever give him any hope.
This is the truth from me." That is what Galang said. That was the
conversation I'm telling you about. My dear son, listen to my advice. The reason for the words is oriented toward Tiku; Tiku is
oriented toward Koto Tangah. When you have bad luck, you have
to be patient. Wait for a sign from Allah. Dear Son, don't let your
heart be worried, don't let your heart be full of disappointment.

UMBUIK MUDO:
Your words are true, Mother. Your advice is right. But I have
something in my heart. Just like your advice. If we move, one step
isn't enough. If we talk, one word is't enough. So, let me try a second one. If two isn't enough, let me try a third. The third time will
be the last. That's the way it used to be done.

MOTHER OF UMBUIK MUDO:
My only son, try to think it over carefully. Listen to this proverb: The children of the crocodile leave when we enter [bad luck sign]. What will you do if good luck won't come? You have to wait.

UMBUIK MUDO:
Don't you feel sorry for your son, Mother? Don't you have mercy for me? It looks like you're running away from this proverb.

MOTHER OF UMBUIK MUDO:
No, I don't hide from this problem, Galang's words were final. It feels like there is nothing left we can do. It is better to wait for a move from Allah.

UMBUIK MUDO:
Why do you want to wait for Allah without doing something? Now it's better if you go there again. Ask her again a last time to make it clear.

MOTHER OF UMBUIK MUDO:
If that's what you ask, let me try. Before the day passes, I will go.

Gurindam
Umbuik's mother has lost
her mind and good judgement.
It is very embarrassing for her
to go back there again.
Because of her love and
compassion for her son,
she goes there one more time.
The big house has nine rooms,
the maiden sits in the *surambi* [waiting room].

How hard it will be.
Just like looking at the highest sky.
She goes to the market and buys something,
but then throws it away.

Bad luck has come to Umbuik.
The sky tumbles and the earth cracks.
She is walking for a long time.
Finally she gets to Puti's house.

SCENE 9

MOTHER OF UMBUIK MUDO:
Oh, dear Mother of Puti Galang Banyak, are you home?

MOTHER OF PUTI GALANG BANYAK:
Don't stand there in the yard any longer. There is water; wash your feet and come in. [*She goes in.*] I think this door has magic powers; after you leave, it can bring you back here again.

MOTHER OF UMBUIK MUDO:
The many colors of the cloth are made in Java, it has been sewn, but it hasn't been washed yet. The reason I come back again is that our discussion is not finished yet. Dear Mother of Galang, listen to me, please. There is a stairway, there is a room, and there is a tray. I came back because I want to repeat our conversation.

MOTHER OF PUTI: We go to the forest, but not to meditate. I don't care; it depends on you.

MOTHER OF UMBUIK MUDO:
I'll role the dice once again. It shakes the gold from Bangko. I try it once again, to change the final words. There is the sound of weapons in Tarusan; there is a war in Limo Koto. I'll tell you the truth. Umbuik wants to be the *sumando* [brother-in-law].

PUTI GALANG BANYAK:
I told you before. We don't put it in the rice fields, we put it on the border. I already told you. Don't put it in your heart, put it on your back. Listen carefully, Mother.
Umbuik cannot have any hope. About your son, even though he is a really good man, and I know it, he is only good because of his borrowed clothes. If he was really rich, I would know. He is rich

because of the gold he brings, it came from his father, but it is not even enough for my ankle ornaments. And now, Mother, don't talk about him any more. Don't start over again. If I touch it and it is rough, let me smooth it. If I broke it, let me take it back. Hearing the name of Umbuik makes my hair stand on end. Do you understand?

MOTHER OF UMBUIK MUDO:
I didn't think it could happen like that. My son will be heartbroken.

Gurindam
The sound of a horse cart is heard,
and someone rides it to Tarumun.
Heartbroken and restless,
[he feels like] hiding under a blanket.
What is life for?
Life for a dead man?
To be dead in the forest
is better than living without love.

It is all about Umbuik Mudo,
he was humiliated by Puti;
his love has been broken by her.
Now his mother,
because of her love for her son,
did what he asked her.
She would do anything for him.

SCENE 10

UMBUIK MUDO:
Dear Mother, why are your eyes all swollen and red? Why is your face changed? Why is your heart so sad? What is your heart made of? I think it is the heart of a banana. Tell me the truth.

MOTHER OF UMBUIK MUDO:
Don't be angry with me. Don't be sad. I will tell you the truth about Galang.

UMBUIK MUDO:
Tell me the truth, quickly. Don't let me wait.

MOTHER OF UMBUIK MUDO:
She said: "About your son, even though he is a really good man, and I know it, he is only good because of his borrowed clothes. If he was really rich, I would know. He seems rich because of the gold he brings, which came from his father, but it is not even enough for my ankle ornaments. And now, Mother, don't talk about him any more. Don't start it over again. If I touch it and it is rough, let me smooth it. If I broke it, let me take it back. Hearing the name of Umbuik makes my hair stand on end." That's what she said to me to tell you. That's why I'm crying.

UMBUIK MUDO [*angry, slapping his fists*]:
Oh, how she must hate me! How bad I must look in her eyes.

MOTHER OF UMBUIK MUDO:
That's why I was reluctant to go there before, and then I was afraid to tell you. It all turned bad. It disturbed the faith in our hearts.

UMBUIK MUDO:
Dear Mother, this is my last request for you. Maybe it will erase the mark on our forehead, if we can submerge the wood in the water.

MOTHER OF UMBUIK MUDO:
My dearest son, what do you think inside your heart? What do you want to ask? Tell me right now, so that it makes me happy in my heart and calm in my mind.

UMBUIK MUDO:
Find me a *parupuak* [magic object] by the water from Lubuk Mato Kuciang. It's not too holy. It just can kill someone that is passing by, the flying bird can fall down dead. And about that parupuak, a big dragon and a dangerous snake guard it and it's on the head of a

big fish. If you can't get that parupuak, it means you don't love me anymore, you aren't sorry for me any more. Let me stab myself, maybe this will make you happy.

MOTHER OF UMBUIK MUDO:
If that is what you want, my son, it's just like eating the *simalakamo* food [poison]. If I go, I will die, if I don't go, you will be angry with me, so I'd rather die. Does that make you happy?

UMBUIK MUDO:
If we get what we want and if our fate from Allah is good, you will be safe to go there.

MOTHER OF UMBUIK MUDO:
Even if we go to the market now, it's impossible to buy it again; if I go now, it's impossible to come back here. How far the bamboo tree is. I don't want to cut it any more. I will leave you, my village, and I will not return.

Gurindam
[melody: Padang Panjang]
Umbuik's mother has gone;
she walks confused;
the earth she steps on is boiling;
the sky over her feels
like it will fall down.

It is a long time on the road;
now she arrives at her destination,
Lubuk Mato Kuciang.
It is a holy pool, but not too holy.
It has rained hard that day,
there is the sound of thunder,
flashes light up the sky.

She prays to Allah there.
Give Umbuik what he wants, please.

Because Allah wants to help,
the rain stops,
the thunder and flashes reside.
She sees the parupuak
floating in the water.

It is no use to make
rendang [food] from peanuts.
It is no use to make
the story any longer;
it is better we make it short.
She gets the only parupuak there.

She runs home, forgetting about
every shame and embarrassment.
She gets home and sees
how happy Umbuik is.
He starts to make a flute right away.
Who knows, it might clear him
from all his shame.

SCENE I I

[UMBUIK MUDO blows the flute, but PUTI GALANG BAN-YAK cannot see him, she is on her way to the *tapian* (bathing place)].

UMBUIK MUDO:
Don't stand any longer on the slopes, we worry that the slope might crumble and make you tumble down.

PUTI GALANG BANYAK:
Oh, you child of the spirits, child of Satan, child of the forest, child without a guide, without education, child without wisdom. You make my bathing place dirty.

UMBUIK MUDO [*She can only hear his voice.*]: The day is too hot, the eagle makes sounds. I am thirsty, and the beautiful maiden has come.

PUTI GALANG BANYAK:
Who is the man with no adat? Who is the shameless one? You'd better leave right away, before I get angry with you and call the guards, before I get you put into jail.

UMBUIK MUDO:
It's no good to get angry with me. The angry one will get old soon. [*Puti Galang Banyak looks at Umbuik Mudo, who comes out from the bushes. She is very angry; she hits the parian (water carrier) that she brought. It breaks.*]

UMBUIK MUDO [*laughing*]:
Everything has fallen down. You go to the spring, but you don't take a bath. You can't use your water carrier any more. To say it in two proverbs, listen to me, dear Sister. A palm is yellow. We take one bunch of the young shoots; suddenly it is taken away by the angels and they eat it. If I don't marry the yellow one, the clouds will collapse, the mountains will crash into each other, the moon will collide with the stars, and love will too. If I get the coconut shoot, I'll plant it by the stairway. If I get true words, I'll take them flying into the sky.

PUTI GALANG BANYAK:
The four rings are only three now. One was lost on the island of Panduah Taji. How crazy friendship is. How will it be if we haven't played it out yet? The children of the ant number less than thirty. Don't use your eyes any longer, because the eyes can get us in trouble. Listen to one more. We plant the *aur* tree, but it turns into bamboo. It grows up in Sigumanti's yard. If both hearts have the same true feelings, maybe we will wait until the sea dries up to get married. Oh, dear lord, because the day has almost passed, give me permission to go home. [*She starts to leave; suddenly she is startled. She looks at Umbuik Mudo.*]

UMBUIK MUDO:
Dearest Sister Puti Galang Banyak, why are you surprised? Why did you stop? What do you think now? What happened in your heart?

PUTI GALANG BANYAK:
I have a big problem.

UMBUIK MUDO:
My dearest sister, what is your problem, please explain it to me.

PUTI GALANG BANYAK:
I am afraid to go home now. It makes my body confused, and makes my parents angry.

UMBUIK MUDO:
Why are you so afraid? What makes your parents angry? Explain it to me.

PUTI GALANG BANYAK:
The veil has four corners, everything I brought is lost and broken. How can I answer my parents? That makes me troubled.

UMBUIK MUDO:
Don't worry about that. Let me make a suggestion. If your father and mother ask you about your belongings, be careful about what you say. I almost died; we almost didn't meet. I saw the buffalo with the long horns; I saw a crazy horse kicking in all directions. The parian broke when I ran away. That is what you should tell them. Listen to this proverb: We go to Sitingkai, we turn right at Simabur, the animals jump around. If you tie the string, don't make it too big; be careful with white lies. Listen again, my dearest sister. We'd better bring onions. Let's give each other our love to make it clear what separation is.

PUTI GALANG BANYAK:
Dear lord Umbuik Mudo, I am still worried and afraid. Why? I can't lie to my parents; it's better if you take me home. You can tell them this story. Tell them I was scared by the buffalo and the horse.

UMBUIK MUDO:
Dear Younger Sister, I am not too lazy to take you home, but I have something in my mind. What if your parents don't believe me and get angry? I have an idea. Just go back home, let me watch you from the back. Let me accompany you with my love.

PUTI GALANG BANYAK:
If that is what you ask, give me permission to leave.

Gurindam
[melody: Talago Biru]
We change the story now,
but it is still the same.
Puti Galang Banyak got sick;
she cannot get up or eat rice.
Rice feels like sand,
water feels like wood.

Many people come to try to cure her;
many dukun come too.
The house is full of medicine.
Many bandages are lying around.
But she is still sick.
After days and weeks the sickness gets worse.
Her father has an idea
and her mother remembers something.
They ask the sick girl what she wants.
What medicine can cure her?

SCENE 12

FATHER OF PUTI:
My dearest daughter, you have been sick too long, many dukun here tried to cure you, but in vain; your sickness has gotten worse. Now I have an idea, my daughter. Tell me what makes you sick.

Maybe I will know what kind of medicine you need or which dukun I should call.

PUTI GALANG BANYAK:
I don't know which part of my body is sick; my body feels like a shadow, my head feels like it is almost broken, my blood is in turmoil. Who knows how I could get better? I am longing for Umbuik. Pick Umbuik up for me.

FATHER OF PUTI:
If that is what you say, it is very clear now. Let me find *umbuik* now, let me pick umbuik up from Ranah Tibarau.

SCENE 13

[No song, just tapuak. Father and villagers walk though the forest and bushes. They look for *umbuik mudo* [bamboo shoots].

VILLAGER 1 [*speaks to himself*]:
We got many umbuik, I hope they can make Puti Galang Banyak feel better. [*He calls.*] Hey, Sutan, Sutan Galinsam, have you got many?

VILLAGER 2 [*loud*]:
Yes, I got enough, a bagful.

VILLAGER 1:
Sutan, let's go home. Where is Galang's father?

VILLAGER 2:
He's waiting down there. [*Villagers 1 and 2 meet.*]

VILLAGER 1 [*while walking*]:
I'm bringing one big bagful.

VILLAGER 2:
I am bringing a bagful too. Maybe Father will bring just as much as we got. That should make her better for sure.

VILLAGER 1:
I don't know.

VILLAGER 2:
What kind of sickness does she have, anyway?

VILLAGER 1: I think she. . . . [*Ad-libbing, they joke around while walking.*]

FATHER OF PUTI [*after he meets the Villagers*]:
I got bored and tired waiting for you. Why are you so late?

VILLAGER 1:
If that's what you ask, you're right. As for me, I got a bagful of um-buik. And he has, too.

FATHER OF PUTI:
I got seven kinds of umbuik; they're all big; please help carry it. Let me carry your small bags.
[*They walk and arrive at home.*]

FATHER OF PUTI:
My dearest daughter, I brought what you wanted, many umbuik from Ranah Tibarau.

PUTI GALANG BANYAK: What kind of umbuik did you bring? How deaf you are, Father! How stupid you are, Father, how silly and dumb! [*She is behaving crazy.*]

MOTHER OF PUTI:
My dearest daughter, don't you have any sense? Don't make any jokes. Don't hide what you really want. I need the final word from you. If you don't tell us clearly, I'll stab myself right now to make your heart happy. [*She takes the kris out, but the father grabs her hand and stops her.*]

PUTI GALANG BANYAK:
Oh, my Mother, oh Father, listen to me carefully. The thunder and the flash kill the *limbeh* fish. The fish is killed by the people from

Kampung Subarang. Even though there are 700 kinds of medicine, the only cure for me is to meet Umbuik Mudo.

<u>Gurindam</u>
[melody: Marantang Abang]
The rice has ripened
in the middle of the town;
take it to make *galu-galu* [food].
Pound it well.
We cannot hide anymore.
The story changes,
but it is still the same.
We change to Umbuik
the true and only cure for Puti.

He has come to her house
because of her father's message.
He rode his horse with the many colors.
Shortly after that, he arrives
there at his destination.
Puti comes down and
she brings water in a tea pot.
She comes directly to Umbuik,
her longing for him was strong
every night and day.

SCENE 14

PUTI GALANG BANYAK:
I am too tired to climb up the stairways. The moon is still without light. I got tired waiting for you; my eyes are pale. And my lord still hasn't come yet.

UMBUIK MUDO:
The young of the *balam* bird sit on the branch of the *dalu-dalu*

plant. The reason I am late is that the road was very long and winding.

PUTI GALANG BANYAK:
Oh, my dearest Umbuik Mudo, don't stand in the yard too long, wash your feet and come in. We can sit and chat inside. [*Umbuik Mudo goes in.*]

PUTI GALANG BANYAK:
If you want to catch a *balam* bird, you have to use one as prey. But the trap has not been put out. Sickness had entered my body and soul. But the medicine did not arrive.

UMBUIK MUDO:
How could I do the impossible? How could I sit comfortably? Listen to my proverb: I have a trap, maybe it is not made from metal. I have seen the medicine, but I don't know if you got it or not.

PUTI GALANG BANYAK:
Even though I got many medicines, the only one that is a cure is to meet you.

FATHER OF PUTI:
Dear Umbuik Mudo, please move, don't sit there. Move to this golden chair, please. It doesn't look good.

UMBUIK MUDO:
Dear father, why should I move? I think I'm sitting in the right place right here. How can I sit on the golden chair? It makes no difference.

FATHER OF PUTI:
Dear child, if I may ask you something, give us what we need, please. We only want you to marry Puti right now.

PANJANG JANGGUIK [*just arrived*]:
Dear Umbuik, follow this, please. Now I will talk to you. This is not just as your teacher. It is also as your father.

UMBUIK MUDO:

Dear Father, teacher, dear elders, who are all sitting in this house now. Forgive me, please. Accept greetings from an unworthy person. I have black skin, and my clothes are of minor quality. I am unworthy and poor, and on top of it I have bad luck. Galang is pure gold, I am just ordinary metal. How can we live together?

FATHER OF PUTI:

Don't speak like that. Think about Galang's heart, please.

UMBUIK MUDO:

Listen to me, Father, teacher, and elders. I look handsome because of my borrowed clothes. I am rich because of the gold from my father, but it is not even enough for Galang's ankle ornaments. And listen to what she said about me before. If I touch her she will cleanse herself right away. If I bring something, she will throw it away. Don't ever say my name twice; it makes her hair stand on end.

FATHER OF PUTI:

Don't repeat yourself. Right now, I ask you. If something was wrong, let me balance it. If there is a debt, let me pay it. Most important is that you marry her right now.

UMBUIK MUDO:

Dear elders of this house. Forgive me, I want to go home now. Please grant me my leave.

FATHER OF PUTI:

Wait for a minute, my son. Wait for the party to be over; drink first.

PANJANG JANGGUIK:

Dear student Umbuik, why do you want to leave so quickly?

UMBUIK MUDO:

If that is what you ask, you are right. The reason I want to go is that I don't have enough education yet. My knowledge is limited; my lessons are not yet finished.

PUTI GALANG BANYAK:
Dear lord Umbuik, what do you feel inside your heart? What is wrong in your eyes? What makes you leave? Explain it to me.

UMBUIK MUDO:
Dear maiden, you'd better not ask me the reasons. It's my bad luck.

PUTI GALANG BANYAK:
If I made a mistake, if my mouth was wrong, don't take it to heart. I need you to forgive me. Listen to this, my dear. The ship of Ali sailed to Indogiri; the ship of Tongga sailed to Balawan. You want to go study. I am left here alone with no friends.

UMBUIK MUDO:
Ask forgiveness from your love. I don't know if I can come back here or not.

PUTI GALANG BANYAK:
Good or bad luck for me is in your hands. If you go, who will stay here with me and be my friend?

UMBUIK MUDO:
What do you want from me? We don't have enough gold and are no use for anything.

PUTI GALANG BANYAK:
What I want in my heart is to be embraced by you. But you refuse. So what can I do?

UMBUIK MUDO:
My sister, think first. You status is high, why do you want to fall? Your clan will be degraded.

PUTI GALANG BANYAK:
My love for you is as plentiful as the hair on my head, and it is in my bones and flesh. Listen to this seriously.

UMBUIK MUDO:
Look at this unworthy person carefully; you cannot see him any longer.

PUTI GALANG BANYAK:
If you go now, perhaps we will never meet again.

UMBUIK MUDO:
If you die before me, wait for me in heaven.

PUTI GALANG BANYAK:
If I cannot see you any longer in this world, how can we meet in heaven?

UMBUIK MUDO:
Just live, Galang. I want to go right now.

Gurindam
[dendang: Risau Lai]
Umbuik Mudo has gone.
He has left Galang.
She is crying heavily
and tossing and turning.
Umbuik arrives at home;
sometimes he goes around alone,
sometimes he is sad and gloomy
because he worries in his heart.

SCENE 15

MOTHER OF UMBUIK MUDO:
Dearest Son, you pass all your time in gloom, sometimes you wander around alone. What is the name of the sickness? What did you get infected with at Puti's house?

UMBUIK MUDO:
Because of your hard work getting the parupuak, we were able to submerge the wood under water. We cleared the shame from our foreheads. But even so, after seeing her crying, I am sorry for her. That makes me so gloomy and I wander around alone.

MOTHER OF UMBUIK MUDO:
Now we have cleared ourselves of the shame she gave us. But there is one other shame. It is about your father, who was killed by the robbers. Now I have an idea. As long as you are still young, before you get married, you have to submerge another piece of wood: carry out your father's last wish.

UMBUIK MUDO:
You are right, Mother, I feel the same. I want to gain more knowledge and wisdom. If Allah allows it, I can find the robbers that killed Father.

MOTHER OF UMBUIK MUDO:
Dear Son, you'd better go right now, before you change your mind. Don't think about her too much. Get ready, take this small pouch of gold. It is for your studies in the rantau. Study hard and seriously. Remember the message from your father. Oh, dear Son, don't come home before you have taken revenge, before you have submerged the wood.

UMBUIK MUDO:
Dear Sister Rambun Ameh, I have a message for you. It is about Puti Galang Banyak. If she dies while I am in the rantau, bring a royal umbrella and a white death cloth. Tell her mother that it is from me. Don't ever forget this.

RAMBUN AMEH:
I will not forget it, don't worry.

UMBUIK MUDO:
Before the day gets hot, I will go. Please help me with the preparations.

RAMBUN AMEH:
Just wait a minute, please. Eat with us first.

Gurindam
[melody: Salawat]

The young man goes merantau,
because he is no use in the home village.
He goes to seek knowledge.
He left his village and nagari behind,
his mother and sister too.
He left his love, Galang.
After a year in the rantau,
he has acquired much knowledge and wisdom.
He is very clever now
for this world and eternity.
After another year, and then another year
he finishes his studies,
but not yet the silek.
He wants to graduate in his silek as well,
so he can use it in the rantau.
He wants to start a trade,
but the real meaning is that he wants to find
his father's murderers.

SCENE 16

UMBUIK MUDO:
Oh, dear master, give me permission, please. I want to talk to you. Give me your forgiveness. I think I have studied hard and learnt a lot. But I still don't know enough silek. If I may ask you, is it time for me to learn more silek now? Please teach me more and the secret parts too.

TUANKU TUO:
Dear student, what is the reason you request that?

UMBUIK MUDO:
Dear master, I am longing to go merantau again. I want to move on to other places to try out my luck. It makes me confused to go, because I don't know enough silek yet; that is what I feel and think.

TUANKU TUO:
If that is what you ask, you are right. If we travel far, we can see much more, if we live long, we can feel much more. It is time for you to see another world. Now, my son, come here please. Wait for me by the forest. Let me finish your silek lesson there.

UMBUIK MUDO:
If that is what you ask, master, I will go now.

TUANKU TUO [*He follows him.*]:
The time has come; we will separate for a while. We cannot meet again for 300 days. Divide the 300 by three. One third you shall spend in this forest in Lurah Situkah Banang, the place where crocodiles and dragons have their home. One third on Gunuang Rayo, the place where the tigers roam. The last third in Bukit Tabun Tulang, the place where robbers eat raw meat. If you survive these days, you can come back again, and we can say a prayer for your safety.

UMBUIK MUDO:
If that is what you ask, master, I will do it with all my heart.

TUANKU TUO:
Before you leave, let's try our silek for a moment.
[*They practice silek.*] Now the time has come. Follow me, repeat after me what I will say. [*They read the prayer of silek graduation.*] Walk slowly, don't ever look back until the sun sets.

UMBUIK MUDO:
Say a prayer for my safety, master.

TUANKU TUO:
So Allah will.

Gurindam
[melody: Ombak Tanjung Cino]

Umbuik graduated from silek,
learned the movement and
the mystic of silek.

He walks slowly,
and his teacher's eyes follow him.

He walks a long distance;
the day has passed.
He arrives at Lurah Situkak Banau,
which is guarded by crocodiles and dragons.
Because of the holiness of his teacher,
Umbuik is safe there;
he wins his fights with all the beasts.

He continues his journey to Gunuang Rajo,
the place of the forest kings.
After looking at Umbuik,
many tigers come to him and try to catch him.
Because of his proficiency in silek.
strikes, and his power,
all the tigers give up.

Umbuik continues to Bukit,
the place of the robbers.
One is Pandeka Langkisau,
and one is Cingahak.
The robbers eat raw food.
They rob everybody who passes by,
they kill everyone they meet.
They don't have any love,
compassion, or mercy.
Seeing Umbuik, they are very happy.
They see his face and
expect much gold and silver.

SCENE 16

PANDEKA CINGKAHAK:
Hey, young man just passing by, where are you from and where

are you going? What's your name and title? Explain it to us to make it clear. If not, your spirit will fly away [you will die].

UMBUIK MUDO:
Oh, dear uncles who just asked me. I am Umbuik Mudo, the child of Ranah Tibarau, I came here just to see the face of some robbers.

PANDEKA LANGKISAU:
What did you say? You want to see robbers? Did you bring any gold and silver with you?

UMBUIK MUDO:
If I may ask you a question, what are your names and titles, three uncles? Did you see any robbers here? Explain it to me.

PANDEKA GARAGASI:
It is us; we are the robbers. Look at us carefully. Do you have a younger sister? Do you want to find a *sumanto* [brother-in-law]?

UMBUIK MUDO:
But you haven't told me your name and title yet. If I like you, I'll take you as my sumanto. If not, I'll let you have my feet [fight you].

PANDEKA LANGKISAU:
My name is Pandeka Langkisau . . . [*ad-libbing and telling everything positive about himself*].

PANDEKA GARAGASI:
I am Pandeka Garagasi . . . [*ad-libbing and telling everything positive about himself*].

PANDEKA CINGKAHAK:
I am Pandeka Cingkahak . . . [*ad-libbing and telling everything positive about himself*]. You know all of us. What's your real intention? Explain it clearly, before you feel my attack.

UMBUIK MUDO:
Listening to your names, it makes me happy in my heart and calm in my mind. I don't have to find another place for revenge.

ALL PANDEKA:
What??

UMBUIK MUDO:
I want to take revenge for my father's death.

PANDEKA LANGKISAU:
What was your father's name?

UMBUIK MUDO:
He was Sutan Saripado, my real father. You robbed him when I was still a young child. He told me your names before he died.
[*All three* pandeka *get angry and swear, ad-libbing.*]

PANDEKA LANGKISAU:
Eh, you brat, you entered our turf; that's more dangerous that entering the tiger's domain.

PANDEKA GARAGASI:
Nobody could ever pass this way and survive! That's why it's called Bukit Tambun Tulang [Hill of Bones].

PANDEKA CINGKAHAK:
Let your spirit and body go, because I want to drink your young blood. [*He takes out his knife and tries to attack Umbuik's neck, chest, and stomach. Umbuik can evade all attacks; at last all three* pandeka *attack him together.*]

UMBUIK MUDO:
I'm tired and bored with defending only; now I will counter. Who is the one who killed my father? Show yourself if you are a real man.

PANDEKA CINGKAHAK:
It is me. Let us try our steps.
[*Umbuik Mudo attacks Pandeka Cingkahak directly and without stopping; he takes his knife away and stabs him with it. Pandeka Langkisau and Pandeka Garagasi see it and come to help him. Umbuik Mudo deflects their attacks.*]

PANDEKA LANGKISAU:
Oh, forgive us, young man, forgive us.

UMBUIK MUDO:
The gold we owe we have to repay with gold; action has to be repaid with action, and spirit has to be repaid with spirit. Now, let your spirit fly. [*He starts to stab the robbers, but suddenly he stops, because he hears the voice of his teacher.*]
Voice of TUANKU TUO: Dear student, forgive them. Ask them to come back to the right way, to Allah's way.

UMBUIK MUDO:
Dear Uncles, if you ask forgiveness from me, I will forgive you. But you have to ask pardon from Allah now. Leave this evil behind; find the good things Allah asks you to do. Do you want to do this?

PANDEKA GARAGASI:
Now you have forgiven us; now we want to request pardon from Allah. Show us how to do it.

UMBUIK MUDO:
If that is what you ask, Uncles, let me stay here and I will teach you so you understand what is right and wrong.

ALL THREE PANDEKA:
How happy our hearts are. The young man wants to stay here for a night and teach us.

Gurindam
After the robbers are reformed
by Umbuik's teaching; they know
about the good and the bad.
Umbuik has gotten new students.
He teaches them how to read the Qur'an.
He asks them to clear the field and
it becomes a small village.
Many people were surprised

that the robbers became farmers
who work in the fields and
founded the small village.

Umbuik Mudo has stayed there for a month,
then for a year.
Then he remembers his home
and wants to go home,
because he has bad dreams.
Who knows, maybe his mother is sick?
Or Puti Galang Banyak has died.

SCENE 17

UMBUIK MUDO:
Dear Mother, are you at home? Sister Rambun Ameh, are you
there? Anybody home?

RAMBUN AMEH:
Dear lord, you are back from the rantau. Why did you stay there so
long, why did you go so far?

UMBUIK MUDO:
Dear Sister, you have grown up. Where is Mother? Is she home
now?

RAMBUN AMEH:
About our mother, her body is still strong now. But she is very
worried about you. She often calls out your name.

UMBUIK MUDO:
Dear Sister, where is she?

RAMBUN AMEH:
Dear Brother, listen to me carefully about her. She is on the way to
the house of Puti's older sisters. The people are praying for a hundred days.

UMBUIK MUDO:
Explain it clearly, dear Sister, who died? Galang's mother or father?

RAMBUN AMEH:
Dear Younger Brother, there was no sign before. Didn't you have any dream? What did your sixth sense tell you? Weren't you longing for my dear sister Puti here?

UMBUIK MUDO:
Explain to me all about her illness. Did you do what I asked you?

RAMBUN AMEH:
After you left her she never got up again. She always called your name and over a long time her body became very thin. She was only skin and bones, she looked like the living death. More than a hundred days ago, my sister Galang asked our mother to be allowed to come to our house. She wanted to sleep in your bed.

UMBUIK MUDO:
Where did she die and where is her grave?

RAMBUN AMEH:
She got better and she started to eat again. She felt refreshment from drinks. Our mother was very happy, and her parents too. She asked about you more and more every day. She asked about what surau you went to. According to her, if her body got stronger, she wanted to go to where you were studying. That was how much she was longing for you. A hundred days ago she asked Mother if there was one of your old blankets left that we used to wrap your body while you were a baby. We looked for it and found it in an old box, but it was very torn up and old. She used this cloth as her blanket. We cried, seeing her like that.

UMBUIK MUDO:
What happened after that?

RAMBUN AMEH:
She asked me and Mother to sleep next to her that night. When we

wanted to give her breakfeast, Galang left. Her lips looked like she was smiling; her face was clear like after taking a bath.

UMBUIK MUDO:
Where is her grave?

RAMBUN AMEH:
We followed your wish.

UMBUIK MUDO:
My dear younger sister, if Mother comes back, tell her I went to Bukit Languang. I want to go to her grave.

RAMBUN AMEH:
Don't stay there too long; come back here soon. You haven't eaten yet. Mother is longing for you.

UMBUIK MUDO:
Before the day passes, I want to go.

Gurindam
Remorse comes to Umbuik's house.
Why did he come home too late?
Why did he let Galang die?
He goes to her grave.
He is worried and
his thoughts are all confused.
His body feels like a shadow.

He is late and arrives when it gets dark.
He looks at her grave and burns incense
and the smoke rises into the sky.
He says a prayer to Allah.
After that he is gloomy and sad.
Tears are rolling down his face,
many tears fall to the ground,
his body is weak and his spirit is gone.

Panjang Jangguik comes there too.
He wants to clean his niece's grave.
Seeing Umbuik there,
he becomes so sad.

SCENE 18

UMBUIK MUDO:
Oh, my dearest love Puti Galang Banyak, forgive me, forgive me, forgive me if you can. I have said the wrong words to you. Now we are in misery together.

PANJANG JANGGUIK:
Oh, dear child, don't be like this any longer, or a *satan* [evil spirit] will get you. Misery will come to you.

UMBUIK MUDO:
Oh, my teacher, because I let my anger lead me, because I felt vengeful, Galang died. There are no bigger regrets than mine. How can I ever make up for that? How can I repay my debt to my beloved sister Puti?

PANJANG JANGGUIK:
Don't be disappointed in yourself. Just strengthen your belief inside. If we live long, we will feel more things. Allah will give us more and more. He is just testing us. About you and Galang, just leave it in Allah's hands. Why? Because anything we receive, meet, or do, and especially death is in the hands of Allah. It is our secret.

UMBUIK MUDO:
I was unlucky all my life, since I was a little child. My father was killed; Galang has passed away because of her longing for me. Oh, teacher, my spirit has gone, my body is weak, I feel like I will not live much longer.

PANJANG JANGGUIK:
Don't say that. Be patient please and strengthen your heart. Make

your spirit stronger. Stay on the straight way. Come on, young man, let's go home.

UMBUIK MUDO:
I have a message for you. If the bad fate comes to me, if I should die, please build my grave here, facing her grave. That will make my spirit happy.

PANJANG JANGGUIK:
I will not forget your message. I will do what you want. But even so, let's go home now, your mother is longing for you. Let me take you to the house.
[*Umbuik Mudo tries to stand up. His teacher holds his hand, but Umbuik stumbles and falls face down; he is too weak to walk.*]

<u>Closing gurindam</u>
Umbuik is sad and tired
His body feels weak
What will he do and where will he go?
All is in the hands of Allah.

The Randai is finished now;
we will play again soon
and tell you how Umbuik finds Puti,
and other things.
If it is in Allah's will,
we shall play again soon.
Blessings unto you.

Notes

1. The few works on randai so far were Anis Nor's *Randai Dance of Minangkabau Sumatra with Labanotation Scores* (1986), Chairul Harun's *Kesenian Randai di Minangkabau* (1991), and Margaret Kartomi's "Randai Theatre in West Sumatra: Components, Music, Origins, and Recent Change" (1981).

2. Minangkabau society is traditionally matrilineal. Islam prescribes a patrilineal social structure, where women cannot inherit property, for instance. The conflict between these two social systems and how the Minangkabau resolve it has been a frequent topic for anthropologists.

3. The name Minangkabau, derived from *pinang kabhu,* more likely means "original home" (Loeb 1935, 97), but the Minangs like the water buffalo story much better, especially since it celebrates their supremacy over the Javanese.

4. If a return is not intended, it is simply called *berpindah* (to move away), referring to permanent migration. (Naim 1985, 112).

5. Loeb 1935, 97; Josselin de Jong 1980, 7–8.

6. According to local legend, adat was created and formalized by two legendary ancestors of the Minangkabau, Parapatih Nan Sabatang and Kjai Katumanggungan. This resulted in two types of adat: one called *adat koto-piliang* (referring to the adat formalized by Katumanggungan) and the other *adat bodi-caniago* (referring to Parapatih). The main difference is that the second one has a more democratic structure and a somewhat milder criminal code than the first. Generally however, there are only minor differences between these two adat systems and most people refer to adat in general, without specifying a particular system.

7. With the advent of Islam and the introduction of the Arab writing system, much of the previously oral literature was written down. In the process, much of the traditional material was changed and reinterpreted by the Muslim writers.

8. See Nancy Tanner and Lynn L. Thomas, "Rethinking Matrilinity: Decision-Making and Sex Roles in Minangkabau," 51ff.

9. This can be illustrated by the fact that the worst insult for a Minangkabau person is to call him or her *kurang beradat* (insufficiently educated about adat).

10. As Prindiville (1985) notes, anthropological research on matrilineal systems has in the past focused almost exclusively on the role of males in the power structure and decision-making processes and has looked at matrilineal systems as an "aberration" of the "standard" patrilineal system in which descending line and authority line are congruous (Schneider 1961; Douglas 1969). Several authors (Abdullah 1966; Schrijvers 1977; Tanner 1971, 1974, 1985; Van Reenen 1996), however, analyze the central role of women in the decision-making processes and power structure. In this context they also challenge the commonly held notion that the matrilineal structure is inherently unstable and prone to be replaced by the more "natural" patrilineal one. The fact that Islam—despite its focus on male leadership and nuclear family structure with the father as authority figure—has not weakened the matrilineal social structure and the inherently strong position of Minangkabau women is a case in point.

11. Males hold the position of *panghulu,* or village chief. This position is the most prestigious and respected for senior men in the community. Inaugurations of a panghulu customarily last three days and are accompanied by the most elaborate ceremonies; typically, randai performances are also held to entertain the participants during these events.

12. The other official religions are Buddhism, Christianity, and Hinduism (mainly in Bali in the form of a unique Hindu-Balinese version), which are found in pockets throughout the archipelago and are tolerated by the Muslim majority.

13. The coexistence of both systems is described in a popular proverb, *Agama mendaki, adat menurun* (religion moves up, customs move down). This refers to the geographical movements of both systems, Islam moving up into the highlands, and adat descending toward the coast. It is implied that both systems retain their integrity in the process.

14. He analyzes conflicts between the patrilineal royal family and the matrilineal commoner family, conflicts between the self-governed village republics in the darek and the rantau, and several others (Abdullah 1966, 4–6).

CHAPTER 2

1. The section on the silek origin is reprinted from *Asian Theatre Journal*

13(2), by permission of the publisher (©1996 by University of Hawaii Press). The section on women in randai is reprinted from *The Drama Review* 157 (Spring 1998), by permission of the publisher (©1998 by MIT Press).

2. Sijobang deals exclusively with the epic about the Minangkabau hero Anggun Nan Tongga (Phillips 1981). The name is derived from the hero's full name, Anggun Nan Tongga Magek Jobang.

3. This is according to scholars (Harun 1992; Zulkifli 1993; Kartomi 1981) and several silek and randai teachers I interviewed in 1994.

4. *Dampeang* (or *dampeng*) is first referred to in a Dutch dictionary (Van der Toorn 1891). It is described as a circular martial arts dance accompanied by singing and hand clapping. Interestingly, the name is used interchangeably with the term *randai*. Consequently, the term *randai* was used to describe a circular martial arts dance accompanied by music *before* it developed into its current dramatic form.

5. I was fortunate to witness a rare mystical event that featured dampeang performances, the *pauleh tinggi* ceremony. This ceremony is only held every twenty-five to thirty years in Sicincin, Pariaman. In this all-male spiritual ceremony, clan elders (panghulu) and Ulu Ambek practitioners from twelve regional clans come together for a three-night ritual intended to establish harmony among the clans and to honor and appease the ancestor spirits. Participants perform Ulu Ambek in pairs as well as in a circular formation (called *Randai Ulu Ambek*, another name for dampeang) accompanied by song and flute music. Ulu Ambek is a martial arts style that relies on magical rather than physical powers. This magic is projected by the practitioner like a protective shield, which stops strikes before they can harm him. Seven to nine performers in a circle employ basic Ulu Ambek movements under the leadership of a senior student or teacher. The most striking feature of this form is its slow, restrained movement and the focus of the performers. They direct their eyes diagonally up, thereby training their peripheral vision and developing a sixth sense necessary for the mastery of Ulu Ambek. (Pauka 1995, 31–33)

6. In the past, dampeang was popular throughout the Minangkabau heartland as well (where it is now rarely found) and was developed from the local martial arts styles. I personally saw only one such performance by members of the silek school *sungai patai* in Sianau Indah.

7. This significant addition is vividly described by local artists. However, some scholars (Nor 1986) maintain that impersonation was not part of randai until the Malay *bangsawan* comedy theater became popular in West Sumatra and gave the impetus to incorporate acting into the (until then nondramatic) randai.

8. Kartomi mentions that by the late 1970s female randai actresses and

singers existed. "In most villages however, women do not take part in randai performances; men still normally play all the female roles" (Kartomi 1981, 23). In 1994, less than twenty years later, all but a very few groups featured female performers, not only as actresses and singers, but even as silek and dance performers.

9. Today, this circular dance is called galombang and still shows features similar to dampeang.

10. Some groups leave the singers and flute player outside the circle, mainly to give the dancers more room to perform, especially if the performance space is rather small.

11. The beginning of the dramatic form of randai is disputed; some local artists uphold the belief that dialogues were developed before outside influences, others claim that randai was nondramatic before the advent of the Malay theater.

12. Randai was "used in the 1971 and 1977 national elections to propagate the ideas of Golkar" (Kartomi 1981, 23). Today, randai performances are often used by the Indonesian government and in these cases incorporate government propaganda and political messages.

13. Ibu Ernilitis, one of the most famous randai actresses and singers, now the leader of the troupe Rambun Pamenan in Sungayang, Tanah Datar, started her career in this way; her first appearance in randai was in 1966, and she claims to have been one of the first female actresses.

14. Cross-dressing of both sexes is condemned by the teachings of Mohammed *(hadith)* (Phillips 1981, 7). Acting is generally condemned as well. This seeming paradox of Islamic prohibition of human portrayal and a thriving theater tradition can be found all over Indonesia, and in other Islamic Southeast Asian countries as well. Also, making women a public spectacle is prohibited by the Qur'an (Phillips 1981, 7). For women, nighttime and outdoor performances are especially undesirable. Nonetheless, female singers continue to be popular during nighttime entertainment.

15. I personally saw only three such groups, and heard perhaps only one other. Of 180 groups participating in the randai festival in August 1994, only one was all-male. Today, performances of female impersonators are received with laughter and mocking comments, especially when a troupe performs outside of its own region. In its home village, such undesired audience reactions are rare, probably because the spectators are familiar with this form and with the actors, and are also less likely to criticize members of their own community.

16. I conducted individual interviews and distributed a questionnaire. See appendix A for additional data.

17. Only few groups, among them Ikan Sakti (Sacred Fish) from Baso in the Agam district, pride themselves for their refusal to use amplification, and rightly so, since the actors' vocal projection is impeccable.

18. Several performers indicated that they would prefer area microphones or wireless clip-on microphones, and they were optimistic that once this technology was readily available, the more interesting movement styles would return. But by the time this technology is affordable for most of these groups, the more traditional and elaborate acting and movement styles might be forgotten completely.

CHAPTER 3

1. Sections of this chapter first appeared in *Journal of Asian Martial Arts* 6(1) (Spring 1997).

2. Indigenous Minangkabau silek styles are styles of Minangkabau origin, contrary to introduced *silat* styles from Java or Bali.

3. Draeger, 1972. The theory of Indian origin is also supported by the elders of the Aliran Puti Mandi in Batusangkar.

4. There may have existed even more different origin myths before the arrival of Islam, but today there is no evidence of such myths left.

5. Aliran Sungai Patai (personal interview with Pak Azul, 20 April 1994).

6. Teachers of the Aliran Silek Lintau in the Tanah Datar district attest to this origin story (personal interviews with Datuk Azir, April and May 1994).

7. This excludes musicians and singers. For female members the expectations are less demanding. If they are actresses in the scenes, they are not required to train in silek, but it is welcomed if they do. If they want to join the circular martial arts dance however, silek requirements are the same for female and male members.

8. Midnight is considered an auspicious time, when magic powers are penetrating the human sphere. It can be both dangerous and rewarding to practice at that time. Many stories relate that a master has acquired some magic skill at midnight, but personally I have not seen any special event at midnight, although I have been present during many midnight practice sessions. For the younger children the training ends around ten o'clock for two reasons: the fear that they might be exposed to dangerous magical powers at midnight, and the more practical consideration that they get enough sleep before attending school the next morning.

9. This becomes more formalized when guests (for example, practitioners from a neighboring sasaran) are present. Then the musicians will wear traditional costume, be seated on a special mat, and play throughout the entire event. For regular training sessions their presence is not mandatory, but is welcomed.

10. I was repeatedly informed that many students are too poor to buy the silek outfit, which cost around 8,000 rupiah, about US$4 in 1994. (The daily pay of an untrained worker is about 5,000 rupiah.)

11. This was different in my case; many teachers went out of their way to explain techniques. When asked for names or concepts of specific movements, they often used proverbs or metaphors, like animal behavior and nature images, to explain a technique.

12. This circular formation in the silek practice, as well as the sound cues, are both also main features of randai, as we shall see below.

13. Randai will normally use the terminology of the local silek style. However, throughout the region of West Sumatra, many schools have different names for similar techniques. I will use the terminology of the *kumango* and *silek tuo* styles unless otherwise indicated, because I am most familiar with these two styles and they are among the eleven major styles in West Sumatra.

14. Often the defender will allow the attacker to escape the defensive lock or hold in order to continue the sequence and practice more variations within a single jurusan. A similar practice is standard procedure in fighting scenes in randai. Here a series of "final" locks is displayed, but in order to continue the performance, the attacker is allowed to escape each one and can attack again.

15. Ulu Ambek relies more on magic and does not emphasize low stances or ground techniques.

16. This is also a standard proverb reiterated by virtuous characters in randai.

17. Personal interview with Pak Azur, teacher of *silek kumango,* Sianau Indah, Tanah Datar, June 1994.

18. The number four is used symbolically in the context of many Asian philosophies (Bertling 1954). In relation to silek it is also often used to refer to four general conditions to be relied on in silek and in life in general. These are given to man through birth by four entities: mother, father, nature, and Allah. (Personal interview with Pak Agung, teacher of *silek gajah badorong,* Baruh Bukit, July 1994). The one given by the mother is further subdivided into four subunits: skin, blood, flesh, and bone. Obtained from the father are: liver, heart, spleen, and kidneys. Nature supplied man with fire, water, air, and land; and Allah gives the soul.

(Ampek dari induak: kulit, daging, urat, tulang / ampek dari ayah: hati, jan-tung, limpo, buah punggung / ampek dari Alam: api, air, angin, tanah / cieh dari Allah: hati.) The number four is probably the most significant in silek, and generally in the Minangkabau culture. Most silek techniques are divided into groups of four (four major attacks, four major defenses, etc.). Similar divisions can be found in randai.

19. It is said that this protective shield can also preempt an attack alto-gether. The best silek master is the one who does not get into fights at all, because his or her potential attackers sense his strength and promptly flee. This is sometimes portrayed in randai as well.

20. I have never witnessed an actual spirit descend into a medium-shaman. The account was described to me in much detail however, and by two independent sources. During my presence a summoning was at-tempted once, but was unsuccessful. It was explained to me that the spir-its are capricious and will not come when a stranger is present, no matter how benevolent one's intention or how unobtrusive one's behavior.

21. However, in the incident I witnessed, it was hard to determine if what looked real was actual dabuih or a theatrical version of it. The weapon was sharp and the impact with which the performers slashed and pierced seemed intense as well. (One clue that no magic was involved might be that my recording tools did not fail that time, normally a "sure" indication that some magic act was about to be performed.)

CHAPTER 4

1. Excerpts from this chapter first appeared in the same article men-tioned in the notes to chapter 2. *Asian Theatre Journal* 13(2).

2. Based on a 1994 survey (see appendix A) and supplementary data from the BKKNI (Badan Koordinasi Kesenian National Indonesia—Or-ganization for the Coordination of the National Arts of Indonesia) in Padang. Of these active troupes, 181 participated in the Fifth West Suma-tra Randai Festival, compared to 165 troupes in the fourth such festival in 1990, and 143 in the third in 1987. Data from the first and second festival are no longer available, but according to the recollections of Ibu Ernilitis (one of the main organizers for all five festivals), the number of partici-pating groups has been steadily increasing. Although the festival statistics may indicate that there are more active groups now than in the previous years, the consensus of randai practitioners is that the increase in the number of festival participants probably only indicates that more and

more groups obtain information about the event and are interested in participating. No firm information on the actual growth or decline of randai is available.

3. Out of sixty-eight performances I observed, only five had a female *pambalok galombang.*

4. This responsibility is a recent development. Before the advance of modern Western film and television, the actors' movements were more frequently based on silek moves. Nowadays, realistic acting is becoming more and more fashionable and the *pambalok curito* is responsible for the creation of a previously unknown acting style.

5. The power and influence of the traditional village leaders has been diminished in the past decades due to the combined influence of the social restructuring under the Indonesian government and the advancing Islamization. The once superior panghulu now has to share his power with government officials on every level of the administration and with the alim-ulama (religious leaders). This loss of power also diminished their material resources to support randai groups, who in the past often relied on donations from the panghulu for their survival.

6. See graph 9 in appendix A. This support can range from actual financial donations to moral support. A mayor might sponsor performances at official events (including food and money donations), and village headmen often provide training spaces. Communities too poor to render financial assistance might nonetheless see their government officials offer moral support in the form of encouraging speeches before a performance in which they state their appreciation of the art form.

7. If anything goes wrong with a performance—for example, if the audience is rude, performers forget their lines or lose their voices, or a performance is drowned out by rain or similar misfortunes—it is quickly blamed on some evildoer who used black magic to disturb the performance. Often the troupe protector has only limited powers; therefore most troupes include in their opening song an elaborate greeting toward the audience asking for their forgiveness and benevolence. This standard request literally asks the audience to refrain from any action that could interfere with the performance: "Please let us stand up now, so that we can perform our best for you." It refers to the belief that black magic can render the performers immobile and incapable of getting up from the crouching position in which they deliver the first song.

8. All members are amateurs. They hold regular jobs and join randai rehearsals and performances as their working schedules allow. Normally, practice sessions tend to be irregular and are not always attended by all

participants. Some group leaders indicated that they meet regularly once or twice a week. However, this might reflect only the intensified rehearsal schedule before the 1994 randai festival.

CHAPTER 5

1. According to Harun, over 500 stories have been performed as randai plays throughout West Sumatra. The repertoire of individual randai troupes is typically limited to one story. Since troupes dissolve and regroup frequently, they tend to start rehearsing a different story as soon as the group constellation changes significantly.

2. Written scripts are a recent phenomenon in randai. Until the 1960s stories were passed on orally. Starting in the sixties the stories were transcribed and collected by local scholars and individual randai leaders with an interest in preserving and documenting their art. A second incentive to record the texts and lyrics has come from the government and other cultural institutions. Starting in the early seventies, the Indonesian government through its local offices (DepPen, DepDikBud) and through its academies for the performing arts (SMKI, ASKI) in West Sumatra encouraged the conservation and documentation of local folk arts. Through this effort, many randai texts and lyrics were written down. Randai groups that have had contact with the local government (mainly through invitations to perform on national holidays or to tour other provinces of Indonesia) are more likely to possess written scripts than groups that are still solely operating in a more traditional village setting. The establishment of the West Sumatra Randai Festival has also required groups to supply a script or at least a written synopsis with their entry. For these reasons, the easily available scripts tend to be modern versions; either newly written stories, or rewritten old tales, frequently spiced with added government messages. To obtain the texts of the more traditional stories, it was necessary to record the live performances and then transcribe the tapes.

3. The habit of chewing betel nut is common throughout Southeast Asia and Oceania and induces mild intoxication. In West Sumatra betel nut is traditionally offered in welcoming ceremonies.

4. Cockfighting and gambling are similarly popular activities for males in many other regions of Southeast Asia, especially Bali, Java, and the Philippines.

5. The scenes cut will typically be those of minor importance, such as the discussion between uncle and parents about the planned purchase of a

buffalo (scene 6), the encounter between the uncle and his imprisoned nephew (scene 7), the business with the parrot (scenes 10 and 11), Manandin's meeting with the strangers on the road (scene 12), and his meeting in disguise with his sister (scene 14).

6. I saw this happen several times—for example, when a performer canceled his participation in a performance on short notice, or fell sick during his scene.

7. This is due to the fact that randai texts preserve an older version of Minang; modern-day Minang is becoming more simplified under the influence of Indonesian, which has no levels.

8. Randai language is similar to the language used in sijobang (Philips 1981, 106)

9. From the play *Siti Nursila*.

10. Room on the upper level of the house, reserved for unmarried daughters.

11. Similar stock phrases referring to a person's body reactions are used in other forms of Indonesian theater, such as in the Javanese *wayang kulit, wayang wong,* and *ketoprak*.

12. From the play *Magek Manandin*.

13. From the play *Mayang Taurai*.

14. When proverbs precede the actual messages they are often chosen for the sound of the last syllables in each line rather than for their content. In that way they are employed to foreshadow the sound of the last syllables of the following statement. Thus they invite the audience to guess what will rhyme with the proverb, catering to their love of word games and puns. Unfortunately this is difficult to reproduce in an English translation.

15. From the play *Mayang Taurai*.

16. From the play *Magek Manandin*.

17. This is especially crucial in traditional social events like weddings, panghulu inaugurations (Errington 1984, 131–34), and harvest celebrations. But it is also perpetuated in other formal gatherings in religious, governmental, administrative, and even military settings.

18. To a much lesser extent, story material is also drawn from introduced Arabic tales and present-day novels.

19. Many storytellers and some singers keep outlines of the stories, but these are typically very brief summaries and don't include fleshed-out dialogue.

20. Older people tend to favor randai based on the old Minangkabau legends, while the young generation is more drawn to modern stories incorporating their own life experiences.

21. As performed in the Payakumbuh area (Philips 1981, 18). Philips also notes that the long epics are rarely performed as a consecutive whole; instead performances tend to be episodic and selective.

22. The earliest example of written literature is a version of *Kaba Cindua Mato,* authored by Pakiah Bandaro in 1831 (Manggis 1980, 16). Most certainly the Minangkabau stories are much older than that, but no written documentation has yet been discovered. I personally was shown a book in the Arab-Malayu language, dated 1838, that also contained the story "Cindua Mato."

23. The same is true for the storytelling tradition of sijobang. Only selected episodes from this epic are narrated. The entire story is almost never performed and few storytellers can even recite it in its entity (Phillips 1981). Randai is even more episodic than sijobang. Often groups select several unconnected episodes from the epic and string them together with songs that summarize what happens in between the scenes.

24. In a different version of this scene, Gondoriah goes willingly with the new admirer, because she suspects that Anggun has tricked her and left her behind on purpose.

25. A standard setup for the creation of a conflict in many randai plays.

26. In a different version she turns into a white gibbon, a highly respected animal, associated with the spirit world.

27. The original kaba has been adapted as a randai script by Chairul Harun, one of the foremost randai leaders and scholars and it is performed by the troupe Umbuik Mudo, named after the title hero. Other versions have been adapted as novels.

28. These recitals are a common practice to teach the pupils the Qur'an, the Arab language, and proper recitation skills.

29. Sometimes the order of scenes is changed. In one version (see appendix C), Umbuik accomplishes all his duties, meets the robbers and educates them, and then returns home to find out Puti has died. Often only fragments of this long story are performed and arranged to suit the occasion. The subplots are treated as individual entities and are easily rearranged.

30. Depending on the preferences of the group, either topic can be more prominent. Thanks to the structure of randai, much of the story can be related through song; therefore time, place, and action are not restricted. Whatever is not appropriate to be acted out, or would take up too much time or focus, is delivered in the song lyrics.

31. This is not the end of the play; several other events follow, such as the confrontation between Sabai and Rajo's wife, and the burial, but they

will be eliminated here, since they are inconsequential for the story and distract from the comparison with the other version of the play.

32. She is supposed to stay indoors with her mother and leave revenge to a male relative.

33. The cloth is used symbolically on two different levels in this scene. First, according to Minangkabau adat, the cloth woven by the woman for her fiancé is a symbol of their agreement to get married; and second, Rajo Nan Panjang hints at a Muslim proverb that advises spouses to be like clothes for each other. His demand for the cloth is a very bold and rude statement in the context of Minangkabau adat and shows clearly that he lusts after her.

34. Pig hunts in Minangkabau are an all-male social activity carried out on a regular basis by large groups of men dressed in ragged clothes and stylish hats, accompanied by expensive dogs and loud noise (Errington 1984, 146ff.).

35. There are many more versions of this play, and most of them can be placed in between these two extremes of an active or passive heroine, although most are closer to the original story in which Sabai actively tricks and shoots Rajo Nan Panjang.

36. One might expect clear differences between troupes from more rural versus troupes from more urban areas, or between troupes from the rantau versus the darek areas. However, such a pattern could not be detected from the scripts available and the performances observed. Both urban and rural troupes perform old and new stories, both elaborate on the important aspects of adat and Islam, and both include government messages when sponsored by government offices or village leaders. The only difference might be that urban troupes are sponsored more often by government officials, so that government messages become a more integral part of the performances of urban troupes. However, to avoid generalizations and oversimplification here, a further detailed study of regional differences would be necessary.

37. Ironically, he is finally beaten at his own game of trickery. Dandomi manipulates him into marriage by promising him the bird.

38. The main betting game is the cockfight, a similar tradition as in Bali. Others include the card game *koa,* and horse and cow races. These are all-male events that are traditionally held during big social festivities like weddings.

39. Similar use of the performing arts can be found on Java, Bali, and most other islands. The local theater genres are used as a loudspeaker for the government.

CHAPTER 6

1. The most startling combination is possibly a female character wearing the traditional Minangkabau gown and augmenting it with U.S. brand-name athletic shoes to demonstrate the character's wealth.

2. This kind of headdress is also worn during ceremonial occasions; it is the bridal crown in a traditional wedding, as well as the decoration worn by the female carrier of offerings during welcoming processions.

3. The hat's shape resembles buffalo horns. It symbolizes the legendary victorious water buffalo that gave the Minangkabau their name. The buffalo horn is a common motif; traditional Minangkabau houses, for instance, have roofs with extremely elongated tips that curve beautifully upward, like horns.

4. Headdresses and jewelry are the most costly pieces of the costume; consequently, the troupes decide on the headdresses depending on the funds available for the purchase of these items. Groups fortunate enough to have a wealthy sponsor are likely to use headdresses and richly ornamented decorations for all characters. The main jewelry pieces are necklaces *(kaluang)*, bracelets *(galang)*, and belts *(ikek pinggang)*. Sometimes the sashes *(sampiang)* are also turned into jewelry through additional embroidery and decorations. To emphasize the high standing of a female character, the actress might also wear shoes.

5. Such two-dimensional masks are used in the performance of the story *Manantang Matohari* by the group Baringin Sati from Tanjung Gadang/Sijunjung.

CHAPTER 7

1. This bamboo flute is played with circular breathing. While exhaling through the mouth, the flutist simultaneously inhales through the nose, thereby producing a continuous sound.

2. Most musicians can play all the instruments of a randai orchestra, although there are many renowned saluang or talempong players that specialize in a specific instrument.

3. These songs are typically laments with highly emotional content, and therefore a more intimate atmosphere is desired.

4. According to some randai leaders, this also makes the galombang performers more aware of which song is being performed and helps them remember which movement sequences they are supposed to execute. It is interesting to note that the simultaneous singing and moving is also part

of the dampeang martial arts dance, which is considered the origin of the galombang.

5. A host might have requested a two-hour performance, but on the night of the performance suddenly change his or her mind and ask for a three- or four-hour performance. The group might then decide to lengthen the songs, since the singers are capable of improvising additional verses. (This would of course also require the galombang dancers to lengthen their dance sequences.) Groups that focus more on the acting might in a similar situation choose to include extra scenes, or allot the clowns more time to improvise and interact with the audience (or both).

6. Around 1990 groups started to adopt these four standard tunes with the growing influence of the West Sumatra Randai Festival, according to Ibu Ernilitis and Pak Chairul Harun, chairpersons of the festival committee (personal interview, 10 May 1994).

7. This is generally true for lively, happy songs *(dendang bagurau)*. Sad songs *(ratok)* are less frequent and include very little percussion. Sad songs are typically accompanied by flute music only, and the galombang dancers occasionally add single soft claps or slaps, but, as a rule, long percussion sequences do not occur.

8. I will use *tapuak* as an inclusive term for both hand claps and pants slapping. In case a differentiation is desired, I will use *claps* when only the hands produce the sound, and *slaps* when the pants are hit by the hands.

9. In performances this subtlety often gets drowned out by the crowds and is more likely to be heard in the somewhat less noisy rehearsal situations.

10. The TUBS (Koetting 1970, 125ff) was first used for the notation of music for African drum ensemble.

11. Female talempong groups outside of randai do still exist. In the past they were even more prominent than the male ones. However, since randai is a newer art form that originated in a time when talempong had already been taken over by males, there are only a very few female talempong musicians in randai.

12. Randai music and dialogue today are also available on cassette tapes and regularly broadcast via Indonesian radio stations. This might contribute to interregional borrowings and a more homogenous style of randai music throughout the Minangkabau region.

CHAPTER 8

1. As an all-male theater form, randai in addition took most of its

story material from the kaba of the traditional storytelling, also an almost exclusively male art form.

2. The function of the principal female role has widened, however, and nowadays often includes speeches about the importance of education, and propaganda for government projects such as family planning. This has resulted in the increased stage presence of female characters.

3. The kinesphere is defined by the body position in space. Wide-open stances with straight legs, extended arms with pointing fingers are typical for a large kinesphere, whereas a small kinesphere is defined by arms close to the body, head bowed, feet close together, and knees bent.

4. These conventions are prevalent in other Asian theater forms with female impersonators—for instance, in Japanese Kabuki theater.

5. It is difficult to draw conclusions on a general acting style of the female impersonators by just two performances. Since I have seen many more female actresses that female impersonators, I can only speculate on the past acting styles by relying on recollections of randai artists.

6. Here, the use of microphones actually enhances the performance and theatricality of the scene. The voice literally comes out of nowhere, especially since the offstage actor hides the microphone and stays quite inconspicuous.

7. According to the actress Ibu Ernilitis, the sobbing has been integrated recently. Before, it was considered sufficient to have a song describe the sadness and despair experienced by the character.

8. In silek as well as in randai this is customarily done four times in four directions, thereby greeting all spectators who surround the performance space. These four repetitions are also intended as greetings toward the four entities: Allah, ancestors and elders, parents, teachers.

9. Often the only consistently used gesture is one hand playing with the cable of the microphone.

10. The anjuang is the room traditionally occupied by the unmarried daughters in the house.

11. This limited contact, especially between the sexes, is understandable considering the restrictions Islam places on female-male interactions. Considering the strict prohibition of physical contact between unrelated males and females, it is surprising to see any touching at all. Interestingly, groups on different occasions humor these restrictions, for instance by placing a handkerchief on the woman's hand before a handshake takes place, thereby insuring visually that no real contact is possible. This normally elicits roaring laughter from the spectators.

12. All weapons used are real, so the excitement and concentration rises considerably in the performers as well as in the audience.

CHAPTER 9

1. Excerpts from this chapter first appeared in the same article mentioned in the notes to chapter 2. *Asian Theatre Journal* 13(2).

2. This is a recurrent feature of other Indonesian theater forms as well—for instance, *wayang kulit* and *wayang wong*.

3. *Maelo rambuik dalam tapuang* literally means "pulling a hair out of the flour." It is a Minangkabau idiom that refers to solving a problem diplomatically, like carefully pulling a hair from a bag of flour, without breaking the hair or spilling the flour.

4. The beginning of a talempong tune in the middle of a scene is a good indication that a fighting scene is about to happen. Another (present-day) hint is that the characters lay the microphones on the ground or pass them to seated members of the galombang circle to free their hands for combat.

5. The terminology is the same as the one used in chapter 3. A brief summary will be included at this point for quick reference:

gelek: a fast turn of the body while the feet stay in place.

jurusan: a standard set of attack and defense moves.

kudo-kudo: a low, wide open stance with the center of weight over the rear foot.

pitunggua: a stance on one leg with the other raised and the foot touching the knee of the supporting leg.

sikap pasang: starting position.

simpia: a very low crouch with legs crossed.

As far as possible, I will use English translations for fighting techniques.

6. I will use A for attacker and D for defender throughout the description of the fighting scenes. If there is more that one of each, numbers will be used (A1 for Attacker One, A2 for Attacker Two, etc.).

7. *Sapik kalo* means "scorpion strike."

8. The kunci mati (death hold) can be lethal in real combat. Obviously, in performance and practice it is not executed fully, instead it is highlighted by a freeze.

9. The knife has been thrown into the center of the circle by one of the galombang members prior to the fourth jurusan. It is simply put there as a prop.

10. This second fight is halted by the sudden appearance of the uncle, Datuak Rajo Mudo, who separates the fighters. He lectures them about the proper way to deal with conflicts, teaching them that diplomacy and forgiveness are the keys to harmony and happiness. All involved apologize to each other and rejoice in forgiveness.

11. The only exception to this progressive development is the very first defense move, the scorpion death hold, which is very difficult and dangerous. It is used dramatically in the very beginning to capture the attention of the audience.

12. There is some improvisation and flexibility in terms of how many and which jurusan are selected for any given performance. But within each jurusan the movement sequence is set. The above example shows one variation of the fighting scene performed by this group. In other performances I saw longer versions that included two additional jurusan for the first pair of combatants. In another version the second pair of fighters never fought and the first pair executed some of the jurusan normally done in the second fight.

13. This is also true for silek practice sessions. In real applications (i.e., in self-defense situations), any of the displayed techniques would be executed to maim or immobilize an attacker. In randai, as in silek practice sessions, the fighters allow each other to escape from a hold or pin in order to be able to continue the practice or performance which, of course, would not be the case in a self-defense situation.

14. To avoid injury, fighting scene with multiple attackers must also be more strictly choreographed than a one-on-one combat.

15. It might look too unreal from the audience's point of view if, for example, the second attacker were to unreasonably delay his movements until the defender was finished with the first attacker.

16. This stabbing was executed with considerable force and the audience shrieked and yelled, and children cried. The knife used was sharp and pointed, and I wondered if the actor playing Sutan Alam wore protective padding underneath his costume or truly had magic inner powers to protect himself.

17. The group called Sutan Budiman resides in Pesisir Selatan (the southernmost tip of the province of West Sumatra). They name their play and group after the honorary title given to the male hero Bujang Baganto, who is killed by Palimo Gagah in the course of the play. The silek style employed is a Pesisir Selatan version of *silek sungai patai*, which originated in Tanah Datar, the heartland of the Minangkabau.

18. This is because the dagger is so powerful and bloodthirsty that it jumps out of its sheath in search of the victim. Since Palimo carries the dagger in his belt, it is also safer for the actors to take it out before the fight becomes too heated and wild. If it were carried in the belt during the hand-to-hand combat section, with its falls and throws, it might injure its bearer.

19. Other styles use the pants slapping during kicks as well, but in its

frequency and strength it is the signature kick of *silek sungai patai*. (Draeger 1972, 149). Often it is used without a kick to scare the opponent, fake a kick, or just plain entertain the audience.

20. No explanation is given in the story.

21. A proverb from another randai script describes the powers of a magic kris given to the young hero by his adoptive father. It starts in typical Minangkabau fashion with an understatement: "It is not a very good knife, but if you wash it in the stream, the fish will die; if you leave it on the grass, the bees will die; if you touch someone's footprints with it, the person will drop dead."

22. Even masters who give public demonstrations of silek refuse to display the technique gayueng angin. The standard reason given for the refusal is that it the technique is too dangerous and will most certainly harm the partner seriously. Ethically, it may only be used in life-threatening situations.

23. Due to merantau there is also a frequent mixture and blending of styles in silek itself.

24. Festivals and touring also facilitate the exchange of other techniques and ideas in randai, such as script variations, song lyrics, and acting techniques.

25. The only exception is during the opening and closing segment of each galombang, where a specific sequence is performed in which the dancers move in straight lines to the center of the circle and back out.

26. The only time silek partners move in unison in a fight is during the opening and closing sequence, including the greeting gestures. In the attack-defense sequences, they might move at a similar pace and with the same intensity, but they typically execute different movements.

27. These new developments occur mainly within groups that are less than five years old. A few older groups however have also started to adapt new dance styles and are adding them into their repertoire.

28. The popularity is increasing so rapidly that the board members of the West Sumatra Randai Festival have taken steps to preserve a more traditional style for randai. Contestants who enter the festival are required to limit the number of pop elements in the galombang: no more than a combination of three dangdut or joget are allowed.

29. In performances that last more than four hours, intermissions are normally inserted after two hours to give the performers an opportunity to rest.

30. Other traditional dances that enrich the movement repertoire of the galombang are *tari barabak* (bird dance), *tari rantak* (forceful dance), *tari payuang* (umbrella dance), *tari pariaman* (Pariaman dance) and *tari*

pasambahan (greeting dance). Like *tari piriang,* these dances are also considered "flowers of silek" *(bungo silek).* The most outstanding and characteristic features of all these dances that filter into the galombang are hand and finger positions, eye-hand coordination, and the fluidity of the arm movements.

31. This is a popular performance feature in the southern Tanah Datar region. A good example is the performance of the story *Sengsara membawah nikmat* (Misfortune turns to blessing) by the group with the same name from Talago Gunuang/Tanjuang Ameh.

32. This is also the case during public displays of silek, when the musicians try to highlight spectacular or well-executed segments to entertain the audiences.

33. In this context it is interesting to note that freestyle fighting is mainly used when a randai performance is given in the home region. On tour, most groups display only the basic jurusan. Two reasons might explain this behavior. The more obvious is that local audiences have seen the performances often and cherish novelty in the form of free fighting, whereas other audiences unfamiliar with the style are easily satisfied with the display of the standard fare. Another, more compelling reason is that in the heat of a free fight a performer might unintentionally "give away" a technique that is considered secret and unique to the style and is jealously guarded by the home aliran. Since the raison d'être for silek is still self-defense, such techniques cannot be shown to outsiders, because they might be needed in the future by one of the practitioners if he or she gets attacked when in a foreign region.

CHAPTER 10

1. Some groups, in which women comprise more than half of the galombang dancers, feature a more lyric dance style, but so do some groups with only male performers. Generalizations about many specific aspects of randai are difficult to draw due to the wide diversity of performance styles.

2. Many randai artists hope that once area microphones or wireless microphones are more widely available, the cumbersome cables can be abandoned and will no longer interfere with the gestures and movement of the actors.

Glossary

adat—customs, traditions

alam Minangkabau—"world of the Minangkabau," consisting of both the original homelands (**darek**) and the new frontier areas (**rantau**)

alim-ulama—religious leaders

aliran—martial arts school

anak randai—lit., children of randai; all active members of a randai troupe

anjuang—sleeping room of the unmarried daughters in a traditional Minangkabau house

antam—front kick in **silek**

bangsawan—Malay comic opera

Bahasa Minang—Minang language

batin—spirit, inner spiritual power, also **kebatinan**

bujang gadih—lit., boy-girl; female impersonator in randai

cancang—overhead strike in **silek**

dabuih—ritualistic self-mutilation executed with sharp weapons; no injuries are inflicted

dampeang—mystical circular martial arts dance used to enhance the practitioners sixth sense and magical powers

darek—Minangkabau heartland consisting of the three oldest districts Tanah Datar, Agam, and Limopuluah Koto; cradle of the Minangkabau culture

datuak—title of a high-ranking male clan leader

dendang—traditional song, specifically a happy song

deta—soft cloth wrapped around the head; part of **silek** and randai costuming

dorong—straight punch in **silek**

dukun—traditional healer and shaman

galombang—circular martial arts dance in randai

gandang—large two-headed drum

gayueng angin—lit., carried by the wind; long-distance **silek** techniques that can be fatal

gelek—fast, evasive body turn used in **silek**

gotong royong—mutual assistance

gurindam—song lyrics, rhapsody

guru—teacher

ilmu batin—(same as **kebatinan**) magic knowledge

jurusan—standardized partner drills in **silek** consisting of attack and defense movements

kaba—lit., news; traditional Minangkabau stories

kabupaten—administrative unit below the provincial level and above the **kecamatan**

karabau—water buffalo

kebatinan—see **batin**

kecamatan—administrative unit below to the **kabupaten** and above the **nagari**

kris—(from Malay keris) traditional Malay dagger with a serpentine blade

kudo-kudo—horse stance; basic stance in **silek**

kunci mati—lit., death hold; technique that terminates a fight or practice session in **silek**

langkah—lit., step

langkah ampeh—lit., four steps; set stepping sequence used in the beginning of **silek** training and randai performances to show respect toward God, ancestors, elders, and teachers

main silek—play **silek**

mamak—lit., uncle; family member traditionally responsible for the upbringing and education of the nieces and nephews

merantau—lit., to go to the **rantau**; customary migration of young Minangkabau men before marriage

nagari—originally an autonomous village republic; today the administrative unit below the **kecamatan**

ninik-mamak—elders

Padri—Islamic extremist movement that fought the royal Minangkabau family and other Islamic movements in Sumatra

pambalok curito—"leader of the story," the one responsible for the story

pambalok galombang—leader of the circular dance

pambalok gurindam—lit., master of lyrics; lead singer in randai

Pancasila—five basic principles of the Republic of Indonesia

pandeka—silek master

panghulu—village chief

pantun—four-lined, rhymed verse used in ceremonial speeches (**pidato**) and in randai

pawang—shaman

pepatah-pepitih—wise sayings

pidato—ceremonial speech used by elders during weddings, inaugurations, and burials

pusako—sacred heirloom

randai silek—general term used for circular martial arts practice formations (see **dampeang**)

randai ulu ambek (same as **dampeang**), circular martial arts practice that employs the movement repertoire of a specific style, **ulu ambek**

rantau—originally frontier regions; now includes all migration destinations outside the heartland, **darek** (see **merantau**)

rebab—two- or four-string fiddle, Arab influenced

rumah gadang—large traditional Minangkabau house with horn-shaped roof tips

sabuah paruik—lit., one womb; smallest unit of a matrilineal clan consisting of one female eldest and all her direct descendants

saluang—large bamboo flute

saluang jo dendang—flute and song

sarawa galembong—pants worn in **silek** and in randai

sarong—wrapped skirt

sarunai—bamboo flute

sasaran—originally the location of silek training; now also an inclusive term for all participants of one school

sijobang—singing of the Minagkabau epic poem *Anggun Nan Tongga*

sikap pasang—starting position in **silek**, with partners on opposite sides of the training ground

silek—indigenous martial arts form of the Minangkabau

sipatuang siriah—shaman protector of a randai troupe

siriah—plant leaves used as ingredient in the chewing of betel nut, traditionally used as offering in ceremonies and placed in a metal vessel

suntiang—tall golden crown worn by the bride in wedding ceremonies or during welcoming parades for high-ranking guests; now also a costume piece in randai

surau—traditionally a special house for boys once they became too old to live in their mother's house; today also used for prayer and other community activities

talempong—musical instrument consisting of bronze kettles and beaten with sticks

tambo—legend (cf. **pantun**)

tangkuluak tanduak—traditional horn-haped hat worn by women; also used as costume piece in randai

tapuak—vocal or other auditory cue

tapuak galembong—lit., pants slapping; sound effects created by the **galombang** dancer

tapuak tangan—hand clapping in the **galombang** dance

tari—dance

tari ilau—mourning dance, believed to be a possible origin of randai

tarikat—secret Islamic brotherhood

tukang—master, craftsman

tukang dendang—master, craftsman of the songs, lead singer

tukang goreh—lit., master of shouts; vocal leader of the **galombang** dance in randai

tukang jajak—master, craftsman of refrain, second singer

tukang kaba—storyteller

ulu ambek—lit., stop before the peak; a mystical martial arts style found primarily in the Pariaman region of West Sumatra

Bibliography

Abdullah, Taufik. 1966. "Adat and Islam: An Examination of Conflict in Minangkabau." *Indonesia* 2: 1–24.

————. 1970. "Some Notes on the Kaba Tjindua Mato: An Example of Minangkabau Traditional Literature." *Indonesia* 9: 1–22.

————. 1985. "Islam, History, and Social Change in Minangkabau." *Change and Continuity in Minangkabau: Local, Regional, and Historical Perspectives on West Sumatra,* ed. Lynn Thomas and Franz von Benda-Beckmann, 141–56. Athens, Ohio: Ohio University Center for International Studies.

Alexander, H. C., et al. 1970. *Pentjak Silat: The Indonesian Fighting Art.* Rutland, Vt.: Tuttle.

Barendregt, B. "Written by the Hand of God: Pencak Silat of Minangkabau West Sumatra." Ms. unpublished ms.

Bertling, C. T. 1954. "Vierzahl, Kreuz und Mandala in Asien." *Bijdragen tot de Taal-, Land- en Volkenkunde van Nederlandsch-Indië* 110: 93–115.

Cordes, Hiltrud. 1990. "Pencak Silat: Die Kampfkunst der Minangkabau und ihr kulturelles Umfeld." Dissertation, University of Cologne.

Damrah, B. 1994. "Manajemen Seni Pertunjukan tradisional pada Teater rakyat (Randai)." *Singgalang* [Padang], 11 July 1994: 7, 8.

Dirajo, D. S. 1987. *Curainan Adat Alam Minangkabau.* Bukittinggi: Pustaka Indonesia.

Djamaris, E. 1991. *Tambo Minangkabau.* Jakarta: Balai Pustaka.

Dobbin, Christine. 1983. *Islamic Revivalism in a Changing Peasant Economy: Central Sumatra 1784–1847.* London: Curzon Press.

Draeger, D. F. 1969. *Comprehensive Asian Fighting Arts.* Rutland, Vt.: Tuttle.

————. 1972. *Weapons and Fighting Arts of the Indonesian Archipelago.* Rutland, Vt.: Tuttle.

Drakard, J. 1993. "A Kingdom of Words: Minangkabau Sovereignty in Sumatran History." Dissertation, Australian University, Canberra.

Echols, J. M., and H. Shadily. 1990. *Kamus Indonesian-Inggeris / An Indonesian-English Dictionary.* 3d ed. Jakarta: Gramedia.

Errington, Frederick. 1984. *Manners and Meaning in West Sumatra: The Social Context of Consciousness.* New Haven: Yale University Press.

Esten, Mursal. 1988. *Sastra jalur kedua: Sebuah pengantar.* Padang: Angkasa Raya.

———. 1993. *Minangkabau: Tradisi dan Perubahan.* Padang: Angkasa Raya.

Frey, K. S. 1985. *Journey to the Land of the Earth Goddess.* Jakarta: Gramedia.

Hakimy, H. I. D. R. P. 1991a. *1000 Pepatah-Pepitih, Mamang-Bdal, Pantun-Gurindam.* Bandung: Penerbit PT Remaja Rosdakarya.

———. 1991b. *Pokok-Pokok Pengetahuan Adat Alam Minangkabau.* Bandung: Penerbit PT Remaja Rosdakarya.

Harun, Chairul. 1992. *Kesenian Randai di Minangkabau.* Jakarta: Gramedia.

Holt, Claire. 1972. "Dances of Minangkabau: Notes." *Indonesia* 14: 73–88.

Jamaan, A. S. K. 1992a. "Kaba, Sumbur Garapan Naskah Randai." Thesis, ASKI, Padangpanjang.

———. 1992b. "Randai Intan Koroang Di Dusun Pauh." Thesis, ASKI, Padangpanjang.

Josselin de Jong, P. E. de. 1980. *Minangkabau and Negri Sembilan: Socio-Political Structure in Indonesia.* The Hague: Nijhoff.

Junus, Umar. 1985. "Political History and Social Change in Minangkabau: Information from Literary Works." In *Change and Continuity in Minangkabau: Local, Regional, and Historical Perspectives on West Sumatra,* ed. Lynn Thomas and Franz von Benda-Beckmann, 181–205. Athens, Ohio: Ohio University Center for International Studies.

Kahn, Joel S. 1980. *Minangkabau Social Formations: Indonesian Peasants and the World Economy.* Cambridge: Cambridge University Press.

———. 1993. *Constituting the Minangkabau: Peasants, Culture, and Modernity in Colonial Indonesia.* Oxford: Berg.

Kartomi, Margaret. J. 1981. "Randai Theatre in West Sumatra: Components, Music, Origins, and Recent Change." *Review of Indonesian and Malay Affairs* 15(1): 1–45.

Kato, T. 1978. "Change and Continuity in the Minangkabau Matrilineal System." *Indonesia* 25: 1–16.

———. 1982. *Matriliny and Migration: Evolving Minangkabau Traditions in Indonesia.* Ithaca: Cornell University Press.

Koetting, J. 1970. "Analysis and Notation of West African Drum Ensemble Music." In *Selected Reports* 1(3), ed. Mantle Hood, 115–46. Los Angeles: UCLA, Institute of Ethnomusicology.

Loeb, E. M. 1935. *Sumatra: Its History and People.* Oxford: Oxford University Press.

Maadis, I. B. A. 1988. "Proses Kelahiran Randai." *Harian Haluan* (Pandang), 14 March 1988: 6.

Manan, A. 1955. *Tambo Alam Minangkabau.* Payakumbuh: Perjetakan Lembago.

Manggis, R. M. 1980. *Kaluak Randai.* Jakarta: DepDikBud.

Marsden, W. 1811. *The History of Sumatra.* London: J. McCreery.

Murad, A. 1980. *Merantau: Outmigration in a Matrilineal Society of West Sumatra.* Canberra: Australian National University.

Naim, Mochtar. 1985. "Implications of Merantau for Social Organization in Minangkabau." In *Change and Continuity in Minangkabau: Local, Regional, and Historical Perspectives on West Sumatra,* ed. Lynn Thomas and Franz von Benda-Beckmann, 111–19. Athens, Ohio: Ohio University Center for International Studies.

Nor, Anis M. 1986. *Randai Dance of Minangkabau, Sumatra, with Labanotution Scores.* Kuala Lumpur: Department of Publications, University of Malaysia.

Pauka, Kirstin. 1995. "Martial Arts, Magic, and Male Bonding: The Pauleh Tinggi Ceremony of West Sumatra." *Journal of Asian Martial Arts* 4(3): 26–45.

———. 1996. "A Flower of Martial Arts: The Randai Folk Theatre of the Minangkabau in West Sumatra." *Asian Theatre Journal* 13(2): 167–92

———. 1997. "*Silek:* The Martial Arts of the Minangkabau in West Sumatra." *Journal of Asian Martial Arts* 6(1): 62–80.

———. 1998. "The Daughters Take Over? Female Performers in Randai Theatre." *Drama Review* 157 (Spring 1998): 113–21.

Peterson, W. 1994. "Minangkabau Dance in West Sumatra: Tradition, Training, and Tourism" SEAMEO Regional Centre for Archaeology and Fine Arts (*SPAFA Journal*) 6(1): 5–12.

Phillips, Nigel. 1981. *Sijobang: Sung Narrative Poetry of West Sumatra.* London: Cambridge University Press.

Prindiville, Joanne. 1985. "Mother, Mother's Brother, and Modernization: The Problems and Prospects of Minangkabau Matriliny in a Changing World." In *Change and Continuity in Minangkabau: Local, Regional, and Historical Perspectives on West Sumatra,* ed. Lynn Thomas and Franz von Benda-Beckmann, 29–43. Athens, Ohio: Ohio University Center for International Studies.

Schmidt, J. 1988. "Der Krieg als Vater der Tanzkunst: Das 'Asian Festival of Theatre, Dance and Martial Arts' in Calcutta." *Ballet International* 6/7: 72–75.

Soelaiman, H. B. 1995. *The World of Minangkabau Custom: The Great Tradition.* Trans. Drg. Widodo. Jakarta: Ikhwan.

Tanner, Nancy, and Lynn L. Thomas. 1985 "Rethinking Matriliny: Decision-Making and Sex Roles in Minangkabau." In *Change and Continuity in Minangkabau: Local, Regional, and Historical Perspectives on West Sumatra,* ed. Lynn Thomas and Franz von Benda-Beckmann, 45–71. Athens, Ohio: Ohio University Center for International Studies.

Thomas, Lynn, and Franz von Benda-Beckmann, eds. 1985. *Change and Continuity in Minangkabau: Local, Regional, and Historical Perspectives on West Sumatra.* Athens, Ohio: Ohio University Center for International Studies, Center for Southeast Asian Studies.

Van der Toorn, J. L. v. d. 1891. *Minangkabausch-Maleisch-Nederlandsch woordenbök.* The Hague: Nijhoff.

Yakub, N. 1987. *Minangkabau Tanah Pustaka: Tambo Minangkabau.* Bukittinggi: Pustaka Indonesia.

Zed, M. A. 1992. "Perubahan social di Minangkabau." Thesis, Universitas Andalas, Padang.

Zulkifli [A.]. 1993. "Randai sebagai Teater rakyat Minangkabau di Sumatera Barat dalam Dimensi sosial Budaya." Thesis, ASKI, Padangpanjang.

Index

Printed and bound by CPI Group (UK) Ltd, Croydon, CR0 4YY

09/06/2025